Barbara Dafoe Whitehead

THE DIVORCE CULTURE

Barbara Dafoe Whitehead writes on family and social issues for many publications. Her *Atlantic Monthly* article "Dan Quayle Was Right" was nominated for a National Magazine Award and won an EMMA (Exceptional Merit in Media Award) from the National Women's Political Caucus and Radcliffe College. She is also the recipient of an editorial award for Magazine Awareness of Global Issues and Concerns from *Folio* magazine and the Cowles Foundation for her *Atlantic Monthly* article "The Failure of Sex Education." She lives in Amherst, Massachusetts.

The Divorce Culture

THE DIVORCE
CULTURE

*Rethinking Our Commitments
to Marriage and Family*

Barbara Dafoe Whitehead

Vintage Books
A Division of Random House, Inc.
New York

FIRST VINTAGE BOOKS EDITION, FEBRUARY 1998

The Library of Congress has cataloged the Knopf edition as follows:

Whitehead, Barbara Dafoe
The divorce culture / by Barbara Dafoe Whitehead. —1st ed.
p. cm.
Includes bibliographical references and index.
ISBN 0-679-43230-2 (alk. paper)
1. Divorce—United States. 2. Family—United States. 3. Children—United States—Social conditions. I. Title.
HQ834.W575 1997
306.89'0973—dc20 96-30180
CIP

Vintage ISBN: 0-679-75168-8

Random House Web address: http://www.randomhouse.com/

Printed in the United States of America
10 9 8 7 6 5 4 3 2 1

For Ralph

For Ralph

Contents

Contents

Acknowledgments

This book had its genesis in an article, "Dan Quayle Was Right," which appeared in the April 1993 issue of the *Atlantic Monthly* magazine. I want to thank Editor in Chief William Whitworth and Senior Editor Jack Beatty for their fearlessness in publishing a piece on a subject bound to rile many readers. I am also grateful to the hundreds of *Atlantic* readers who took time to write to the magazine or to me after the article appeared.

I want to acknowledge my intellectual debt to William Galston, whose writing on the family in the mid-1980s inspired my interest in the changing nature of family life. Jack Beatty offered insightful comments on an early draft of the book, as did my colleague and friend David Popenoe. I am grateful to Norval D. Glenn, Leon Kass, and Don S. Browning for their help and suggestions on chapters in progress. The Woodrow Wilson International Center for Scholars provided office space and research support, including the capable services of my research assistant, Kaitlin E. McKelvie, during a crucial stage in the writing of this book. My thanks to Larry Smith for his friendship and kindnesses; to Vesna Neskow for the happy evenings we spent talking about our respective writing projects; to my agents, Glen Hartley and Lynn Chu, for their faith in the book; and to my editor, Jane Garrett, for her expert guidance. My children, Ann, Sarah, and John, did me the favor of remaining incurious about this book and helped me keep a sense of perspective. It cannot be easy to live with a woman who thinks incessantly about divorce, but my husband, Ralph, cheerfully endured and gave me the benefit of his unflinching criticism and unwavering support from beginning to end.

The Divorce Culture

The Making of
a Divorce Culture

DIVORCE IS NOW PART of everyday American life. It is embedded in our laws and institutions, our manners and mores, our movies and television shows, our novels and children's storybooks, and our closest and most important relationships. Indeed, divorce has become so pervasive that many people naturally assume it has seeped into the social and cultural mainstream over a long period of time. Yet this is not the case. Divorce has become an American way of life only as the result of recent and revolutionary change.

The entire history of American divorce can be divided into two periods, one evolutionary and the other revolutionary. For most of the nation's history, divorce was a rare occurrence and an insignificant feature of family and social relationships. In the first sixty years of the twentieth century, divorce became more common, but it was hardly commonplace. In 1960, the divorce rate stood at a still relatively modest level of nine per one thousand married couples. After 1960, however, the rate accelerated at a dazzling pace. It doubled in roughly a decade and continued its upward climb until the early 1980s, when it stabilized at the highest level among advanced Western societies. As a consequence of this sharp and sustained rise, divorce moved from the margins to the mainstream of American life in the space of three decades.

Ideas are important in revolutions, yet surprisingly little attention has been devoted to the ideas that gave impetus to the divorce revolution. Of the scores of books on divorce published in recent decades, most focus on its legal, demographic, economic, or (especially) psychological dimensions. Few, if any, deal fully with its intellectual origins. Yet trying to comprehend the divorce revolution and its consequences without some sense of its ideological origins, is like trying to understand the American Revolution without taking into account the thinking of John Locke, Thomas Jefferson, or Thomas Paine. This more recent revolution, like the revolution of our nation's founding, has its roots in a distinctive set of ideas and claims.

This book is about the ideas behind the divorce revolution and how these ideas have shaped a culture of divorce. The making of a divorce culture has involved three overlapping changes: first, the emergence and widespread diffusion of a historically new and distinctive set of ideas about divorce in the last third of the twentieth century; second, the migration of divorce from a minor place within a system governed by marriage to a freestanding place as a major institution governing family relationships; and third, a widespread shift in thinking about the obligations of marriage and parenthood.

Beginning in the late 1950s, Americans began to change their ideas about the individual's obligations to family and society. Broadly described, this change was away from an ethic of obligation to others and toward an obligation to self. I do not mean that people suddenly abandoned all responsibilities to others, but rather that they became more acutely conscious of their responsibility to attend to their own individual needs and interests. At least as important as the moral obligation to look after others, the new thinking suggested, was the moral obligation to look after oneself.

This ethical shift had a profound impact on ideas about the nature and purpose of the family. In the American tradition, the marketplace and the public square have represented the realms of life devoted to the pursuit of individual interest, choice, and freedom, while the family has been the realm defined by voluntary commitment, duty, and self-sacrifice. With the greater emphasis on individual satisfaction in family relationships, however, family well-being became subject to a new metric. More than in the past, satisfaction in this sphere came to be based on subjective judgments about the content and quality of individual happiness rather than on such objective measures as level of income, material nurture and support, or boosting children onto a higher rung on the socioeconomic ladder. People began to judge the strength and "health" of family bonds according to their capacity to promote individual fulfillment and personal growth. As a result, the conception of the family's role and place in the society began to change. The family began to lose its separate place and distinctive identity as the realm of duty, service, and sacrifice. Once the domain of the obligated self, the family was increasingly viewed as yet another domain for the expression of the unfettered self.

These broad changes figured centrally in creating a new conception of divorce which gained influential adherents and spread broadly and swiftly throughout the society—a conception that represented a radical departure from earlier notions. Once regarded mainly as a social, legal, and family event in which there were other stakeholders, divorce now became an event closely linked to the pursuit of individual satisfactions, opportunities, and growth.

The new conception of divorce drew upon some of the oldest, and most resonant, themes in the American political tradition. The nation, after all, was founded as the result of a political divorce, and revolutionary thinkers explicitly adduced a parallel between the dissolution of marital bonds and the dissolution of political bonds. In political as well as marital relationships, they argued, bonds of obligation were established voluntarily on the basis of mutual affection and regard. Once such bonds turned cold and oppressive, peoples, like individuals, had the right to dissolve them and to form more perfect unions.

In the new conception of divorce, this strain of eighteenth-century political thought mingled with a strain of twentieth-century psychotherapeutic thought. Divorce was not only an individual right but also a psychological resource. The dissolution of marriage offered the chance to make oneself over from the inside out, to refurbish and express the inner self, and to acquire certain valuable psychological assets and competencies, such as initiative, assertiveness, and a stronger and better self-image.

The conception of divorce as both an individual right and an inner experience merged with and reinforced the new ethic of obligation to the self. In family relationships, one had an obligation to be attentive to one's own feelings and to work toward improving the quality of one's inner life. This ethical imperative completed the rationale for a sense of individual entitlement to divorce. Increasingly, mainstream America saw the legal dissolution of marriage as a matter of individual choice, in which there were no other stakeholders or larger social interests. This conception of divorce strongly argued for removing the social, legal, and moral impediments to the free exercise of the individual right to divorce.

Traditionally, one major impediment to divorce was the presence of children in the family. According to well-established popular belief, dependent children had a stake in their parents' marriage and suffered hardship as a result of the dissolution of the marriage. Because children were vulnerable and dependent, parents had a moral obligation to place their children's interests in the marital partnership above their own individual satisfactions. This notion was swiftly abandoned after the 1960s. Influential voices in the society, including child-welfare professionals, claimed that the happiness of individual parents, rather than an intact marriage, was the key determinant of children's family well-being. If divorce could make one or both parents happier, then it was likely to improve the well-being of children as well.

In the following decades, the new conception of divorce spread through the law, therapy, etiquette, the social sciences, popular advice literature, and religion. Concerns that had dominated earlier thinking on divorce were now dismissed as old-fashioned and excessively moralistic. Divorce would not harm children but would lead to greater happiness for children and their single parents. It would not damage the institution of marriage but would make possible better marriages and happier individuals. Divorce would not damage the social fabric by diminishing children's life chances but would strengthen the social fabric by improving the quality of affective bonds between parents and children, whatever form the structural arrangements of their families might happen to take.

As the sense of divorce as an individual freedom and entitlement grew, the sense of concern about divorce as a social problem diminished. Earlier in the century, each time the divorce rate increased sharply, it had inspired widespread public concern and debate about the harmful impact of divorce on families and the society. But in the last third of the century, as the divorce rate rose to once unthinkable levels, public anxiety about it all but vanished. At the very moment when divorce had its most profound impact on the society, weakening the institution of marriage, revolutionizing the structure of families and reorganizing parent-child relationships, it ceased to be a source of concern or debate.

The lack of attention to divorce became particularly striking after the 1980s, as a politically polarized debate over the state of the American family took shape. On one side, conservatives pointed to abortion, illegitimacy, and homosexuality as forces destroying the family. On the other, liberals cited domestic violence, economic insecurity, and inadequate public supports as the key problems afflicting the family. But politicians on both sides had almost nothing to say about divorce. Republicans did not want to alienate their upscale constituents or their libertarian wing, both of whom tended to favor easy divorce, nor did they want to call attention to the divorces among their own leadership. Democrats did not want to anger their large constituency among women who saw easy divorce as a hard-won freedom and prerogative, nor did they wish to seem unsympathetic to single mothers. Thus, except for bipartisan calls to get tougher with deadbeat dads, both Republicans and Democrats avoided the issue of divorce and its consequences as far too politically risky.

But the failure to address divorce carried a price. It allowed the middle class to view family breakdown as a "them" problem rather than an "us" problem. Divorce was not like illegitimacy or welfare dependency, many claimed. It was a matter of individual choice, imposing few, if any, costs or consequences on others. Thus, mainstream America could cling to the comfortable illusion that the nation's family problems had to do with the behavior of unwed teenage mothers or poor women on welfare rather than with the instability of marriage and family life within its own ranks.

Nonetheless, after thirty years of persistently high levels of divorce, this illusion, though still politically attractive, is increasingly difficult to sustain in the face of a growing body of experience and evidence. To begin with, divorce has indeed hurt children. It has created economic insecurity and disadvantage for many children who would not otherwise be economically vulnerable. It has led to more fragile and unstable family households. It has caused a mass exodus of fathers from

children's households and, all too often, from their lives. It has reduced the levels of parental time and money invested in children. In
sum, it has changed the very nature of American childhood. Just as no
patient would have designed today's system of health care, so no child
would have chosen today's culture of divorce.

Divorce figures prominently in the altered economic fortunes of
middle-class families. Although the economic crisis of the middle class
is usually described as a problem caused by global economic changes,
changing patterns in education and earnings, and ruthless corporate
downsizing, it owes more to divorce than is commonly acknowledged.
Indeed, recent data suggest that marriage may be a more important
economic resource than a college degree. According to an analysis of
1994 income patterns, the median income of married-parent households whose heads have only a high school diploma is ten percent
higher than the median income of college-educated single-parent
households.[1] Parents who are college graduates *and* married form the
new economic elite among families with children. Consequently, those
who are concerned about what the downsizing of corporations is doing to workers should also be concerned about what the downsizing of
families through divorce is doing to parents and children.

Widespread divorce depletes social capital as well. Scholars tell us
that strong and durable family and social bonds generate certain
"goods" and services, including money, mutual assistance, information, caregiving, protection, and sponsorship. Because such bonds endure over time, they accumulate and form a pool of social capital
which can be drawn down upon, when needed, over the entire course
of a life. An elderly couple, married for fifty years, is likely to enjoy a
substantial body of social and emotional capital, generated through
their long-lasting marriage, which they can draw upon in caring for
each other and for themselves as they age. Similarly, children who
grow up in stable, two-parent married households are the beneficiaries
of the social and emotional capital accumulated over time as a result of
an enduring marriage bond. As many parents know, children continue
to depend on these resources well into young adulthood. But as family
bonds become increasingly fragile and vulnerable to disruption, they
become less permanent and thus less capable of generating such forms
of help, financial resources, and mutual support. In short, divorce con-

sumes social capital and weakens the social fabric. At the very time that sweeping socioeconomic changes are mandating greater investment of social capital in children, widespread divorce is reducing the pool of social capital. As the new economic and social conditions raise the hurdles of child-rearing higher, divorce digs potholes in the tracks.

It should be stressed that this book is not intended as a brief against divorce as such. We must assume that divorce is necessary as a remedy for irretrievably broken marriages, especially those that are marred by severe abuse such as chronic infidelity, drug addiction, or physical violence. Nor is its argument directed against those who are divorced. It assumes that divorce is difficult, painful, and often unwanted by at least one spouse, and that divorcing couples require compassion and support from family, friends, and their religious communities. Nor should this book be taken as an appeal for a return to an earlier era of American family life. The media routinely portray the debate over the family as one between nostalgists and realists, between those who want to turn back the clock to the fifties and those who want to march bravely and resolutely forward into the new century. But this is a lazy and misguided approach, driven more by the easy availability of archival photos and footage from 1950s television sitcoms than by careful consideration of the substance of competing arguments.

More fundamentally, this approach overlooks the key issue. And that issue is not how today's families might stack up against those of an earlier era; indeed, no reliable empirical data for such a comparison exist. In an age of diverse family structures, the heart of the matter is what kinds of contemporary family arrangements have the greatest capacity to promote children's well-being, and how we can ensure that more children have the advantages of growing up in such families.

In the past year or so, there has been growing recognition of the personal and social costs of three decades of widespread divorce. A public debate has finally emerged. Within this debate, there are two separate and overlapping discussions.

The first centers on a set of specific proposals that are intended to lessen the harmful impact of divorce on children: a federal system of child-support collection, tougher child-support enforcement, mandatory counseling for divorcing parents, and reform of no-fault divorce laws in the states. What is striking about this discussion is its narrow focus on public policy, particularly on changes in the system of no-fault divorce. In this, as in so many other crucial discussions involving social and moral questions, the most vocal and visible participants come from the world of government policy, electoral politics, and issue advocacy. The media, which are tongue-tied unless they can speak in the language of left-right politics, reinforce this situation. And the public is offered needlessly polarized arguments that hang on a flat yes-or-no response to this or that individual policy measure. All too often, this discussion of divorce poses what *Washington Post* columnist E. J. Dionne aptly describes as false choices.

Notably missing is a serious consideration of the broader moral assumptions and empirical claims that define our divorce culture. Divorce touches on classic questions in American public philosophy—on the nature of our most important human and social bonds, the duties and obligations imposed by bonds we voluntarily elect, the "just causes" for the dissolution of those bonds, and the differences between obligations volunteered and those that must be coerced. Without consideration of such questions, the effort to change behavior by changing a few public policies is likely to founder.

The second and complementary discussion does try to place divorce within a larger philosophical framework. Its proponents have looked at the decline in the well-being of the nation's children as the occasion to call for a collective sense of commitment by all Americans to all of America's children. They pose the challenging question: "What are Americans willing to do 'for the sake of *all* children'?" But while this is surely an important question, it addresses only half of the problem of declining commitment. The other half has to do with how we answer the question: "What are individual parents obliged to do 'for the sake of their own children'?"

Renewing a *social* ethic of commitment to children is an urgent goal, but it cannot be detached from the goal of strengthening the *individual* ethic of commitment to children. The state of one affects the standing of the other. A society that protects the rights of parents to easy, unilateral divorce, and flatly rejects the idea that parents should strive to preserve a marriage "for the sake of the children," faces a problem when it comes to the question of public sacrifice "for the sake of the children." To put it plainly, many of the ideas we have come to believe and vigorously defend about adult prerogatives and freedoms in family life are undermining the foundations of altruism and support for children.

With each passing year, the culture of divorce becomes more deeply entrenched. American children are routinely schooled in divorce. Mr. Rogers teaches toddlers about divorce. An entire children's literature is devoted to divorce. Family movies and videos for children feature divorced families. *Mrs. Doubtfire*, originally a children's book about divorce and then a hit movie, is aggressively marketed as a holiday video for kids. Of course, these books and movies are designed to help children deal with the social reality and psychological trauma of divorce. But they also carry an unmistakable message about the impermanence and unreliability of family bonds. Like romantic love, the children's storybooks say, family love comes and goes. Daddies disappear. Mommies find new boyfriends. Mommies' boyfriends leave. Grandparents go away. Even pets must be left behind.

More significantly, in a society where nearly half of all children are likely to experience parental divorce, family breakup becomes a defining event of American childhood itself. Many children today know nothing but divorce in their family lives. And although children from divorced families often say they want to avoid divorce if they marry, young adults whose parents divorced are more likely to get divorced themselves and to bear children outside of marriage than young adults from stable married-parent families.

Precisely because the culture of divorce has generational momentum, this book offers no easy optimism about the prospects for change. But neither does it counsel passive resignation or acceptance of the culture's relentless advance. What it does offer is a critique of the ideas behind current divorce trends. Its argument is directed against the ideas about divorce that have gained ascendancy, won our support, and lodged in our consciousness as "proven" and incontrovertible. It challenges the popular idea of divorce as an individual right and freedom to be exercised in the pursuit of individual goods and satisfactions, without due regard for other stakeholders in the marital partnership, especially children. This may be a fragile and inadequate response to a profoundly consequential set of changes, but it seeks the abandonment of ideas that have misled us and failed our children.

In a larger sense, this book is both an appreciation and a criticism of what is peculiarly American about divorce. Divorce has spread throughout advanced Western societies at roughly the same pace and over roughly the same period of time. Yet nowhere else has divorce been so deeply imbued with the larger themes of a nation's political traditions. Nowhere has divorce so fully reflected the spirit and suscep-tibilities of a people who share an extravagant faith in the power of the individual and in the power of positive thinking. Divorce in America is not unique, but what we have made of divorce is uniquely American. In exploring the cultural roots of divorce, therefore, we look at our-selves, at what is best and worst in our traditions, what is visionary and what is blind, and how the two are sometimes tragically commingled and confused.

CHAPTER ONE

The Problem of Divorce

IN THE AMERICAN EXPERIENCE divorce has posed a classic problem: how to expand individual freedoms without encouraging individual license. From the nation's beginnings until recent decades this problem shaped thinking about divorce. The challenge for a democratic people was to uphold the freedom to divorce without inspiring promiscuous divorce.

Compared with other Western societies, Americans have a strong tradition of divorce. To some degree, that tradition was shaped by the experience of political rebellion. New England colonists saw the highly restrictive and cumbersome procedures of English divorce law and practice as a sign of the Crown's illegitimate authority, which they sought to defy by liberalizing colonial divorce practices. This tradition also had roots in religious dissent. Puritan dissenters took issue with the conservatism of the Church of England in retaining Roman Catholic doctrines respecting divorce. Not surprisingly, the Puritan strongholds of Massachusetts and Connecticut had the most liberal provisions for divorce as well as the most divorces in the seventeenth century.[1]

In general, the early liberalizing of English legal traditions focused on two areas. For one, colonists treated marital dissolution as a civil rather than a church matter, shifting authority over divorce from the ecclesiastical courts to legislative or judicial bodies. For another, New England colonists broadened the grounds for divorce beyond those permitted in England. In Massachusetts, between 1692 and 1786, 110 divorces were granted on grounds not permitted by English ecclesiastical courts at a time when the colony's population never exceeded 250,000.[2]

Divorce in America was never linked to aristocratic status, as it was in European societies. In England, divorce was so difficult and expensive that it was possible only for the highborn and well-connected. By contrast, in America it was available to the middle and lower classes. Between 1785 and 1815, for example, 38 percent of divorce petitioners in Pennsylvania came from the middling ranks of society, while 17 percent reported even humbler backgrounds.[3] This democratic pattern prevailed in other states as well. Indeed, early American divorce records conjure a picture of a democratic yeomanry—barbers, carters, farmers, and cordwainers—enjoying a privilege available in the Old World only to a handful of aristocrats. And, in another sharp contrast with English tradition, this picture of early American divorce includes women. American women were awarded divorces more than a century before their British counterparts.[4]

American political ideology also contributed to a more liberal disposition toward both marriage and divorce. A philosophical preoccupation with the terms of union and disunion was central to republican thinking on both family and political relationships. Indeed, as Jay Fliegelman points out in his study of American revolutionary ideology, the two were closely intertwined. During the pre-Revolutionary period the political press showed an extraordinary concern with the nature of marriage. Robert Aitken's *Pennsylvania Magazine* and Isaiah Thomas's *Royal American Magazine*, the only two American magazines published in the years 1774 and 1775, were filled with discussions of the subject. Fliegelman observes that "the theme of domestic tyranny of all sorts preoccupied the American mind on the eve of Revolution. As the British government sought to prevent colonists not only from becoming independent but also from entering into a voluntary and inviolate union among themselves, British tyranny was, in its own way, nothing less than interference 'in the great article of marriage.' "[5]

The editor of, and a major contributor to, the *Pennsylvania Magazine* was Thomas Paine, who had himself left an unhappy marriage in England. Paine devoted many pages of the magazine to a consideration of the right reasons for entering a marriage. In "Reflections on Unhappy Marriages," published in 1775, he argues against marriages based on either unruly physical passion or cold calculations of greed or advantage. "Matches of this kind are downright prostitution," he writes.[6] Such corrupt alliances belonged to an Old World tradition of forced, arranged, or clandestine marriages. Republican marriage, on the other hand, was a union of the heart, created through the pledges of mutual affection and the voluntary commitment of one to another, a relationship freely chosen and independent of the interests or claims of others.

This ideal of voluntarism, with its elements of choice and mutual affection, lay at the heart of republican thinking on both marital and political unions. Freedom did not mean abandoning social or political bonds altogether but, rather, gaining the freedom to choose one's bonds. As Fliegelman acutely observes, "psychologically it was vital for the colonists to believe that they were fighting not the cause of a licentious freedom but of a glorious voluntarism."[7]

Republican notions of "glorious voluntarism" in both marital and political relationships also contained the argument for dissolution of such bonds. "Bands" of love and friendship could be broken when the heart turned cold or tyrannical. Thus, the ideal of affectionate marriage introduced an element of conditionality into relationships: True marriage lasts only as long as mutual affection endures; once the affections sour, then the union is broken, and, as Paine writes, "we instantly dissolve the band."[8]

Five years after the Revolutionary War a pamphlet entitled *An Essay on Marriage, or the Lawfulness of Divorce* argued that the freedom to divorce was an expression of republican liberty. Announcing itself as the first pamphlet on the subject to appear in the new Republic, it describes the suicide of a wife "on account of some infelicity in marriage." The pamphleteer, reflecting on the "misery of marriage in those who are unsuitably united," invokes the spirit and lessons of republicanism: In America, a nation "famous for her love of liberty," should not "that same spirit of indulgence" extend to "those united together in the worst bondage?"[9]

The founding of the nation brought about a burst of divorce, one clear sign that these political ideas influenced private as well as public behavior. According to historian Nancy Cott, the number of women filing for divorce in Massachusetts between 1775 and 1786 was nearly double the number in the preceding decade, a development that suggested a new personal outlook emphasizing initiative and independence.[10] Though marked regional differences in divorcing remained, with the South more cautious and restrictive than the North, the overall trend in the early years of the Republic was toward liberalizing divorce provisions.[11] Important too, the association of divorce with women's freedoms and prerogatives, established in those early days, remained an enduring and important feature of American divorce.

Despite a more liberal outlook, however, Americans worried about divorce and feared its spread. In the republican tradition, notions of virtuous behavior encompassed private as well as public life. John Adams was expressing common opinion when he observed that "the foundation of national morality must be laid in private families."[12] As the central institution of family life, marriage served as a bellwether of virtuous conduct and the model of social union. On the eve of the American Revolution an article in the *Royal American Magazine* drew the connection between virtuous marriage and a virtuous people: "[I]n proportion to the increase in learning, politeness and virtue, in every nation the importance of matrimony to the public welfare has appeared; and without this virtuous union, there cannot be prosperity and happiness in a community or among individuals."[13]

Moreover, precisely because marriages in the new republic were based on mutual affection and individual choice, they were likely to be more virtuous than Old World marital arrangements. It is in the very voluntariness of union that Paine locates the source of lasting commitment and permanence: "[W]e make it our business to oblige the heart we are afraid to lose." Because spouses are at liberty to choose each other, they are rarely inclined to exercise "the liberty to separate."[14] Thus, while the freedom to disband was implicit in the freedom to choose, marriages bound by affection were less likely to dissolve.

For this reason, marital dissolution, whether caused by desertion or divorce, provoked anxiety and concern, suggesting a worrisome lapse from virtue as well as a falling-out between spouses. Even when divorce was rare, it aroused fears of contagion and rapid spread. If the freedom to divorce ran unchecked, it might undermine the very ideal of virtuous marriage and introduce the corruptions of the Old World into the new Republic.

The association of divorce with both freedom and license persisted throughout most of the nation's history. Until very recently, each rise in the levels of divorce revived fears about moral decadence and social disorder. At the end of the nineteenth century, for example, when the daughters of rich American industrialists began to marry fortune-hunting European dukes, counts, and barons, the popular press breathlessly reported on their fabulous weddings. Later, when the marriages fell apart, the press returned to tell the tale of the equally fabulous divorces between "American dollar princesses" and their adulterous "dollarless princes."[15] Like today's tabloids, the popular press got to have it both ways: It reveled in the romance of these storybook weddings and then turned with equal relish to the squalid details of the divorce. But the association of divorce with Old World licentiousness touched on deeper strains in American thinking as well: The aristocratic observance of the mere form of marriage without any true affection offended republican notions of matrimonial virtue and right conduct.

Americans also identified divorce with the homegrown corruptions of the marketplace. The commercial exploitation of divorce began in the mid-nineteenth century with the founding of divorce colonies in western states. Divorce colonies followed the frontier, moving from Indiana in the 1860s and 1870s to Illinois in the 1880s to the Dakotas in the 1890s and on to Wyoming, Nebraska, and especially Nevada. As western legislators and entrepreneurs discovered, short residency requirements could attract divorce-seekers from states that required a year's residency or more before granting divorce. The transcontinental railroad proved a boon to the divorce colonies, attracting divorce-seekers from the East.[16] With legal residency periods lowered to as little as ninety days, remote states like Nevada and South Dakota could attract Easterners for short stays and quickie divorces.[17] In the meantime, while waiting out the residency period, divorce petitioners could amuse themselves by spending their dollars in western hotels, bars, shops, and restaurants.

At the end of the century the *Nation* magazine condemned the divorce trade in South Dakota as a disturbing sign of the invasion of the money world into the domestic sphere. Rapacious capitalism had barged into the marriage bower. "[M]any cases of flaunting shame are recorded," the magazine observed, with "rich profligates consorting openly with the women whom they are to marry as soon as the decree of the court makes them free to do so, scattering money with lavish hand in the shops of jewellers and florists, and even endowing local charities, enriching hotel proprietors and unscrupulous lawyers."[18]

For Americans, therefore, divorce was problematic not only because it offended conventional morality but also because it excited republican fears of corruption and license. Even modest levels of divorce aroused fears of a spread of promiscuous behavior, and conjured up images of aristocratic decadence. Moreover, the commerce in divorce suggested a worrisome intrusion of marketplace values into the realm of family relationships.

Democratizing Divorce

Two important new features characterized American divorce in the twentieth century. One was that divorce became a mass phenomenon. The second was that secular opinion replaced religious thinking as the source of expertise on marriage and divorce.

Among advanced Western societies, the twentieth century is the great century of divorce. Earlier, the barriers to divorce were high and it remained relatively rare. But during the present century, despite sporadic efforts to maintain the restrictions upon it, the social, economic, and legal barriers came down. Divorce became both more affordable and more thinkable for people in the middle and lower ranks of society. As a result, after World War I it became a mass phenomenon and an "integral part of the social and demographic system in Western societies."[19] Even so, during the first two-thirds of the century, the progress of divorce was uneven. The divorce rate slowed during the Great Depression, increased sharply after World War II, and then slowed again for the next two decades. It was not until the last third of the century that divorce truly gained momentum and spread rapidly throughout the Western world.

For most of the century American attitudes toward divorce took two contrasting yet complementary forms. The first was to decry its spread and deplore it as a menace to social stability. Each surge in the divorce rate prompted new expressions of concern about this growing social problem. At the turn of the century, when the rate stood at a mere three divorces per thousand marriages, many of the nation's clergy joined scholars in the infant social sciences to condemn the rising tide. Presenting the latest numbers on divorce, one Indiana statistician referred to his table of figures as "the repulsive exhibit."[20] Similar reactions occurred following each of the two World Wars. Some critics compared divorce to a natural disaster, while others used epidemiological metaphors—cancer or infectious disease—to denote what they feared was its rapid spread through society.

Public concerns were deepest when it came to divorces involving dependent children. In fact, even the most ardent defenders of divorce consistently pointed to its harmful impact on children. During most of the twentieth century, both popular and social-scientific opinion emphasized the hardships of growing up in a broken home, including low income, delinquency, poor relationships with a father, and emotional adjustment problems. During a polio epidemic one social-work professor argued that divorce posed a greater threat to children than this dread infectious disease: "Imagine 300,000 children stricken in one year by infantile paralysis. Yet the chances of these children in divorce being crippled emotionally are far greater than the chance for physical crippling by poliomyelitis."[21] The view of divorce as a source of disadvantage to children persisted until the mid-1960s.

The second response was to adopt a more liberal and "scientific" approach to the issue of divorce, and to formulate a rationale for its acceptance as a legitimate part of modern social life. The body of thought which established this perspective emerged in such diverse and disparate fields as literature, etiquette, and the new disciplines of the social sciences. It sought to recognize divorce as a social fact, to integrate it into modern marriage, and to establish its importance as a "safety valve" protecting marriage itself. Early in the century, the advice writer Dorothy Dix noted that contemporary Americans "see that no good purpose is achieved by keeping people together who have come to hate each other."[22] If too many cold and loveless marriages were forcibly preserved, then the entire cultural ideal of affectionate marriage would be weakened and compromised. Better for the presumably few such bankrupt marriages to dissolve than for the credibility of the institution itself to be damaged. Secular opinion also attempted to regularize divorce by admitting it into the social world. With more Americans divorcing, it no longer made practical sense to ignore or ostracize divorced people.

Yet this emerging body of secular opinion also reflected the classic tension in the American response to divorce. Although these experts sought greater social acceptance of divorce, they also tried to keep it in check through a set of largely informal and increasingly mild social sanctions and controls. If divorce no longer should be viewed as a disgrace, it was nothing to cheer about either—especially when it came to the welfare of children. In a society that provided easy routes to divorce, expert opinion seemed to argue, some measure of social disapprobation was required in order to slow the rush to the exits.

Vulgar Divorce

The first decades of the twentieth century brought a rise in the divorce rate. Between 1910 and 1920 divorce increased from 4.5 to 7.7 per 1,000 marriages, with the steepest rise occurring in 1919–1920, immediately after the First World War. Wartime brought sudden disruptions of marriages and families. With greater mobility and anonymity caused by war, the traditional social and familial constraints on men and women weakened, and rates of illegitimacy, desertion, and divorce typically rose during war and its immediate aftermath.

After World War I, divorce became more common—"vulgar," in the original sense of the word. According to historian Roderick Phillips, the flood of divorces after the war "increased the exposure of ordinary people to divorce on a scale unthinkable ten years earlier."[23] The proportion of divorced men and women among those married in the 1920s was twice that among those married before the war, and middle-class Americans were more likely to know someone who had been divorced than in the past.

Although World War I had the most immediate and direct impact on the divorce rate, broader social and economic forces figured in the steady vulgarization of divorce. The early twentieth century and especially the years after the First World War saw the rapid expansion of a consumer economy. As a mass market for consumer goods developed, expectations rose concerning the material standard of living. Within the household economy, wives and mothers gained new authority and power as domestic purchasing agents. Their tastes and preferences became a matter of intense interest and concern to marketers. They were courted by advertisers, wooed by merchants, fussed over by purveyors of personal services. The consumer economy paid special attention to women's physical appearance, exploiting feminine vanities as well as creating new anxieties about hair, makeup, and costume.

The rising material aspirations of middle-class wives and their growing sovereignty in the realm of domestic consumption prompted new ideas of what constituted basic needs. Commercial advertising convinced middle-class Americans that what had been luxuries to their grandparents were now essentials of life. These essentials included consumption itself. In a successful 1920 divorce petition between an insurance salesman and his wife, the wife was awarded three dollars a month for her "personal recreation," one sign that courts recognized consumption and amusement as necessities of life for modern women.[24]

The redefinition of wants as needs influenced expectations about acceptable levels of support. As historian Elaine Tyler May points out, popular definitions of the words "support" and "provider" changed in the early decades of the twentieth century even as the cultural consensus that husbands must be good providers remained in force.

May's study of divorce petitions in California and New Jersey in the early decades of the century shows the growing prevalence of issues concerning money. "By 1920," she writes, "it was no longer clear precisely what constituted adequate support on the part of a husband, and a number of bitter conflicts erupted over the issue."[25] Similarly, in the Indiana community famously known as Middletown researchers noted that money issues were becoming central in divorce petitions. Between 1890 and 1929 two-thirds of divorces were granted on the grounds of nonsupport. "Talks with the women interviewed would seem to indicate that economic considerations figure possibly more drastically than formerly as factors in divorce. This does not mean that a husband has failed to provide food and shelter for his wife, but it does indicate that in some way their economic adjustment has broken down. . . ."[26]

The growing importance of money issues in divorce suggested a strong relationship between a wife's economic expectations and her marital satisfaction, especially in periods of prosperity when expectations were rising.[27] Failure to meet these expectations could sour a marriage. Thus, husbands came under greater pressure to provide not only the necessities of life but also the outward signs of financial and social success. Although the pattern of economic restlessness and discontent was pervasive across socioeconomic groups, the pressure may have been especially severe among urban wage earners at middle to lower levels, where the struggle to earn was intensified by aroused appetites to buy and consume.

According to May, even working-class husbands were subject to rising concerns about status. One New Jersey working-class wife left her husband, a railroad brakeman, after she became dissatisfied with the family's standard of living. Her husband won a divorce on the grounds of desertion, testifying that his unhappy wife "insisted upon telling me how much more the neighbors had than she had, and what the neighbor's husband did, and what they didn't do."[28] Complaints of economic neglect sometimes linked a husband's shortcomings as a provider to his abject failure as a man. One blue-collar wife's divorce petition argued: "You have had ample time to *make a man of yourself* in all these six years, if you cared for your wife and baby, instead of driving a wagon for twelve dollars a week. You would not take work offered you at twenty-one dollars a week, so it is not because you could not find better."[29]

Marital disputes over money often centered on management and control of the paycheck. Although the husband's duty was to provide, many wives expected to share decision-making control over how the paycheck was spent. Indeed, a husband's status as a good provider involved not only the size of his paycheck but his willingness to turn the money over to his wife. Working-class wives defined a "good provider" by the criterion of faithfulness to this duty, an attitude that persisted well into the present century. One housewife in the 1950s said proudly: "I have the final say-so on our money. My husband just signs his checks and gives them to me."[30]

Of course, discord over money often masked underlying issues of power in many marriages. Control over money and spending was one way for wives to exert influence at a time when women had limited opportunities to express themselves outside of the domestic sphere. For their part, husbands might thwart their wives' desire for greater authority by claiming full and exclusive control over the family's income, an approach that some women accepted, others quietly resented, and still others angrily and openly resisted.

The small but growing number of employed wives also threatened traditional husbandly prerogatives and authority. A paycheck meant women could more readily leave a bad marriage. As one divorced man plaintively observed, "Why should a woman stay married if she don't like a man and can get a job? Why, there's so many working it's getting so a man can't get a woman to fry him a piece of meat or bake a pie!"[31]

Criticizing Vulgar Divorce

Although divorce was spreading among the middle and lower classes during the early twentieth century, it remained culturally identified with the vulgar excesses and display of the monied class, especially the newly and boisterously rich. The contemporary critique of divorce combined two classic themes: the invasion of middle-class family life by marketplace values, and the association of wealth with immorality. One of the leading critics of divorce, Episcopal Bishop William Hare, was shocked by the commerce in marriage partners among the wealthy faithful. Attending a dinner in his honor in South Dakota, he discovered that the host had a brand-new wife and that the dinner guests included the host's first wife and her new husband.[32] Apparently, the rich dealt in spouses as brashly as they traded in stocks and bonds.

The clergy were not the only critics of vulgar divorce, however. For progressive secular thinkers, vulgar divorce was a problem because it posed the threat of corrupting the virtuous middle class with capitalist values. In an article thick with sarcasm, the *Nation* condemned the rich whose lusts and ambitions wrecked marriages and mocked middle-class habits of marital fidelity. The middle class does not aspire to more than one living wife at a time, the magazine scornfully declared, nor can men of "bread-and-butter disposition" afford more than one wife. Middle-class husbands and wives go about family life "in their unimaginative way, [making] the best even of a matrimonial bad bargain and contentedly pursu[ing] the plodding task of domestic compromise and adjustment."

Perhaps the wealthy will find a way to sell divorce to the laboring classes, the magazine goes on; "the business might be a profitable side venture for building and loan associations and bond or indemnity companies. One could imagine a combination life, endowment, accident, sickness, homestead, burial and divorce policy that might . . . extend the blessings of experimental marriage to the very proletariat."[33]

Other critiques of divorce drew the same connection between divorce and commercial transactions. In a 1921 *Good Housekeeping* article one expert quipped: "The modern age runs much on the instalment [*sic*] plan, and we are applying the same plan to matrimony . . . if present tendencies continue much further a divorce coupon for the convenience of the couple will be attached to each marriage license."[34]

"Cheques, Nothing but Cheques"

Early in the century there was no shrewder chronicler and critic of vulgar divorce than Edith Wharton. Her 1913 novel *The Custom of the Country* offers a devastating portrait of divorce as a vehicle of social ambition and economic mobility. Its heroine, Undine Spragg, is an arriviste from the Midwest who pursues her interests in New York society by divorcing up, climbing the economic ladder with each new divorce. Undine's morality is Wall Street morality. Under her ruthless application of its laws, divorce becomes the domestic equivalent of acquisitive capitalism, motivated by the same principles of power, self-interest, and competitive advantage.

In Wharton's fictional world, marriage is no longer safeguarded by custom, morality, or tradition. Indeed, her novels challenge the very notion of a private domestic sphere, separate from and morally superior to the sphere of the marketplace. Like commercial transactions, marriage exists to be exploited for personal gain and advantage. As a member of Undine's social set drawls: "Marriage has its uses. One couldn't be divorced without it."

In a 1922 novel, *The Glimpses of the Moon*, Wharton describes a marriage contracted for the most unsentimental of reasons: mutual advantage. The clever and penniless heroine, Susy Branch, proposes a deal to her equally threadbare lover, Nick Lansing. "Why shouldn't they marry: belong to each other openly and honourably, if for ever so short a time, with the definite understanding that whenever either of them got the chance to do better he or she should be immediately released?"

Nick has never thought of marriage as a way to improve his personal fortunes, and he finds Susy's proposal as "mad as it was enchanting." Nonetheless, her "arguments were irrefutable, her ingenuities inexhaustible." At first, of course, Nick believed she had in mind "all the wedding presents. Jewels, and a motor, and a silver dinner service"—wasn't that what she meant? "Not a bit of it! She could see he'd never given the question proper thought. 'Cheques, my dear, nothing but cheques. . . .' "

In *The Glimpses of the Moon*, marriage and business contracts are identical in purpose. Both seek to maximize individual interest, and both require a brisk, loss-cutting approach to a change in personal fortunes. Another jaded and oft-divorced entrepreneur later tells Susy: "A man can get out of a business partnership when he wants to . . . why not get out of marriage the same way?"

Edith Wharton's own unhappy marriage ended the year she published her novel of divorce, *The Custom of the Country*. As Cynthia Griffin Wolff notes in her biography of Wharton, the failure of the writer's marriage was a defining experience: "[I]t is probable that nothing else she ever did—save perhaps the momentous commitment to her career as a writer—affected her with such deep and painfully contradictory feelings."[35] Wharton's divorce raised again, in Wolff's words, the "haunting problems" associated with an ethic of feminine "niceness" and passivity: ". . . the particular problem that was increasingly thrust to the top of her mind was that of initiative. As a woman—a successful, ambitious woman—did she have the right to a self-determined, autonomous, even competitive life?"[36]

By the 1920s other American women were asking that question, and their struggle to assert their opinions, choices, and desires in the public sphere was beginning to bear fruit. In addition to winning the right to vote, women were moving into higher education, the professions, and leadership roles in social and reform movements.[37] As women gained greater opportunities to engage the world outside the home, they also continued to take steps toward greater independence in the domestic sphere. For centuries, Roderick Phillips observes, men had expectations of marriage and their wives that were higher than their wives' expectations of marriage and their husbands. Too, men had long expressed their dissatisfaction with marriage by acts of violence, adultery, or desertion, while women were far less likely to resort to such expressions of discontent when their marriages broke down.[38] However, as women's opportunities for greater independence in their economic and political lives grew, so too did their expectations for greater freedom both in marriage and in the dissolution of marriage. During the century, therefore, divorce became an increasingly important measure of women's political freedom as well as an expression of feminine initiative and independence.

For Wharton herself, the problem of initiative was successfully resolved in her professional life as a writer. According to Wolff, she was able to resist the social imperative of feminine passivity and "niceness" by achieving recognition as a distinguished novelist and tough literary professional, capable of making money and managing her literary affairs. As a writer she also asserted her prerogatives by taking up themes "that required her to enter the forbidden areas where questions of initiative and competition had their origins."[39] Divorce was such a theme.

In Undine Spragg, Wharton created a woman defined by energy and initiative. Voracity and drive are Undine's distinguishing features. Like the tornadoes that sweep across her home state of Nebraska, she propels herself into New York society with blind energy and force. Undine is free of the social constraints imposed by the society she invades. She resembles a foreigner with a phrase book; her task is to acquire enough knowledge about the language and customs of the country to get what she wants. Driven by opportunism, she picks up "an intonation here, a vocabulary there, a set of moral sensibilities of one sort, a set of aesthetic norms of another."[40]

In her pursuit of great fortune Undine's ambitions are fulfilled, her initiative is rewarded. Unlike Lily Bart, the heroine of Wharton's earlier novel *The House of Mirth*, who kills herself when her marital schemes fail, Undine is brilliantly successful in her maneuverings. At the end of the novel she has married up and divorced up until she has reached the "top of her game." After a whirlwind Reno divorce and marriage she has captured her richest-ever husband: Elmer Moffatt, a midwesterner of obscure background whose energies and entrepreneurialism propel him to financial heights unattainable by proper old New Yorkers. Moffatt is her doppelgänger, and she marries him twice.

Undine's second marriage to Moffatt—her most successful divorce gambit—enlarges her. To her eight-year-old son, Paul, who visits the newlyweds in their opulent Paris apartment, his mother appears physically taller and more handsome than ever. But unlike for her spouse, Moffatt, whose popping shirtfronts suggest contentment, even satiety, Undine's size and physicality do not reflect an inner sense of satisfaction. Even as she is engrossed and aggrandized through her marital conquests, she is tormented by old hungers. Even when she appears outwardly to have fully satisfied her cravings for wealth and distinction, her appetites remain curiously unappeased.

It is not Undine's protean energy, the force of her ambition, that draws Wharton's criticism; it is the conventions of a social world that require ambitious women to express their drive and initiative in the domestic sphere. Like her husband, Moffatt, Undine has a talent for buying and selling; denied that outlet, she ends up marrying and divorcing. According to Wolff, Undine and other ambitious Wharton heroines "reflect the perversions" of a world where everything is for sale. "What they market is simply themselves. Marriage and divorce are no more than their means of bartering."[41] In these transactions women become battle-hardened. The shrewd ones, who know the custom of the country and play by its rules, "act with inhuman indifference to the feelings of others."[42]

For this reason, Wolff explains, almost all of Wharton's men seem more appealing to us than the women; as psychological entities the men are more coherently developed because they inhabit and operate in a world where their choices are ordered and their ambitions and energies chastened and disciplined by the conditions and order of the business and public world. By contrast, Undine (and other self-seeking divorcées like Undine's childhood friend Indiana Frusk) have the drive, the energy, the ambition, the imagination of entrepreneurs, but not the concrete testing and harnessing that go on in the marketplace.[43]

However, the most calamitous consequence of Undine's misdirected ambition lies in her inability to mother her son, Paul. The plight of children enmeshed in their parents' vulgar divorces is a recurring theme in Wharton's fiction. Like her contemporary Henry James, who earlier dealt with the same problem in his novel *What Maisie Knew*, she presents a devastating portrait of children whose rich parents discard them as easily as they leave lovers and abandon marriages. In her 1928 novel *The Children* Wharton describes the peripatetic lives of the negligent rich whose "marriages are just like tents—folded up and thrown away when you've done with them," and whose children, unschooled, unmannered, and unloved, bounce around from watering spot to watering spot, awaiting the next exchange of spouses as their parents watch for the next dip in the Dow.

But it is more than carelessness toward children that Wharton criticizes in *The Custom of the Country*. Here she introduces her second criticism of vulgar divorce: its damaging impact on the mother-child bond. Undine is a terrible mother because she has lost her capacity for feeling, and therefore access to maternal tenderness. From the moment of her son's birth she is incapable of loving him. He is an annoying and distracting presence; his nursery is moved because his scamperings disturb her sleep. She cannot bear to carry him because his weight pulls her skirts into the mud. She forgets his first birthday. Away from her child for months, she writes occasionally but never makes a single suggestion for his care. To other adults Paul appears quite delightful, and throughout the novel he wins the scattered attention and sporadic affections of assorted relatives and stepfathers. Yet to his mother Paul is a drag.

In the final chapter of *The Custom of the Country*, Wharton resumes her commentary on the divorced mother–child relationship, but this time from the child's perspective. A boarding school student, Paul arrives at his mother's newly purchased and lavishly appointed Paris apartment to spend the Easter holidays, only to discover that his mother and her new husband, Moffatt, are out, looking at a house they may rent for the summer. Paul is disappointed but not surprised by the news: Undine and Moffatt "were always coming and going; during the two years since their marriage they had been perpetually dashing over to New York and back, or rushing down to Rome or up to the Engadine: Paul never knew where they were except when a telegram announced they were going somewhere else."

After a "solitary luncheon served in the immense marble dining room," Paul wanders around, from his room, "in which there was not a toy or a book, or one of his dear battered relics," to the library, where rare books are locked behind gilt trellised doors, to the dining room, where servants are making early preparations for a dinner party. In this household of strangers he finally finds a familiar face: Mrs. Heeny, his mother's longtime masseuse. The old retainer carries in her vast bag the gossip columns of New York newspapers, including clippings describing Undine's Reno divorce and marriage to Moffatt. "Paul . . . had the feeling that Mrs. Heeny's clippings . . . might furnish him the clue to many things he didn't understand and that nobody had ever had time to explain to him. His mother's marriages, for instance: he was sure there was a great deal to find out about them." Mrs. Heeny unearths a clipping from a gossip column with the following headline: DIVORCE AND REMARRIAGE OF MRS. UNDINE SPRAGG-DE CHELLES. AMERICAN MARQUISE RENOUNCES ANCIENT FRENCH TITLE TO WED RAILROAD KING. QUICK WORK UNTYING AND TYING. BOY AND GIRL ROMANCE RENEWED.

What captures Paul's eye is the description of his mother's testimony: "[A]t the trial Mrs. Spragg-de Chelles, who wore copper velvet and sables, gave evidence as to the brutality of her French husband, but she had to talk fast as the time pressed. . . ."

Wharton is having great fun satirizing the Reno divorce, where the high-speed divorce-trial-and-marriage-ceremony of the railroad king and his new queen was accomplished in less than an hour. But this scene offers no comic relief, because Paul has received a cruel blow. He learns for the first time that his mother has accused his French stepfather, the only father he has ever known and loved, of cruelty. "In the dazzling description of his mother's latest nuptials one fact alone stood out for him—that she had said things that weren't true of his French father. . . . She had got up and said before a lot of people things that were awfully false about his dear French father. . . ."

At that very moment Undine and Moffatt return. As Paul looks down upon the couple from a staircase, he sees the great heirloom

tapestries that once covered the walls of his French stepfather's ances-
tral home, and that through deception and huge sums of money his
mother and Moffatt have contrived to carry off for their own apartment. To Paul, the tapestries symbolize his mother's betrayal.

Catching sight of her son, Undine theatrically embraces the boy
and then dashes off to get ready for her party, leaving Paul with his
newest stepfather. With bluff good nature, Moffatt observes that he has
gotten a good deal on the tapestries. "Paul flushed up, and again the
iron grasp was on his heart. He hadn't hitherto disliked Mr. Moffatt,
who was always in a good humour, and seemed less busy and absent-
minded than his mother; but at that instant he felt a rage of hate for
him. He turned away and burst into tears."

This final scene—the first and only time that we see Undine from
Paul's vantage point—offers the novel's harshest view of the heroine.
Paul realizes that his mother has sold him out; she has deliberately sac-
rificed his interests on the altar of her ambition. Her failures as a
mother are not, as Moffatt consolingly tells him, a consequence of her
busyness but, as Paul now understands, the essence of her business—
the trading of affections for material and social advantage, a commerce
in which a small son's feelings figure scarcely at all.

In her portrait of Undine as a mother Wharton underscores the
second theme in her critique of vulgar divorce: The relentless pursuit
of divorce makes women hard and unfeminine, destroying motherly
feelings and wrecking the maternal bond itself. In a larger sense, Wharton seems to suggest, motherhood and divorce are incompatible,
creating irreconcilable tensions between initiative and nurture, an independent self and dependent children, between the obligations of the
home and the ambitions of the marketplace.

Regulating Divorce

Because divorce was so rare before the twentieth century, it was largely
ignored as an event affecting social relationships and conduct. But as it
became more common, this view changed. The arbiters of polite conduct could no longer maintain a rigid silence on divorce or ignore the
growing presence of divorced people in everyday life. A democratic society must find ways to accommodate divorce. At the same time the

conduct experts could not go overboard in their acceptance of it; too enthusiastic an embrace might weaken the institution of marriage and encourage frivolous divorce. If, then, divorce was to be admitted into the social world, it must submit to regulation by that social world.

In the early twentieth century, middle-class Americans increasingly turned to secular experts for advice on how to behave. Although books on manners were vastly popular in the nineteenth century, it was not until the twentieth century that a mass market for etiquette instruction developed.[44] Unlike earlier generations, an urbanizing and industrializing middle class no longer turned to the study of good manners in order to "gain admittance into the homes of the rich." Rather, it turned to etiquette experts for advice on how to succeed in business and romance. This new craving for guidance in matters of conduct reflected intense social anxieties and insecurities, which were cleverly exploited by the emerging advertising industry. The early twentieth century was the age of B.O., halitosis, and dandruff. According to one chronicler of the period, "The assumption was that the country teemed with eager young people who were woefully ignorant of social amenities, rules of bodily cleanliness and general information of Eighth Grade standard."[45] Estranged from rural traditions and local opinion, thrust into a social world of shifting boundaries and blurring distinctions, worried about their taste and their odor, middle-class Americans sought expert guidance in the rules of proper conduct.

No one was more influential in calming the social fears of middle-class Americans than Emily Post. In many ways Emily Post resembled her contemporary Edith Wharton. She was part of the New York social elite, trained for a life of elegance and ease, but as a young woman she had ventured into writing and had successfully published novels, travel books, and magazine articles by the time she was in her early thirties. Like Wharton, Post was divorced after a difficult marriage; and it was partly as a result of her reduced economic circumstances that she turned to writing as a professional pursuit. From 1922, when she published her first edition of *Etiquette*, until her death in 1960, Emily Post was recognized as the nation's leading authority on proper conduct. Through her communications ventures as well as through her correspondence bureau, the Emily Post Institute, she expanded the popular audience for etiquette. Her *Etiquette: The Blue Book of Social Usage* sold more than five hundred thousand hardbound copies in its first twenty years. The first edition topped the nonfiction best-seller list shortly after its publication, displacing the popular *The Life of Christ*. It was followed by fourteen later editions, continuing after her death and spanning more than seventy years of American social life. In millions of American households the fat blue-bound volume, best known simply as "Emily Post," became as familiar and well thumbed as the family's favorite cookbook.

During the 1930s Post became a media personality, appearing three times weekly on a national radio show sponsored by General Electric and emceed by Ralph Edwards. After he began his Fireside Chats, President Franklin Roosevelt reported that his listeners sometimes complimented him for being "as good as Emily Post."[46] For years she wrote regular columns for *McCall's* and the *Ladies Home Journal;* her syndicated newspaper column appeared in 200 newspapers with a circulation of more than 6.5 million and, combined with her radio broadcasts, drew 250,000 letters a year.[47] In her use of the mass media, moreover, Emily Post set the model for the modern advice columnist. Her immediate successor, Amy Vanderbilt, followed in her footsteps, writing monthly columns for *McCall's* and the *Ladies Home Journal* and a syndicated newspaper column, and hosting her own radio program, *The Right Thing to Do.*[48] Meanwhile, the Post tradition continues to the present day: The fifteenth edition of *Etiquette*, compiled by Emily's granddaughter-in-law Elizabeth Post, was published in 1992.

The immediate inspiration for *Etiquette* was a 1920s New York advertising campaign with the theme "Everybody Tittered." Each ad featured a young man or woman caught in a social gaffe: "Everybody Tittered When I Ate My Oysters from a Spoon." "Everybody Tittered When I Took an Olive with My Fork." "Everybody Tittered When I Said, 'Mrs. Jones, Meet My Boyfriend.' "[49] As Emily Post's enterprising publisher saw it, there was a popular audience for a book on how to avoid the torment of titterers. And to judge from the behavior proscribed in the first edition of *Etiquette*, there was indeed a compelling need for such instruction. For example, Miss Post gently advises men that "a discussion of underwear or toilet articles and their merit or their use" is unpleasant in polite conversation.[50]

Emily Post's larger ambition was to school Americans in the philosophy as well as the practice of good manners. She took issue with the popular notion that etiquette concerned only "high society," and challenged the idea that rules of proper conduct were rigid and artificial. As she explained, manners, like the law, changed over time in response to changes in society. The analogy of manners with the law was well established in American culture. As one nineteenth-century writer argued, "The rules of etiquette are by no means a system of torture; they are to society what civil law is to a country; and, as in the exercise of civil law only the offenders are punished, so in the exercise of social law only those find it unpleasant who violate its requirements."[51] Yet manners, like the law, were subject to revision. In her 1942 edition, which devoted much attention to adjusting manners to fit wartime circumstances, Miss Post noted with a hint of pride: "It is this increasing fusing together of the new with the old that has kept this book from becoming a collection of dry-dust maxims. . . ."[52]

Changes in the rules of etiquette were also essential in ensuring obedience to a code of behavior that was strictly voluntary. If social rules departed too drastically from the social world they sought to govern, then such rules would not be enforceable. They would seem not only dusty but phony. For etiquette, the great pitfall was hypocrisy, and the great danger a loss of credibility and thus of moral authority.

At the same time the philosophical basis of etiquette was unchanging. It was rooted in a set of ethical principles, most notably sympathy, kindness, and consideration for the feelings of others. "Manners are made up of trivialities of deportment," Emily Post writes. ". . . Etiquette must, if it is to be of more than trifling use, include ethics. . . ."[53] In this context her frequent resort to the word "pleasant" was never weak or insipid but wonderfully precise: to please others, to place the comfort and interests of others above one's own. Beginning with the seventh edition and continuing thereafter, *Etiquette* entreats readers to work toward the goal of impersonality—"keeping our thoughts away from every trend that is sentimentally focused upon ourselves by thinking of something else—never mind what."[54] Later editions, written by Elizabeth L. Post, reaffirm this guiding principle.

Though the rules of conduct might resemble the laws of a civil society, there was one crucial difference between the two: Laws were mandatory while manners were voluntary. Etiquette governed through example and moral suasion. It was rooted in the optimistic proposition that people wanted to get along with one another; its appeal was to the better angels in people's nature. At the same time, this system of regulating behavior was circumscribed and limited by its very voluntary character. It had nothing to say to people who were determined to be rude or disagreeable. Similarly, it exerted no sway over those who wanted to assert their individual interests or rights over others. Radical individualism was an enemy of etiquette, because it allowed no place for the rule of social opinion. Indeed, once individuals ceased to care about the good opinion of others, etiquette lost all authority to regulate behavior. Its arbiters had to hand over the gavel to the lawyers.

In the difficult matter of divorce, the philosophy of etiquette assumed that divorce was a social as well as a legal event and that social "others" had interests in the dissolution of marriage. In practice, this meant that Emily Post and other experts had to invent a new set of rules for managing social relationships in a nation where divorce was becoming more common. If the growing numbers of divorced Americans should no longer be ostracized, how should their presence be handled at family get-togethers, their children's weddings, and social gatherings of friends from their old married days? How should divorce be governed?

For Emily Post, the subject of divorce was personally painful as well as socially delicate. In 1906 she was divorced after fourteen years of marriage and two children. According to her son and biographer, Edwin, the circumstances were humiliating. After a scandal sheet discovered her socially prominent husband, Edwin Post Sr., in a love nest with a showgirl, it threatened blackmail. With his wife Emily's knowledge and support, Edwin refused to be blackmailed, and in retaliation the publisher ran the lurid story. Edwin Post later testified against the publisher, and the story filled the New York press for months.[55] Yet in later years, following her own rule about "impersonality," Emily Post never alluded to the unhappy circumstances of her divorce. Nor did she attempt to turn her personal experience to professional advantage. During her long career she steadfastly refused to offer advice to the many Americans who wrote asking for help in dealing with their own troubled marriages.

In editions of *Etiquette* spanning more than twenty-five years, Miss Post compares divorce with both natural disaster and epidemic disease, writing that "the epidemic of divorce which has been raging in this country for the past forty years must be rated as a catastrophe along with floods, dust bowls and tornadoes."[56] Yet divorce cannot always be avoided, she acknowledges. A spouse's moral turpitude or cruelty can turn into hatred so destructive of homelife that it is best for all concerned, including children, that the marriage end. Therefore, divorce must be accepted as part of modern social life. There is no reason to treat it as socially shameful, and it should no longer carry a stigma or prompt social ostracism.

The most compelling reason to admit divorce into the social world was to reduce enmity between parents. In the past, when it was assumed that divorce was the result of only the most grievous and bitter injuries, social convention required that divorced people meet in public as "unspeaking strangers." Miss Post called for a repeal of this convention "for the sake of the children": "In the thousands of cases where children are involved, it is far, far better that the parents make every effort to remain on friendly terms. Nothing in all the world is so devastating in its destruction of character and of soul as living in an atmosphere infused with hatred. Anything is better for children than that!"[57]

Underlying this change in rules was a larger principle: In divorce, just as in marriage, parents must place children's family happiness and security above their own. Implicitly this principle suggested that children's interests in the marriage might be different from the interests of warring spouses. Explicitly it argued that children were the injured parties in divorce. In 1940 Emily Post observed: "There is no use in pretending that there is any *good side* from the children's point of view to divorce, excepting in a case where they are protected from a cruel parent or from the influence of a dissolute one. . . . But to the thousands of children who love both parents equally and who can therefore never have more than half a home at a time, the feeling of devastation is quite as great as that caused by enemy bombings of mere buildings abroad."[58] For more than half a century, each edition of *Etiquette* closed its discussion of divorce with this uncharacteristically effusive statement:

At present the breaking up of homes is so widespread it may be that those who grow up never having known the completeness of home will find it unessential. Or will it be the other way around? Perhaps the children of today's divided houses will be twice as earnest in their efforts to provide their own children with the priceless security of a father and mother together in one place called HOME![59]

Despite its greater acceptability in polite society, however, divorce must remain a private matter. In editions spanning almost fifty years, *Etiquette* declared that it was in the worst possible taste to trumpet the news of divorce. "A divorce is a failure, even though both people may agree that it is best, and there is little reason to be proud of a failure." Then too, public announcements of divorce were likely to hurt at least one partner in the marriage. "There is almost invariably one injured party," Miss Post counsels, and "it is surely rubbing salt in his wound for the other to shout publicly, 'hooray, I'm free!'"

Friends too must not inquire closely into the circumstances of the breakup. Though they should never criticize or censure the divorcing couple, they should avoid "prying [into] or questioning the reasons for or mechanics of the divorce."[60] And divorced people themselves should refrain from discussing their divorce. Again, *Etiquette* issued a double-edged admonition: "Don't dwell on your problems with everyone you see, but don't be ashamed to mention your state."[61]

In the prohibition against public disclosure there was an implicit obligation to work to preserve the marriage for the children's sake. "There could never be any argument with the fact that if there is any chance of maintaining a civil relationship, if not a deeply loving one, it is far better to do so, not only for the couple but most especially for the children."[62]

Similarly, separation was not to be viewed as a halfway step toward divorce, but rather as a chance to reconsider and possibly to rehabilitate a damaged marriage. A proper separation was both private and provisional, and the couple was advised to preserve the appearance of married life. In the case of a separation, Emily Post counseled, the woman continues to use her husband's name and wears her wedding ring. He quietly moves out of their home, possibly on an extended "business trip," or she may take her children for a "visit" to her family. Separated couples "refuse invitations that come to 'Mr. and Mrs.', although if they accidentally meet, they should act as friendly and normal as possible."

This double prohibition against stigmatizing as well as publicizing divorce maintained the tension between approval and disapproval in the social world. As *Etiquette* explains, "there is no stigma attached to divorce in this country, but neither should anyone approach it lightly."

The rules of etiquette also sought to locate divorce within the larger jurisdiction of marriage. Divorce did not exist in an independent domain but as a necessary, if minor, aspect of a modern marriage system. For this reason etiquette protected the symbols and meaning of marriage by drawing a distinction between the divorced and the non-divorced in wedding ceremonies and rituals. Remarriage must not resemble first marriage but instead must take on a more private character, a ceremony at home followed by a small reception. Similarly, it was not proper for a divorced woman to appropriate the virginal symbols of a traditional white wedding dress or a bridal veil. Nor should she carry orange blossoms.

Post frowned on the practice of divorced or remarried parents sending out joint announcements of their daughter's wedding. Like the evil fairy at the ball, parental divorce cast a shadow on the young couple's marriage: "To have our attention called to their shattered and rehashed pledges upon the same sheet of paper that calls upon us to witness the solemn taking of these same breakable pledges by their daughter would not seem to be giving the latter's marriage a fair chance at the start."[63] A divorced father who was on unfriendly terms with his ex-wife was allowed to escort their daughter down the aisle but was not permitted "even a glimpse of her after the ceremony," nor was he welcome at the wedding reception, hosted by the bride's mother and possibly her new husband. This ban extended to all members of the divorced father's family.[64]

The centrality of marriage was further reinforced by the way divorce was treated in the conduct manual itself. *Etiquette* cast divorce in the category of the marginal and miscellaneous. In the first edition, published in 1922, it is mentioned briefly in a section titled "Fundamentals of Behavior," and then only in the most glancing way: A man of honor should "let his wife get her freedom on other than criminal grounds, no matter what her conduct," while disaffected wives are encouraged to seek privately the advice of their "wisest and nearest" relatives. Subsequent editions place divorce at the back of the book. For example, the 1960 edition discusses the problems of divorce in one of the last chapters of the more than seven-hundred-page volume. This chapter, oddly titled "Our Contribution to the Beauty of Living," might more properly be called "Exhausted Advice Writer Offers Thoughts on Miscellaneous Topics That Don't Fit Anywhere Else in the Book." Divorce is thrown into the chapter along with "In-Law Situations," "Tact," and "The Old House Coat Habit." A later edition places divorce in a chapter devoted to "Happy Marriage." It is not until the 1975 edition that divorce is treated independently of marriage.

In short, in *Etiquette*'s first fifty years very little expository energy is devoted to the subject of divorce. Revealingly, too, the word "unhappiness" is never used to describe the failed marital relationship during this period. A divorcing couple might be described as mismated or ill-fated, but never as merely unhappy. Indeed, according to Post, unhappiness is not sufficient cause for married couples to break up.

In her 1940 book *Children Are People and Ideal Parents Are Comrades*, however, Post hints that social practice may be changing. "The world of yesterday would never have given countenance to any woman who left an inculpable husband and devoted father, taking the children with her for no reason except that she was finding life less glamorous than she had expected it to be. Still less could any man who claimed to be a gentleman, bring himself to announce to his blameless wife that he no longer loved her, and therefore intended to marry someone else." Nevertheless, she makes it clear that "the children's right to an unbroken home" remains more important than "whether Father or Mother might themselves be finding happiness in marriage."[65]

Within the larger framework of social relationships, therefore, the experience of divorce remained ill-defined, unelaborated, and unmediated. The very meagerness of the associated vocabulary had a dampening and isolating effect. Too, admonitions about parental obligations to preserve marriage for the children's sake, whenever possible, remained consistent and strong. Even more centrally, the conduct literature did not see personal unhappiness as a "just cause" for divorce. Taken together, the social rules of divorce reflected the ongoing effort to maintain some balance between the social acceptance of divorce and ready resort to it.

Divorce and Marriage Counseling

In another secular domain of expertise the emerging class of marriage counselors wrestled with the question of how to preserve the institution of marriage in the midst of a growing trend toward divorce. At about the same time that Emily Post published the first edition of *Etiquette*, Ernest R. Groves created the first course on family life for college students and later the first marriage-preparation course. Groves was one of the pioneers of professional marriage counseling, and the author of a number of practical marriage books: *Wholesome Marriage* (1927); *Sex in Marriage* (1931); *Preparation for Marriage* (1936); *Conserving Marriage and the Family* (1944). Like others trained in the new academic discipline of sociology, Groves came from a generation schooled in religion as well as science. Educated at Yale Divinity School and strongly influenced by the teachings of Freud, he sought to combine traditional morality with the new insights into human psychology and behavior, and thereby to develop a more scientific approach to marriage and marital problems.

Central to his thinking was the idea that marriage was becoming increasingly fragile as an institution. Because Americans regarded marriage as an affectionate partnership rather than an economic or social necessity, modern marriage was particularly vulnerable to disruption. Thus, divorce should be regarded as part of the marriage system rather than as an offense against it. Divorce was not a moral transgression but a social finding, the "pragmatic recognition" that marriage is hazardous.[66] As a consequence, Groves argued, a certain, albeit unspecified, level of divorce must be expected.

Like others in the emerging social-scientific disciplines, Groves looked to enlightened legislation and scientifically based formal instruction on marriage, rather than religious or moral opinion, to preserve this essential but fragile institution. In his view, the law lagged behind popular opinion and practice when it came to recognizing divorce as a part of the modern marriage system. In many states, the law continued to view divorce as a moral offense, requiring the assignment of fault, even as popular opinion increasingly treated it as a practical remedy for marital incompatibility. Consequently, the legal system actually harmed the institution of marriage by requiring couples to engage in subterfuge and deception in seeking its dissolution. Groves wrote: "The getting of the divorce is bad enough, but when the only relief for an impossible domestic situation appears to be through false accusation or trickery because of inherent incompatibility between the legal system and the mores of the people, the risk of demoralization becomes all the greater."

Groves called for liberalizing divorce laws in order to bring legal norms into closer relationship with social practices. Nonetheless, his strenuous advocacy for divorce law reform was linked to his ambitions for the improvement of marriage. He did not endorse divorce as the answer to marital problems, and he took pains to warn unhappily married couples against pursuing divorce as a route to greater happiness. Throughout his long career as a marriage expert and counselor he consistently treated divorce as a last and least-favored remedy for marital dissatisfaction. At worst, he warned, divorce brings on a host of new troubles; at best it may "only partly close the gateway to discontent."[67]

In developing a scientific approach to marriage counseling, Groves drew upon the insights of the new discipline of psychology. Marital breakdown was caused not by moral weakness or characterological defects but by individual personality problems. In his 1944 book *Conserving Marriage and the Family: A Realistic Discussion of the Divorce Problem*, Groves argues that divorce is most common among people who cannot grow up, who fail to separate from their parents, and who cling to their own selfish desires. Marriage tests an individual's capacity for emotional growth, and too many spouses, unable to meet its demands, flee into divorce court. To divorce-seekers, he poses this rhetorical question: "Has marriage proved itself a failure merely because it has brought obligations, the demand for self-control and the need that you emotionally readjust yourself to your parent?"[68]

By contrast, Groves saw marriage as the pathway to maturity. The habit and practice of married life led the individual away from egocentrism toward mutual regard and consideration for the happiness of others. Implicit in his view was the notion of the marital relationship as psychologically dynamic. Far from promoting emotional stunting or stagnation, marriage led to emotional growth. It encouraged an individual orientation toward flexibility and compromise, often coaxing more immature and underdeveloped personalities into the habit of giving as well as taking. In Groves's words, successful marriage led to a "miracle of character reconstruction." By enlisting in the marital institution, one got the chance to grow up. On the other hand, a rigid and immature personality was likely to resist the change and "the responsibilities and limitations associated with intimate fellowship."

One expression of the immature personality was an inability to shift from courtship to a partnership view of marriage. Courtship has its delights, but also "carries a certain amount of deception." Similarly, an immature spouse could get stuck in the honeymoon phase. "It may be that marriage has an emotional glow in the first weeks or months or years on account of its new experience of physical passion," Groves wrote. However, he continued, since intercourse is "a merely physical association, it is by nature limited. . . . This shows why some people find marriage for a brief period almost an emotional intoxication and then drift into a dreary monotony and finally decide to separate."[69] The failure to move beyond the early sexual and romantic intoxications of the courtship and honeymoon toward deeper satisfactions of marital fellowship leads to dissatisfaction and perhaps divorce.

Like Emily Post, Groves viewed "unhappiness" as an insufficient reason for divorce, arguing that unhappiness is far too global a feeling to attach to the marital institution itself. Too, chronic unhappiness may be a sign of the self-absorbed personality. "If . . . you are willing to turn away from yourself and look at others, it will be easier to see that happiness as a rule is something that one has in every part of one's life or not at all. We are happy all over or everywhere life seems disappointing. This shows how unconvincing a reason for divorce being unhappy generally is."[70]

Too, like Emily Post, he believed that divorce caused enormous suffering for children. When he contemplated the plight of children caught up in divorce, Professor Groves dropped his professionally dispassionate tone. Resorting to old-fashioned moral rhetoric, he wrote: "It is only when one becomes acquainted with the evils resulting from divorce, as they affect the life of children, that one realizes in full measure the necessity of society's making every effort by education and legislation to prevent marriage failure, and the great need of providing the best possible means of reconciliation and settlement for those in matrimonial difficulty."[71]

In his work and writings Groves contended with the divorce problem by arguing for its greater acceptance as a social fact of life while at the same time holding out the hope of scientifically based counseling as a way to teach individuals about the emotional and social responsibilities of marriage. His faith in social science as a means of improving society led him to the optimistic view that a science of marriage could reduce, if not eradicate, divorce. Moreover, since marital failure grew out of personality maladjustments, such problems could be corrected, even avoided, through the interventions of the professional marriage counselor.

Despite his more psychological orientation, however, Groves's bias as a marriage counselor favored the institution of marriage rather than the individual. He recognized that marriage must be rooted in enduring spousal affection if it was to meet modern expectations of marital success, and he cast the spousal relationship in psychologically dynamic terms. At the same time he never departed from the notion that marriage serves social purposes larger than the self, indeed that it is the central institutional means for mobilizing individual interests and desires toward more altruistic goals. The notion that the institution should promote individual satisfaction and interests was utterly absent from his thinking.

GI Divorce

Vulgar divorce faded with the advent of the Great Depression and economic hard times. As families struggled to keep food on the table, divorce again became unaffordable and unthinkable.[72] But, although many Americans saw the slowdown in divorce as one of the few "good" things about the national ordeal of the Great Depression, it was only temporary. During the Second World War the divorce rate again spiked upward, doubling between 1940 and 1946.[73] As husbands and fathers left home to serve in the military or to find lucrative work in wartime industries and as women moved from the home into the workforce, spouses separated and lived apart. For unhappily married husbands and wives, wartime separation created a kind of de facto divorce. When World War II ended, many couples took legal steps to end an already irretrievably broken relationship, thus causing a postwar surge in divorce. The wartime climate of emotionalism and hedonism also contributed to both hasty wartime marriages and quickie postwar divorces.

As GIs returned to domestic life after the Second World War, Americans worried about how to get soldiers to honor the marriages made hastily and impulsively during ten-day furloughs. Experts appealed to the soldiers' sense of patriotic duty and military discipline: Men could repay the sacrifice of their buddies left behind on the battlefields by staying married to the girls they had left behind.

Popular articles and books aimed at returning GIs, still giddy with their freedoms and tempted to bolt from wartime marriages, lectured men on their responsibilities as fathers and on their children's need for paternal guidance.

Postwar America mobilized to pressure men into assuming responsible roles as dutiful husbands and fathers. Just as Rosie the Riveter had to forsake the workplace for the home, GI Joe was called upon to fulfill his patriotic duty by returning to his wife and children. The romantic recklessness of wartime had to be abandoned in favor of marriage and monogamy; soldiers must "remain attached to one girl, remain true to one vow, and contribute to a normal family unit." Moreover, men must drop some of the habits of military life. "Since the marriage is a union between equals," writes the author of *The Veteran and His Marriage*, "the conception of a 'boss' who 'dominates' is offensive."[74] Yet military training could also help returning GIs curb their wayward and irresponsible impulses: "Army discipline should help the veteran . . . use such discipline in his home where to succeed means so much."[75]

The postwar campaign for domesticity, combined with a generous package of government benefits for married GIs, probably helped lower the divorce rate for a while. The divorce rate dropped to pre-1940 levels in the 1950s and remained stable throughout that decade and into the 1960s, lower than projections based on long-term trends would suggest. Only 20 percent of the men and women born between 1933 and 1942 would see their marriages dissolve by the tenth wedding anniversary.[76]

As the combined result of declining mortality and low divorce, marriages lasted a long time, even a lifetime. Throughout the 1950s and into the early 1960s, the women's pages of local newspapers regularly reported celebrations of fiftieth or even sixtieth wedding anniversaries.

Not until the 1960s did divorce rates begin to climb sharply in Western nations. From the mid-1960s until the mid-1980s divorce increased dramatically throughout Europe, Australia, and Canada before dropping slightly or continuing to rise at a slower rate. In America the patterns were similar. Between 1965 and 1975 the divorce rate doubled, peaking at twenty-two divorces per thousand married women in 1979 and then dropping slightly and stabilizing at the 1994 rate of twenty divorces per thousand married women, the highest rate among all advanced Western societies.[77]

The spread of divorce can also be described by a look at the experience of all Americans who married in a given year, projecting the likelihood of divorce for those married in more recent years. According to one estimate, half of all marriages made in the mid-1970s will end in divorce. As for marriages made more recently, demographers project that as many as 64 percent will end in divorce.[78]

Yet what has been called the divorce revolution cannot be captured in demographic trends alone. In the history of American divorce the last third of the twentieth century marks a time of profound discontinuity and rapid change. Indeed, the cultural fault line, the B.C. and A.D. of American divorce, can be drawn somewhere in the mid- to late 1960s. Before that time, divorce was contained within a system of marriage and subject to its jurisdiction. After that time, divorce moved outside the government of marriage and established its own institutional jurisdiction over family relationships. Before the mid-1960s, divorce was viewed as a legal, family, and social event with multiple stakeholders; after that time, divorce became an individual event defined by and responsive to the interests of the individual. Consequently, to chart the progress of divorce in the last third of the century is to describe two separate but closely related migrations. In one, divorce breaks free from its place within a marriage system and establishes itself as an independent institution governing the lives of parents and children. In the other, divorce moves from the domain of the society and the family into the inner world of the self.

CHAPTER TWO

The Rise of
Expressive Divorce

LIKE THE ERA OF VULGAR DIVORCE, the new divorce era began in a period of economic ebullience and restlessness and at a time when women were gaining new freedoms and opportunities in the world of work and public life. Both factors figured prominently in the growing disposition to divorce. But two features defined this new era of divorce as truly revolutionary. The first was that the nation's most dramatic and sustained divorce "high" was unaccompanied by any sense of crisis. Earlier in the nation's history, even when the rate of divorce was negligible by contemporary standards, Americans fretted over the problem of broken homes; after the mid-1960s, as divorce swept across the social landscape, Americans showed remarkably little concern about its impact or spread. The old fears about the social havoc caused by unchecked divorce, the concerns about the damaging impact of divorce on children, the anxieties about freedom tipping into license, all but vanished. After the mid-1960s, divorce ceased to be defined as a problem.

Second, in the last third of the century divorce was harnessed to new ambitions and purposes. Underlying the growing disposition to divorce was an entirely new conception of the nature and purpose of divorce itself. The transformation in the idea of divorce occurred as the result of an inner revolution that took place among postwar Americans. This revolution created a new way of thinking and talking about divorce. It also created a new rationale for divorce as an expressive as well as a legal freedom.

In the postwar period, the nation experienced two decades of steady and widespread economic growth. The rise in the standard of living was unparalleled in American experience, as breadwinners' rising wages sustained homemakers' spiraling consumption. For postwar American families it was a sweetheart deal. Earning and spending advanced hand in hand, creating what seemed like an economically ordained union between the separate spheres of work and family life.

The experience of sustained material affluence served to unleash a sense of psychological affluence. Americans began to feel economically invulnerable, and the widespread optimism about economic prospects encouraged a more expansive outlook about individual opportunities in noneconomic spheres of life.[1] The social analyst Daniel Yankelovich observes that the experience of affluence began to cut into the American psyche in the late 1960s; it was then that people began to believe that the economic good times would continue indefinitely and that they could begin to "live for today and for their own self-satisfaction."[2]

According to the authors of The Inner American, a social-scientific study of the emotional well-being of postwar Americans, this shift represented nothing less than a "psychological revolution." In the period between 1957 and 1976 Americans began to look at the world and themselves in a new way. They turned their attention toward the inner world of self. The link between economic well-being and personal happiness weakened; people were less likely to cite economic reasons as the cause of unhappiness than they had been twenty years earlier.[3] Instead, their sense of individual well-being became more dependent on the richness of their emotional lives, the depth and quality of feelings, and the variety of opportunities for self-expression.

The psychological revolution contributed to a change in conceptions of what made for a good and successful life. Middle-class ambitions shifted from climbing the economic ladder to moving up the happiness scale. It was psychological mobility—a boost in emotional and expressive satisfactions, a chance to be a more fulfilled person—rather than economic mobility that engaged American energies and appetites from the 1970s on.

Increasingly Americans tended to view happiness as a subjective feeling rather than a set of objective economic or social conditions. Similarly, they displayed a growing readiness to define "unhappiness" as psychological rather than situational in nature, caused by a decline in personal satisfaction rather than a shift in personal or social fortunes. Americans were also more willing to talk about their personal problems and to seek help from mental health professionals rather than from doctors and clergy, the professional help givers whose advice had been most commonly sought in the 1950s.[4] And as interest in the inner life increased, so too did its apparent richness. The geography of the inner life turned out to be far more complex, intricate, and differentiated than once imagined. Upon closer investigation, it also turned out to be more difficult to negotiate solo, without the assistance of an expert guide.

Consequently, the psychological revolution created a growing market for psychological expertise and services. The demand for therapy, once concentrated mainly in an urban and "egghead" class, moved into the suburbs and the middle class. According to psychologist William J. Doherty, the late 1970s marked the beginning of the "golden age of therapy": "[L]egions of therapists entered a field that offered plentiful jobs, the promise of private practice incomes, and a high degree of professional autonomy."[5] Perhaps more surprisingly, social work professionals, whose traditional mission was to help poor people deal with such social problems as joblessness and homelessness, began to flock to more lucrative individual counseling practices aimed at middle-class Americans with insurance coverage. In *Unfaithful Angels*, a critique of social-work trends, Harry Specht and Mark Courtney write: "For the most part, professional associations of social workers and schools of social work are active participants in the transformation of social work from a professional corps concerned with helping people deal with their social problems to a major platoon in the psychotherapeutic armies."[6] By the 1990s about 40 percent of social work professionals were in private practice serving middle-class clients.[7]

As Specht and Courtney point out, many of these psychotherapists functioned as professionals in the "personal happiness" business. Their practices were set up to treat problems of psychological well-being rather than to deal with mental illness: "Many—perhaps the majority—of people who are seen by psychotherapists cannot be characterized as sick. Rather, they are the 'worried well': middle class young adults and young middle-aged, who are primarily professionals and primarily Caucasian, who are unhappy, unfulfilled and unsatisfied."[8] (A quick scan of the yellow-page listings for therapists bears out their observation. Many of the therapists advertise practices devoted to "relationships," "decision making," "women's issues," "midlife adjustment," "couples counseling," "stress-anxiety," and "grief and loss." These are important and legitimate areas of concern, to be sure, but not the standard specialties for dealing with the mentally ill.)

With respect to the problems of marriage, there was a corresponding shift in help-seeking behavior. In the past Americans usually turned to family members and friends for advice on troubled marriages. Among those who sought professional help, the vast majority sought the help of clergy. The next most commonly consulted professional was a medical doctor, though not a psychiatrist. Officially, doctors offered expert advice on the sexual problems of marriage, but unofficially, trusted family doctors often listened sympathetically to patients struggling with difficult marriages and sometimes ventured an opinion that was not strictly medical. Only one or two adults in one hundred ever sought the professional advice of anyone other than a doctor or clergyman. Marriage counselors, according to a national mental health study published in 1960, were judged the least effective of all sources of help.[9]

With the psychological revolution, however, Americans began to see marriage and family relationships as part of the domain of mental health. Psychotherapeutic thought and practice began to invade marriage counseling. Even pastoral marriage counseling began to acquire a more psychotherapeutic orientation. Indeed, as Specht and Courtney observe, "ministers and priests have come to look and act more and more like psychotherapists, just as psychotherapists have come to look and act more and more like priests."[10] Mainline religious denominations led the procession into psychotherapy. Pastoral counseling began to take a client-centered approach that required clergy to stay within the client's "value system." Pastors (and congregations) retreated from theological challenge to an individual's values on the psychotherapeutic ground that such a challenge would be damaging to the individual's selfhood and would come across as "preachy" and "moralistic." Perhaps more surprisingly, psychology made inroads into the evangelical denominations. Unlike the mainliners, evangelicals tended to use psychology to support traditional religious teaching on marriage and the family, although over time they too came to view marital dissolution in more psychological terms.[11]

The disciplinary shift toward a psychotherapeutic canon among helping professionals meant that the traditional experts in matters of marriage—family doctors or clergy—ceded authority to those trained in one of the more than 250 varieties of psychotherapy. Therapists became the teachers and norm-setters in marriage and then, later, in the dissolution of marriage.[12]

As a result, in the post–World War II period, marriage counseling steadily migrated from the church and nonprofit institutions, the domain of the civil society, to the professional service sector and the domain of the marketplace. In contrast with the earlier practitioners of marriage counseling, who offered their services as part of their vocation, therapists sold their services in the marketplace. Moreover, since private therapy was relatively unregulated, its practitioners were highly sensitive to the incentives of the market, including the expanding and lucrative market of Americans whose marriages were on the rocks. Fears about the commercial exploitation of divorce disappeared as its commercial potential grew.

Most Americans did not rush to seek professional help for their family problems, of course, but many began to talk and think in a language influenced by popular psychotherapeutic disciplines. In Robert Bellah's now-familiar phrase, this was the language of expressive individualism. Americans talked about self-esteem and self-validation, about finding oneself and feeling good about oneself. As Bellah and his colleagues also point out, expressive individualism had an ethical dimension. It defined commitment as a form of self-commitment: One's first and most important obligation was to oneself. Psychologist Fritz Perls captured the new expressive ethic in his famous Gestalt Prayer:

> *I do my thing, and you do your thing,*
> *I am not in this world to live up to your expectations*
> *And you are not in this world to live up to mine,*
> *You are you and I am I,*

And if by chance, we find each other, it's beautiful.
If not, it can't be helped.[13]

Marital Discontent in a Psychological Age

The emphasis on seeking personal happiness in relationships had a profound impact on women's family lives. Just as rising economic expectations had bred material dissatisfaction earlier in the century, so now rising emotional expectations fostered a growing sense of emotional dissatisfaction and restlessness in marriage. In a psychological age the pressures on marital partnership as the source of deep emotional rewards intensified. This was especially true for women, who placed greater emphasis on the relational and affective side of marriage than did men. And as the expectations for marital satisfaction increased, so too did the potential for deep disappointment and disaffection.

As one of the defining documents of the period, Betty Friedan's *The Feminine Mystique* captures this sense of psychological discontent and restlessness, a yearning for emotional fulfillment after material wants have been brilliantly satisfied. Indeed, it is the very achievement of material well-being, the comfortable house in the suburbs, the successful husband, and the college-bound children, that creates women's sense of emptiness and aimlessness.[14]

Although it is widely regarded as the founding document of the modern women's movement, *The Feminine Mystique* is not a conventional work of political analysis and criticism. Its language is drawn almost entirely from psychology, and women's plight is described in psychotherapeutic terms. The "problem that has no name" is experienced vaguely as an inner feeling, a yearning, a restlessness, a malaise; its symptomatology is as hard to pin down as its name. But the cause of the problem, Friedan makes clear, is the stunting of women's opportunities for personal growth. Borrowing from the work of Abraham Maslow, the psychologist who established the concept of a "hierarchy of needs," she argues that women's domestic roles keep them from moving up the scale of needs toward personal fulfillment and therefore prevent them from realizing their full human potential.

Contrary to popular belief, Friedan did not attack men as the source of women's discontent, nor did she say that marriage itself caused women's inner restlessness. Her central insight was that the lack of paid work opportunities outside the home blocked the pathway to women's personal growth. Shrewdly she recognized the expressive, besides the economic, rewards of work outside the home. For her primary audience, college-educated middle-class women who were economically comfortable but emotionally and intellectually starved, the message that paid work could offer psychological satisfactions struck a powerful chord.

However, other feminists soon pointed to marriage as the source of women's stunted growth and personal unhappiness. The main contours of the feminist critique of marriage are found in *The Future of Marriage*, a 1972 study by the sociologist Jessie Bernard. A well-respected scholar and a self-described "pioneer" in sociological research on marriage, Bernard had earlier written influential studies on divorce, remarriage, and sexuality. *The Future of Marriage* was heralded as an instant classic, generating widespread attention and debate. An article based on the book appeared in an early issue of *Ms.* magazine, and Bernard became a frequent guest speaker at women's conferences.

Bernard argued that marriage was good for men and bad for women. While marriage conferred health and happiness on men, it had the opposite effect on women. Marriage could make women sick. Compared with unmarried women, Bernard claimed, married women were more likely to suffer from a host of mental and physical problems, including insomnia, trembling hands, nightmares, fainting, headaches, dizziness, phobias, and heart palpitations. Thus, the marital institution itself was pathological. "To be happy in a relationship which imposes so many impediments on her, as traditional marriage does," Bernard wrote, "a woman must be slightly ill mentally."[15]

Bernard's description of marriage as embodying separate and unequal "his" and "her" marriages reflected the feminist view of the marital state as an institution of patriarchal power and dominance which kept women in a subordinate and inferior status, and in the concluding chapter of her book she acknowledges her debt to feminist thinking. "I did not start out with the conviction that marriage was bad for wives. Nor did I expect this book to turn out to be a pamphlet on the destructiveness for women of marriage. . . ." But, she continues, "the message of the radical young women had reached me."[16]

Nonetheless, Bernard added an important psychotherapeutic dimension to the feminist critique of marriage. As *The Future of Marriage* makes clear, marriage is not only the source of separate and unequal status for women but also the source of diminished physical and emotional well-being, even mental illness. In short, marriage is unhealthy as well as unjust.

Not all scholars agreed with Bernard. Especially disputed was one key point: that the high level of reported happiness among married women was an artifact of social norms and expectations and thus reflected not true psychological well-being but adjustment, even resignation, to married status. Sociologist Norval D. Glenn observed that "if, as Bernard implies, the thousands of American young women who, with typical eagerness, marry each year are acting against their long-term interests, their behavior is a phenomenal example of mass irrationality which has implications for all major theories of human behavior."[17] The authors of *The Inner American*, too, rejected Bernard's argument as "extreme." Like Glenn, they found no difference in husbands' and wives' reports of marital happiness or in their feelings of equity in their relationships.[18] However, the survey evidence pointed to other key differences between men and women. Compared with husbands, wives were more likely to be irritated and resentful of their spouses' lack of help in meeting the responsibilities of housework and child care. Too, according to the 1970s data, women held more liberal views of marriage than men; they were more likely to describe their marriages as "two separate people" and to approve of divorce.[19] Therefore, Bernard's notion of separate marital stakes and experiences captured, however distortedly, some of these attitudinal differences. But perhaps more important, her argument suggested, at least implicitly, a therapeutic imperative for women: Get better by getting out.

At the same time that marriage was coming under attack as detrimental to women's emotional health, it was also weakening as an economic arrangement. With greater educational and job opportunities in an expanding economy, women could look forward to a growing measure of economic independence. No longer did they have to endure marriage to abusive, alcoholic, or unfaithful spouses out of sheer economic necessity. Moreover, as middle-class women entered the paid workforce, the association of breadwinning with male heroism began to erode. The ritualized celebration of the breadwinner's return to the family each night—Daddy's home!—lost its gendered meaning. Mommy struggled home after a hard day's work as well. Nor was breadwinning exclusively identified with male achievement. Women knew how to bring home a paycheck too.

When it came to the dissolution of marriage, the economic grievances that preoccupied men and women in the era of vulgar divorce faded, and attention to the financial hardships of divorce receded. It was not that economic factors ceased to be important or "real." Indeed, as studies of the economic impact of divorce later showed, divorce could be economically devastating for women and children. But in the early years of the divorce revolution, economic concerns became subordinate to the psychological imperative of greater personal happiness and satisfaction in marriage. As Roderick Phillips notes, "domestic relative deprivation in modern western society simply does not have the public character of poverty in traditional society, and fears of the economic consequences of divorce in modern times may be overridden by expectations of generous property settlements, alimony, child support payments and social welfare assistance, even though many of these may turn out to be chimeras."[20] Moreover, by the 1980s the psychological revolution had gained cultural momentum even as the economic high that had given it impetus began to fade.

Under these changed conditions, marriage became more fragile as the main institution of family life. From the mid-1960s on the affectional requirements for marriage ratcheted upward, the demands for emotional satisfactions in family life escalated, the pursuit of love connections took on a manic intensity. Marital happiness, like the definition of a good provider, turned out to be a highly elastic notion.

The Rise of Expressive Divorce

As it altered views of marriage, the psychological revolution changed the conception of divorce. First, it redefined divorce as an individual experience. Before the psychological revolution Americans regarded divorce mainly as a legal, social, and family event, with far-reaching consequences for others; the impact of divorce on the individual remained a subordinate concern. After the psychological revolution they tended to define divorce as an individual event; the impact of divorce on others became far less important. Second, the psychological revolution changed the locus of divorce, from the outer social world to the inner world of the self. Before the 1970s Americans rarely associated divorce with the inner life or talked about it as a complexly faceted emotional journey. After the psychological revolution, however, divorce became a subjective experience, governed by the individual's needs, desires, and feelings. Third and perhaps most important, the psychological revolution redefined the family, once the realm of the fettered and obligated self, as a fertile realm for exploring the potential of the self, unfettered by roles and obligations. Divorce was recruited in the service of this new expressive goal. Thus, the psychological revolution cast the sad business of marital dissolution into a new and more positive light. According to this new conception of divorce, leaving a marriage offered opportunities to build a stronger identity and to achieve a more coherent and fully realized sense of self.

Not only did this psychological conception transform the meaning of divorce, but it also changed the purpose of divorce. Once the last and least desirable remedy for a failed marriage, divorce now became the psychologically healthy response to marital dissatisfaction. This new rationale for divorce established a far more permissive standard for seeking divorce. It also ensured that divorce would become far more widespread since marital dissatisfaction in a psychological age proved to be a fairly common experience.

The Inner Divorce

The new way of thinking about divorce is clearly evident in the large body of popular divorce literature, which first emerged in the 1970s. Written mainly by divorced therapists or women who had been through therapy during their divorces, this literature locates divorce in the inner life of the individual and depicts the breakup of a marriage almost exclusively as a set of bewildering and disorienting feelings—fear, anger, hate, grief, loss, love, denial, regret. Many advice writers also speak of a "crazy period," usually a brief time when individuals become emotionally unhinged: "You find yourself doing crazy things . . . playing detective . . . spying on your ex. Forgetting whether the red light means stop or go."[21] In her divorce book, *Crazy Time*, the *Washington Post* writer Abigail Trafford expands on this idea: "The world is turned upside down; you've lost your center of gravity. You can't get your feet back on the ground. Instead you flip-flop in slow motion like astronauts in space. You don't seem to go in any particular direction; not forward, not backward. You just float and sink, float and sink again. . . . You go to a therapist who tells you what you already know: Divorce is a disorienting experience."[22]

Yet, according to these writers, the emotions engendered by divorce are not as disorderly as they seem. There are common patterns in the psychological experience of divorce, a progression of stages that must be endured and negotiated during the "emotional divorce." Trafford identifies five distinct phases of divorce craziness: relief/disbelief; deep shock; anger; ambivalence; and depression. Other writers invent other typologies. A Presbyterian minister and therapist sees "Five Divorces" taking place, beginning with the nearly unconscious experience "of one or both partners losing the motivation and energy needed to sustain a marriage" and ending with the achievement of "divorce with freedom." The fifth and final divorce brings a full sense of being single again internally and emotionally.[23]

Moreover, although the psychological experience of divorce is difficult and painful, it can also be transformative. At the end of the "crazy time," Trafford notes, comes the "emergence of self." Unlike the bad feelings engendered by death, prolonged illness, or chronic joblessness, the bad feelings of divorce can lead to good things. Divorce can trigger a kind of emotional counterresponse, a marshaling of inner resources to ward off the assault on the self. As the author of one popular divorce book writes, "After being in a long-term marriage in which they tended to deny so much of themselves, divorce gives many women their first chance to validate their reality, to explore who they are, to cherish newfound identities, to heal old wounds, and ultimately to take care of themselves."

However traumatic, therefore, the divorce experience carries the potential for personal growth. "Divorce is about change," one advice book observes; ". . . it is emotional pain that sets in motion the wheels of growth and change. . . ."[24] At the end of the emotional divorce is the "phoenix" phase. "As a Phoenix person, you have written a new script for yourself. You have enough confidence from discovering your own individuality that you don't feel crushed by the past reasserting itself. . . . You can gain more control of your life and take greater charge of the present. You change jobs, get married again—or not; you take piano lessons, become a minister. You finally become you."[25]

Both the popular and the scholarly literature draw a distinction between the "emotional" divorce and the "legal" divorce. Divorce is seen as comprising two separate events—the inner breakdown of affection and commitment, and the official dissolution of the marital partnership. The "inner divorce" begins with a psychological awakening, the stirring of feelings of discontent expressed variously as unhappiness, distance, mistrust, alienation, anger, hurt, or disinterest. Sometimes the inchoate feelings of unhappiness and discontent remain buried or hidden from one's spouse; other times they erupt in acts of infidelity, fighting, or violent conflict. In either case, these feelings cannot be denied or deferred; once they surface, the individual must take the initiative to declare that the bonds of love, trust, and affection have been broken.

The emotional divorce precedes the legal divorce, often by years, and sometimes is not completely over with until long after the marriage has legally ended. But it is the psychological, rather than the legal, ending of marriage that marks the "true" divorce. The legal divorce merely ratifies the emotional divorce.

Here, again, divorce is associated with the exercise of feminine initiative and agency, as it had been in the novels of Edith Wharton. But this time, the earlier identification of divorce with assertiveness and risk-taking is fused with the newer notion of divorce as a form of psychological entrepreneurialism.

A New Birth of Freedom

After the psychological revolution, Americans began to use the language of expressive individualism to describe their divorces. Divorce had long been identified with legal freedoms, but in the last decades of the twentieth century it became associated with psychological liberation as well. According to one small but revealing study of 104 divorcing adults (half men and half women), both men and women said that leaving a marriage gave them a newfound sense of freedom and control over their personal lives. Nevertheless, the meaning of freedom differed for men and women. Men saw freedom as an escape from the exacting standards of intimacy and responsibility in family relationships, while women talked about the freedom to acquire a stronger sense of self, a "wholeness" and a sense of greater confidence and competence. The study's author, sociologist Catherine Riessman, observes that "more than half of the women in the sample, particularly those separated less than a year, actively engaged in reconstructing a self, emphasize this outcome. They say they 'got born,' have 'the freedom to be myself,' feel 'more like a free person.' "[26]

In describing their economic lives, these men and women emphasized the new expressive opportunities and freedoms unleashed by divorce. Leaving a marriage brought economic as well as personal freedom. But again, their accounts emphasize different aspects of this newfound freedom. While men report a new freedom to spend more lavishly on expensive hobbies, trips, sports, or even hair transplants, buying things that "make them feel good," women speak proudly of their newly acquired sense of competence and control at earning a paycheck and "handling" the bills. Of the fifty-two women in the study, one-fourth (thirteen) "spontaneously expressed happiness at their greater control over money." Thus, Riessman concludes, "rather than being victims of their poorer circumstances, women present themselves as active agents, taking charge by opening bank accounts, establishing credit, and deciding how to spend what they have. Like fixing toilets, managing money is both a symbolic and a tangible way to measure freedom and to project a new and positive self."[27]

The popular divorce literature also reflected the gendered nature of the understanding of divorce as a form of initiative and freedom. The literature aimed at men emphasized the sexual and romantic freedoms that came with easy divorce. Whereas men were once socially pressured to conform to the norms of monogamous marriage and responsible fatherhood, the new freedoms of divorce provided cultural dispensation from these obligations even as postdivorce arrangements often made it harder for men to meet these obligations. With greater liberty to divorce, men were freer to escape and likelier to fail at their prescribed duties as family men. However, popular writers devoted little effort to ascribing positive meaning to men's divorcing behavior; rather, the message of expressive divorce was that men no longer need feel guilt or shame about what was once considered bad conduct.

Likewise, there is a gender gap in the metaphorical language of divorce. The contemporary divorce literature aimed at men combines the conception of divorce as an expressive pursuit with the traditional male metaphor of combat. Divorce is characterized as a battle, a game, an adversarial struggle with a winner and a loser. Typical titles include: *The Fighter's Guide to Divorce: A No-Holds-Barred Strategy for Coming Out Ahead*; *The Lion's Share: A Combat Manual for Divorcing Males*; and *How to Dump Your Wife.*

In *Winning Your Divorce: A Man's Survival Guide*, lawyer Timothy J. Horgan tells his readers that "every word is dedicated to assisting you in emerging from your divorce with your sanity and economic assets relatively intact." Horgan's recommended tactics include: delaying divorce until your income and assets are at a low ebb; selling valuable coin or stamp collections to a friend for a nominal sum with an understanding that you will repurchase after the divorce settlement; quietly videotaping each room in the house to document all items that your wife might try to sell; "talking down your income, moaning about your expenses," and doing everything you can to reduce your wife's personal spending before the divorce. As for the divorce trial, Horgan says, men have a competitive advantage because they are socialized for combat. He writes: "[W]inning at trial demands coolness under fire, steady nerves and the ability to absorb and deliver punishment. My frequent use of military analogies in this book is not unintended."[28]

Cast in the metaphor of combat, such divorce accounts emphasize control, even denial, of the feelings. While Horgan encourages men to seek therapy to deal with the emotional upheaval of divorce, he reminds them that the larger goal is to ignore or suppress feelings. "How successful the outcome of your divorce will be," he notes, "depends on how well you can control your emotions . . . no one can negotiate successfully out of emotion."[29]

By contrast, the much larger body of advice literature for women casts divorce in the metaphor of an emotional journey. Earlier in the century, the small body of advice literature on divorce for both men and women was notably unimaginative and utilitarian. Books on divorce tended to emphasize the practical mechanics of dissolving a marriage: *Should I Get a Divorce and How?* ran one typical title. Other titles—*Life After Marriage*, for example—suggested a reticence about the very word "divorce." Still others warned readers that they would not be amused by the subject. One book began, "You will not find this book entertaining, because there is nothing entertaining about divorce."[30] But the contemporary advice literature invites women "to step into the [picture] frame, view and review their lives in a new light, and, finally, to become Players, starring in their own stories."[31]

Consider, for example, the opening passages in three popular divorce books. "Twelve years ago my marriage ended," writes Stephanie Marston in *The Divorced Parent*. "It's been nearly twenty years since my marriage cracked open on a gray Christmas afternoon," Abigail Trafford's *Crazy Time* starts off. "My divorce, seven years ago, left me reeling from all the changes I had to make in my life . . . ," Catherine Napolitane says in *Living and Loving After Divorce*.[32] Like "Once upon a time," these incantatory and closely parallel passages draw us into a story. Already we are caught up in signs and portents: holidays turned gray and lives sent reeling. Each of these introductory sentences also makes clear that this is a story rooted in the tradition of women's romantic novels, even as it turns that tradition on its head. Thus, the traditional ending of the romantic novel—"Reader, I Married Him"—is slyly replaced with the beginning "Reader, I Divorced Him." In these advice books, a woman's life is well and truly launched not with marriage to her beloved suitor but with her divorce from a despised spouse.

Moreover, this advice literature links the culturally powerful themes of freedom with the theme of an emotional journey. Sometimes the journey is described in therapeutic terms: from sickness to health. Other times it is characterized in political terms: from slavery to freedom. Occasionally it is cast in spiritual terms: from darkness into the light. Health writer Abigail Trafford writes, "The decision to separate is like Martin Luther nailing his theses to the door. . . . You start on your emotional reformation."[33] Another author writes of "wandering in the wilderness" before setting out on the pilgrimage of divorce. In some of these books, there is also an undertone of apocalyptic expectation—a marital end-time followed by a glorious reawakening. But unvaryingly the narrative is that of an odyssey. At the center of virtually every book is the questing self, seeking and eventually achieving a new identity.

This literature does not ignore the emotional and social upheaval of marital breakup, nor does it minimize the anger and grief that accompany divorce. However, the authors of the books view grief as a temporary and transient condition, marking the first step in the journey toward greater self-awareness and strength. Indeed, as one writer explains, "almost all growth takes place in the imperative of unhappiness." This message is reflected in upbeat titles: *Divorce and New Beginnings*; *Growing Through Divorce*; *Divorced Women, New Lives*; *Our Turn: Women Who Triumph in the Face of Divorce*; *The Best Is Yet to Come*.

In broad outline, the typical divorce narrative goes roughly as follows: A young woman enters marriage blindly or mistakenly or, as the Marxists say, with false consciousness. She has been duped by "the romantic counterrevolutionary image of Grace Kelly surrendering to her prince," or coerced by social pressures to conform to a narrow role.[34] As a result, she falls into a kind of psychological stupor, insensible to her own innermost wishes and desires. But she is shaken out of her somnolent state by reading feminist literature or by taking a women's studies course.[35] Intimations of a better life come to her, slowly at first but with gathering speed and force. As she awakens, she recognizes her true self as distinct from the inauthentic self defined by the roles of wife and mother.

The turning point in the drama comes as the woman realizes that her marriage, based as it was on mistaken ideas or false choices, is fraudulent. In fact, the decision to marry was made by a lesser self, a self that has now vanished. To remain committed to the marriage is to cling to an inauthentic self. "There is no reason," writes Lynette Triere in *Learning to Leave*, "that a woman should be bound for life to a mistaken choice she made at age 18, 24, 33 or 41."[36]

Thus, the awakened woman must take the initiative to end the marriage. As a woman moves out of a relationship that has become involuntary and therefore a kind of servitude, she accomplishes her personal transformation. She opts for freedom, and in the exercise of her freedom she becomes at last, like Pinocchio, a real person.

In divorcing, the self is not only made new but also made whole. Marital breakup brings about a coherent and integrated identity. As one writer puts it, "When being a victim is no longer an option, we are free to discover our own abilities, strengths and creative solutions."[37]

In this advice literature, themes of individual initiative, choice, and independence inevitably invite themes of protest and revolt. In order to express initiative, to overcome passivity and dependency, the self requires something to push against, an opposing and resistant other. The idea of the revolutionary self is not new to expressive divorce. As sociologist Ann Swidler observes, notions of rebellion are central to traditional love ideology: "Identity is symbolized through choosing whom to love and remaining true to one's choice against all opposition. The love relationship that defies convention, family or class barriers asserts the autonomy of the individual."[38]

Yet in the traditional ideology of love and marriage, romantic revolt leads to commitment, both to the chosen beloved and to the social roles and obligations defined institutionally through marriage. If the revolutionary self is expressed in acts of initiative and choice, then the social self is confirmed through marital commitment. Writes Swidler: "What the traditional ideal of love accomplished was to fuse the two conceptions of self together in one overriding achievement. One could follow his deepest impulses to find his true self and embed that self in an institutional commitment."[39]

In this advice literature, however, marriage itself becomes the focus of romantic protest. Women are cloistered in a "cozy cocoon" of marriage, "casualties of a marital subculture that crushed their emerging identities."[40] The literature engages in a rhetorical shift as well, turning divorce, rather than marriage, into the symbol of a mature and accomplished identity. It is divorce, not marriage, that defines a sense of self and leads to greater maturity and self-knowledge. It is divorce, not marriage, that is stimulating and energizing and growth-enhancing. Thus, divorce becomes the defining achievement of women's lives, the great article of their freedom.

Single Motherhood as an Expressive Pursuit

Until the era of expressive divorce, both the expert and popular literature emphasized the hardships of postdivorce life for mothers and
their children. The notion of a shared plight had its roots in nineteenth-century notions of motherhood that saw the mother-child
bond as the most important and durable of all family attachments. A
child's welfare depended on secure and unbroken bonds with the
mother, and this nurturant relationship argued for close physical ties
and maternal custody of the young child—the so-called "tender years"
doctrine. It also required mothers to identify with children emotionally, to assume responsibility for their offspring's pains and sorrows as
well as their physical health and safety.

Because of this ideal of maternity, the family status and identity of
mothers and children were deeply intertwined. Social reformers in the
nineteenth and early twentieth centuries often treated mothers and
children as interchangeable, sometimes conflating child abuse and
wife-battering.[41] Efforts to improve the legal and social status of unwed
mothers were based on the premise that mothers and children share
identities and fates; therefore, liberal reformers argued, eliminating the
stigma of illegitimacy would also remove this social taint not only from
mothers but from their children.

The notion that mothers and children share a common status and
fate in family life also shaped thinking about the impact of divorce on
women throughout the nineteenth and during most of the twentieth
century. Popular magazines and books emphasized the shared difficulties of postdivorce life for mothers and their children. Emotional distress, economic struggle, and social isolation, if no longer social
ostracism, would be their common lot.

Before the last third of the twentieth century, three themes commonly recurred in the expert and popular literature. The first was that
life after divorce was limiting and "unliberating," tying mothers to new
and burdensome economic responsibilities. Worse, even after the marriage was over, there was no breaking free from a despised ex-spouse.
In the tasks of caring for children after divorce, women found themselves miserably bound to their ex-husbands in a state of continued

dependency. As one writer notes, child support payments "chain a divorced couple together" and serve as a source of continuing conflict: "[T]he father often resents them and the mother is often angry because they seem to her to be too little or too late."[42] Even the children's faces remind a mother of her bonds to her ex-spouse. "His nose will stare at you incessantly from the center of Susan's face," one advice manual warned, "and his ears stick out at you from either side of Jimmy's head."[43]

A second recurring theme was that children suffer emotionally from the absence of a father in the family household. Making this point in his classic 1956 study of divorced mothers, sociologist William J. Goode observes: "[A]t every developmental phase of childhood, the child needs the father (who is usually the absent parent) as an object of love, security or identification, or even as a figure against whom to rebel safely. This is the case for both boys and girls."[44]

The popular literature also suggested that mothers would lose their children's affections as a result of divorce. Not only did children experience deep, often unresolved anger and grief at the loss of their fathers, the literature observed, but the children might idealize the father as the special and yearned-for visitor, blaming their mother for his departure.

Experts warned that postdivorce visitation arrangements often led to conflict and distress for children, who must witness emotional scenes between parents and must spend their lives "bouncing back and forth between parents, homes and loyalties."[45] Moreover, the visiting between father and child gave former husbands the opportunity to snoop into, even disrupt, their ex-wives' newly achieved private lives.

A third theme was that mothers would bear the burden of their children's suffering. Because the mother held herself responsible for the child's emotional as well as physical well-being, the child's unhappiness would serve as a constant and nagging reminder not simply of marital failure but, more devastatingly, of maternal failure. Guilt was the divorced mother's constant companion. Divorce might also engender resentment and anger toward the children, diminishing maternal competence and causing deep confusions about the maternal role itself. Thus, divorce could drive a wedge between mothers and children.

As late as the early 1970s, therefore, expert advice, though not unsympathetic to the plight of unhappily married mothers, took an unsentimental, even hard-boiled view of the impact of divorce on women. The gist of the message was: "Don't fool yourself, kid. You may have to get a divorce, but it is tougher than you think. Your children will suffer." All of these arguments obviously placed pressures on women to remain in unhappy, even dangerous marriages "for the sake of the children," as well as to devote themselves to fixing or enduring, rather than exiting, the marriage.

With the rise of expressive divorce, this view of divorced motherhood changed. In studies based on personal interviews, middle-class divorcing mothers report a new sense of control and "a seeming zest and delight" in their new identities as single mothers. Even in the traditional tasks of nurturing, some mothers cite a greater sense of freedom. Without the fathers' presence, they are able to relate to their children "in their own ways."

Many divorced mothers testify that their divorces have given them the opportunity to acquire new competencies and to "develop their instrumental side." In a large government survey 60 percent of divorced mothers said that their career opportunities were better after divorce, and 54 percent reported that their overall situation for caring for their children had improved. The researchers concluded that despite heavier work and child care burdens, the majority of these divorced mothers enjoyed an improved outlook on their lives.[46]

By requiring mothers to pursue jobs, to acquire additional education, or to set up their own businesses, marital breakup could lead to the development of new skills and opportunities. Divorce nurtured competencies that meshed with the demands of the work force and propelled women into a world where their intelligence, initiative, and risk-taking were likely to be recognized and rewarded. After divorce, one advice book explained, women "develop management skills, learn the facts of economic life that they have previously ignored, and take risks that will help them grow."[47]

The notion that divorce and single-motherhood provided the opportunity for mothers to gain new competencies that had value in the larger world of work overturned the earlier conception of divorce as a source of hardship and disadvantage to divorced mothers and their children. If divorce contributed to women's achievement of autonomy, control, and freedom, then it assumed far greater cultural significance and centrality in a society committed to expanding women's opportunities than if it were simply a legal remedy for irretrievably broken marriages. Moreover, if divorce provided a way for women to develop their instrumental side, if financial control and independence were more important than income itself, then there were hidden incentives to divorce that might offset the economic disincentives traditionally associated with it. Finally, if divorce gave mothers the opportunity to gain such psychological benefits as self-esteem, a sense of control, and a stronger identity, why should anyone interfere with the acquisition or development of such valuable personal assets?

CHAPTER THREE

The Divorce Ethic

THE PSYCHOLOGICAL REVOLUTION'S first contribution to the new conception of divorce was scientific. It applied, usually in popular form, knowledge that was generated by the academic and professional disciplines of psychiatry, psychology, and psychotherapy. It was this knowledge that contributed to the notion of an inner life that could be described in secular and clinical terms, the sense that this inner life could be enhanced by the use and application of psychological insights, and finally, the notion that divorce has its genesis in the inner life of the individual.

The psychological revolution's second and more significant contribution to the new conception of divorce was ethical. It took the notion of divorce as an inner experience and placed it under the sway of the ethic of expressive individualism. Arguably, it was possible to apply a knowledge of psychology to divorce without taking the additional and separate step of embracing the expressive ethic, but this did not happen. Instead the ethic of expressive individualism became the ethic of divorce. Its governing principle was that one's first obligation in the dissolution of marriage was to oneself.

The divorce ethic radically changed established ideas about the social and moral obligations associated with divorce. In the past Americans assumed that there were multiple stakeholders in the unhappy business of marital dissolution: the other spouse, the children, relatives, and the larger society. All these stakeholders held an interest in the marital partnership as the source of certain goods, goods that were put at risk each time a marriage dissolved. At particular risk were children, who were the most likely to experience severe losses as a consequence of divorce, especially the loss of the steady support and sponsorship of a father. In divorcing, spouses also jeopardized their own relationships with their children and put at risk the children's relationships with grandparents, relatives, and even family friends. Moreover, since married parents had the central social responsibility for preparing the next generation for useful lives as citizens, workers, and future family members, the dissolution of a marriage was an event in which the society claimed an interest.

However, the notion of divorce as the working out of an inner life experience cast it in far more individualistic terms than in the past. Because divorce originated in an inner sense of dissatisfaction, it acknowledged no other stakeholders. Leaving a marriage was a personal decision, prompted by a set of needs and feelings that were not subject to external interests or claims. Expressive divorce reduced the number of legitimate stakeholders in divorce to one, the individual adult.

If expressive divorce excluded the idea that there are other parties at interest in the "divorce experience," it also overturned earlier notions about one's moral responsibilities to others. An individual's right to divorce was rooted in the individual's right to have a satisfying inner life to fulfill his/her needs and desires. The entitlement to divorce was based on the individual entitlement to pursue inner happiness.

Like all entitlements, the psychological entitlement to divorce was jealously guarded and protected. No one, including the divorcing individual's children, had a "right" to intervene in this intensely private experience or to try to disrupt the course of an emotionally healthy journey toward divorce. Nor were there morally compelling arguments for considering the interests and claims of others in the marriage. If divorce was an entirely subjective and individual experience, rooted in a particular set of needs, values, and preferences, then there was no basis for making judgments about the decision to divorce. The new ethic of divorce was morally relativistic: There could be no right or wrong reasons for divorce; there were only reasons, which it was the task of therapy to elicit and affirm.

Taken together, the conception of divorce as an inner journey of the self and the ethical imperative to put one's interests and needs first had one far-reaching consequence: It weakened the rationale for the legal or social regulation of divorce. If the divorce experience was an inner journey of the sovereign self, what right had anyone to place impediments in the way?

Deregulating Divorce

With the advent of expressive divorce, the argument for regulating divorce collapsed. Americans increasingly believed that individuals are entitled to seek divorce for their own reasons without outside interference. This thinking clearly shaped attitudes about legal impediments to divorce. As one scholar observes, the emerging legal consensus maintained that "individuals who are unhappy in their marriage have a 'right' to get a divorce and that it is unfair and inappropriate for the state to erect legal barriers to prevent them from exercising that right."[1]

The shift to a system of no-fault divorce both reflected and contributed to the new conception of divorce. For a couple who had come to a mutual decision to end a marriage, the traditional practice of finding and assigning fault to one spouse often required fabricating some offense like adultery and thereby tainting the reputation of one partner. No-fault divorce was designed to eliminate this legal playacting and thereby to make divorce more honest. California enacted the nation's first no-fault statute in 1970, and other states soon followed; by 1980, all but two states had no-fault divorce laws on the books. Fault no longer sullied divorce or tarnished reputations; in this sense, the legal dissolution of marriage had become a "cleaner" as well as an easier process.

However, no-fault divorce fully supported the single-stakeholder theory of expressive divorce. It established a disaffected spouse's right unilaterally to dissolve a marriage simply by declaring that the relationship was over. Characterizing standard legal practice in the states, legal scholar Mary Ann Glendon has observed: ". . . the virtually universal understanding . . . is that the breakdown of a marriage is irretrievable if one spouse says it is."[2] Even more consequentially, no-fault gave one parent the unilateral power to disrupt at will and without cause the other parent's affective relationship with his or her child.[3]

The removal of legal impediments to divorce was accompanied by the removal of the remaining social impediments. From the mid-1970s on the secular experts of marriage and divorce began to deregulate divorce. Their goal was to remove even modest and informal social sanctions against divorce involving children, to lift the encumbrances that stood in the way of the individual right to divorce.

Etiquette, one source of more conservative opinion on divorce, came to reflect this new mandate. As the divorce rate began its historic climb, the etiquette literature remained consistent in its view of divorce as a failure and continued to counsel Americans against publicly expressing relief or happiness over the dissolution of marriage. Yet with the psychological revolution and the rise of expressive divorce, two important changes occurred in the conduct literature. First, divorce was decoupled from marriage. Instead of treating divorce as part of an institutional system governed by marriage, as it had in earlier years, Elizabeth L. Post's *Etiquette* placed divorce in the category of "relationships," and later in the even more generic category of "interrelationships." Simultaneously marriage lost its privileged status in the social world and was demoted to the status of an intimate relationship, equivalent to divorce and living together. In the 1994 edition the chapter titled "Interrelationships" includes what might be called relationship formation—rooming together, dating, cohabiting, marrying, remarrying, adopting, and choosing to bear a child on one's own—as well as relationship dissolution—moving out, separating, and divorcing. It also attends to managing relationships, including such family matters as explaining divorce to children, introducing a "new relationship" to children, and informing your child's school about a new living-together arrangement. ("I want you to know that Jenny's home situation has changed. Don Phelps is living with us.")

A second and striking change in the conduct literature was the gradual shift away from conduct itself. After 1975 *Etiquette*'s focus turns from rules on "how to behave" in divorce to rules on "what to say" about divorce. Propriety no longer takes the form of right conduct but of good explanations. In brief, psychological norms replace social norms, and therapeutic correctness becomes the new standard of good behavior. This shift is particularly strong when it comes to divorces involving children. Editions after 1975 exhibit great solicitude for

children troubled by divorce or remarriage and profess consideration
for their feelings. But the literature drops its injunction that parents
should seek to preserve marriage "for the sake of the children." Instead, the 1994 edition of *Etiquette* instructs parents not on how to
avoid behavior that might be damaging to their children but on how
to tell children about the decision to divorce or to "solo-parent." It
also offers guidance on how children should describe a parent's "living
together" relationship as well as how to console children over the loss
of a live-in lover: "We lived together as long as we were able to help
each other be happy but when Joan [or Bill] and I couldn't do that any
more, we had to leave each other. . . . Let's try to remember how nice it
was for a while and find other ways to be happy now."[4]

A similar but more dramatic shift occurs in the literature and practice of marriage counseling. By the 1970s the elimination of fault in
most of the states' divorce laws made the sorting out of responsibility
for marital breakup a psychological rather than a legal endeavor. Considerations of fault did not disappear so much as change venue; fault
was not assigned by the courts but worked out in therapy. Achieving a
constructive "emotional" divorce became a dominant goal of marriage
therapy.

Nonetheless, according to therapeutic precepts, the fault for marital breakup must be shared, even when one spouse unilaterally seeks a
divorce. In essence, counseling established a joint-fault system aimed
at persuading each individual to accept responsibility for the breakup.
As one study of therapeutic opinion notes, "the strategy which most
clearly differentiates divorce therapy from marital or family therapy is
what we have labelled orchestrating the motivation to divorce." This
may include "openly arguing for the advantages of the divorce as opposed to continuing marital unhappiness and trial separation." The
goal here was to accept responsibility for the failure of the marriage
and thereby to achieve a new level of self-understanding. "To view
oneself as innocent victim is thus to engage in fundamental distor-
tion," the study goes on, "the consequence of which is a high proba-
bility for an equally bad remarriage."[5]

Such therapeutic reasoning defied a more commonsense view of
right and wrong, however. Many husbands and wives who did not seek
or want divorce were stunned to learn from their therapists that they

were equally "at fault" in the dissolution of their marriages. The notion of fault apparently had a moral basis which endured even after the notion of fault had been eradicated in law and mores.

Therapeutic opinion shifted dramatically with respect to the earlier goal of "saving the marriage." Marriage therapists now adopted a formal posture of neutrality on whether or not to work for marriage preservation. As one therapist explained in a newspaper interview, "I don't think it's my job to decide whether it's a good marriage or a bad marriage, so I can't decide whether a couple should stay in it. My job is to help each of them see what they do that limits them or prevents them from getting what they need and want."

Despite the posture of therapeutic neutrality, its practical effect was not true neutrality but a bias toward divorce. In *One Man, Hurt*, a divorce memoir written in the 1970s, the pseudonymous author recounts his experience in marriage counseling. Reluctant to divorce, this husband and father of four young boys entered therapy in hopes of salvaging his marriage. But he soon discovered that therapy actually increased the disposition to divorce:

> The counseling itself pulled us further apart rather than bringing [*sic*] us closer together. Yes, it did put us in touch with ourselves, it did enable us to see our needs better, and it did encourage us to fulfill them. But that is what is dreadfully wrong . . . the tragic result is that people caught in the emotional chaos and upheaval of marital crisis can seldom look beyond the tough, unpalatable, excruciating steps of rebuilding the relationship. It is easier to say that no basis for the rebuilding exists or that it is not his or her need.

When he voiced his deep desire to preserve his marriage, his marriage therapist invoked the ethic of expressive divorce: "We are in the business of saving individuals, not marriages."[6]

One consequence of this individualistic approach was its neglect of marriage as the domain of obligation and commitment, particularly to children. Not only did marriage counseling ignore the spousal relationship, it also excluded children as stakeholders in the marital partnership. Intentionally or not, it relieved divorcing couples of their responsibilities for considering their children's well-being. In *Soul Searching*, a critique of psychotherapeutic trends in recent decades, William Doherty defends self-interest as one component of marital commitment. But he notes: "Many therapists will dismiss as a copout a client's statement that he or she is staying married 'for the children's sake,' or because I made a commitment for 'better or worse.' These reasons for staying in a marriage are seen as excuses to avoid making a hard decision based on one's needs."[7]

Books and articles on divorce routinely encouraged parents to make the decision about divorce on the basis of their own individual situations and interests rather than on the wishes or needs of their children. In a 1985 book entitled *Quality Time: Easing Children Through Divorce*, one psychiatrist writes: "All the comments about the needs of children for intact families should not cause any divorcing parent to consider reconciliation for the sake of the children."[8] In brief, psychotherapeutic thinking in the 1970s and 1980s largely dismissed commitment to children as a reason for trying to "save" a marriage. Commitment to self was all.

Though the rules of etiquette and the practice of marriage therapy drew upon different traditions and focused on different dimensions of human behavior and experience, their responses to divorce were remarkably convergent after the 1970s. Each moved away from the social and familial world in the direction of individual expressive freedom. Each retreated from the notion that parents have an obligation to put children's interests and well-being above their own needs. Each sought to weaken or remove the outer obstacles and constraints to divorce.

The idea that social rules are obstacles to the individual's pursuit of life satisfactions dramatically changed the role and influence of the experts themselves. In order to accommodate expressive divorce, experts had to abandon their own professional traditions. Many marriage counselors disavowed marital counseling altogether, because counseling on marriage suggested a commitment to the institution, with its larger social purposes, rather than to individuals. Instead they became divorce counselors, whose professional goal was to help individuals in the management of the "inner divorce." Similarly, the conduct experts had to accept a diminished role in the social regulation of divorce in order to comply with the new rules of expressive divorce, which, by their very nature, rejected outside governance and thus the authority of the social arbiters. Finally, the experts retreated from their traditional defense of children as stakeholders in their parents' marriage. The idea that every effort should be made to preserve and improve marriage "for the sake of the children" was abandoned. The individual psychological well-being of adults, based on the subjective self-reports of grown-ups, became the new measure of family well-being.

Applauding Divorce

Expressive divorce did not simply argue that the social world should remove the impediments to divorce and remain neutral about its practice. It made a more presumptuous claim: It sought the good opinion of others. One of the leading academic exponents of this argument was University of California therapist Constance Ahrons, author of the 1994 book *The Good Divorce.* According to Ahrons, it is not divorce itself but "divorcism"—a set of harshly discriminatory and cruelly stigmatizing attitudes and stereotypes—that makes divorcing so personally traumatic.

Though imprecise and inconsistent in her nomenclature, Ahrons seems to equate stigma with negative stereotyping, the social labeling of divorced people as a deviant group.[9] This labeling takes several forms. First, there is divorcist language: Divorced families are characterized as "broken," "deviant," and screwed up. Second, there are the negative stereotypes associated with divorce: unhappy single mothers; distressed and disruptive children; economically threadbare households. Third, there is widespread misuse of research studies to blame and to burden further families that experience divorce. Ahrons points to politicians (unnamed) who use studies of the negative economic consequences of divorce "to support more punitive, regressive divorce laws." Too, the media focus on the worst and most conflictual divorces—Burt Reynolds and Loni Anderson, for example—rather than on the most harmonious and successful divorces. Finally, the legal system of divorce "is still embedded in the old moralities," perpetuating negative stereotypes and thus damaging the well-being of divorcing couples and their children. Ignoring a substantial body of evidence to the contrary, Ahrons writes: "Emotionally, legally, and socially, divorce is difficult to get."[10]

According to Ahrons, disapproval of divorce carries harmful social consequences. It can lead to discrimination against divorced people. For example, many personal information forms or applications have a "divorced" box to check. "Why do they want this information?" Ahrons asks. "I can imagine an account executive saying 'Hmm, divorced. Who's responsible for paying the bills?' Or a doctor attributing an ailment to the stress of divorce."[11] What's more, stigma encourages denial of the social reality of divorce. The fact is that divorce is "here to stay," and we might as well learn to live with it, even incorporate it into "our visions of the good life." But the worst consequences of stigma are psychological. The external labeling affects internal feelings. Social disapproval of divorce makes people feel bad about themselves; it contributes to anger, self-doubt, low self-esteem. It is "dangerous to the soul."[12] Because the social disapproval associated with divorce is so psychologically debilitating, it must be eradicated.

Accordingly, Ahrons proposes an agenda for changing the rules, roles, and rituals of divorce, including a cultural overhaul of language, customs, and habits. One recommended change is the ritualization of divorce. As a desirable ritual she cites the wedding ring–smashing ceremony invented by a New Mexico entrepreneur specializing in "Freedom Rings: Jewelry for the Divorced."[13] This ceremony involves hitting the wedding ring with a sledgehammer and then creating a new bauble (at various price ranges) from the smashed metal. If such rituals were to become more common, Ahrons argues, they could become part of the emotional healing process.[14] Similarly, we might smash divorcist language. "The negative language so common to divorce imprisons families by making them feel that they are bad or unacceptable," she writes. Why not reform our "nuclear-centric" vocabulary? Why not refer to divorced families as "binuclear" instead of "broken"; why not call ex-relatives and near relatives "fuzzy kin" rather than "exes" and "steps"? (However, she does not call for changing the stigmatizing stereotype of "deadbeat dad.") More persuasively, Ahrons argues for unburdening children of divorcist stereotypes. "The negative effects on children could be minimized if they could be assured that their family life was not dependent on their parents' marriage."[15]

Nowhere is her appeal for approval more passionate than when she describes her own divorce, which took place in 1965, after considerable and prolonged travail. "I was the one who left," she tells us, "and for two miserable years, my husband and I battled constantly over custody, visitation, and child support. There were private detectives, a kidnapping, several lawyers, and two years of legal fees that took me the next ten years to pay off."[16] Moreover, she suffered from the attitudes of well-meaning relatives who told her no one in the family had ever been divorced, and from the prejudices of her children's teachers, who assumed her kids would be troubled. She also faced a problem concerning her right to maintain a residence in married student housing after she left her husband, though college housing officials eventually relented and permitted her to stay.

One can sympathize with Ahrons's troubles, but the idea that the vicissitudes of her divorce were caused by *society's* bad behavior is hardly credible. Clearly, she and her ex-husband had at least something to do with their messy breakup. Nonetheless, her argument is revealing of the imperious claims that expressive divorce makes on the larger social world. In order to help divorced people to feel good about themselves, society in general must feel good about divorce and incorporate it, in Ahrons's words, into "our dreams of the good life."

This view represents a historic departure from previous thinking about the proper social response to divorce. Earlier in the century experts had argued that in order to protect the interests of children and to promote greater harmony between divorced parents, society should not ostracize the divorced. By contrast, the new argument called for the end to social disapproval of divorce in the name of individual psychological health. According to this perspective, what was placed at risk by divorce was not the children's well-being or the family's stability as an institution for child-rearing but the individual's inner sense of well-being. Thus, the argument for "good divorce" goes well beyond the reasonable bid for conscientious efforts to lessen the hardships of divorce for children or to improve the legal process for divorcing parents or to encourage more parental cooperation in child-rearing after divorce. In essence, it shifts the burden of responsibility for proper conduct and right thinking to the other members of the society. The unobligated self places obligations on others. As one woman told Ahrons, "I'm sick and tired of being blamed for taking a step I think was healthy for me!"[17]

The Expressive Ethic and the Spirit of Capitalism

Though academics like Ahrons saw their efforts to free divorce from social regulation as consistent with liberal ideology, they were actually moving away from the earlier strain of liberal thought which saw divorce as exploitative of family relationships. As the progressive critics of vulgar divorce understood, divorce fostered a marketplace approach to family and social obligations, encouraging individuals to use divorce as a means of advancing their social and economic fortunes.

Like vulgar divorce, expressive divorce regarded marital breakup as a vehicle for self-improvement. But whereas vulgar divorce emphasized the material resources that might be freed through divorce and an economically strategic remarriage, expressive divorce saw one's inner resources as a block of capital, to be developed and deployed to maximum advantage. The deeper logic of expressive divorce was the logic of capitalism. Just as the ideology of the market called upon the owner of capital to maximize resources, so the expressive ideology of divorce urged the proprietor of psychological capital to do the same. Just as the astute investor of financial capital shrewdly moved resources from commercial relationships that yielded a relatively lower rate of return to commercial relationships that offered a higher return, so the investor of psychological capital should do the same, though the relationships in this case were personal rather than commercial. In order to maximize profits, capital had to be mobile; like financial capital, psychological capital should not be fettered or bound by relationships that did not yield high returns. To accept such fetters was stupid and led, as the divorce books had it, to a stuporous existence, the psychological counterpart of what the investment world would describe and decry as the lazy use of capital.

The logic of expressive divorce also suggested that relationships themselves—especially relationships that are binding or permanent—

are risky investments. The most reliable form of investment thus becomes the investment in the self. The logic of expressive divorce argued not only for building one's own psychological capital, therefore, but also for keeping it "liquid." A self not tied down by permanent bonds and obligations was a self that could take advantage of new opportunities as they came along.

Once divorce had been redefined as an inner experience that could yield important psychological assets, all barriers to the commercialization of divorce fell. Marketplace values of choice, unfettered freedom, contingency, and dynamic change were the values of expressive divorce. Moreover, the marketplace was better suited to respond to individual needs and preferences in the dissolution of marriages than were the traditional institutions of the civil society, such as the church, the voluntary nonprofit organization, and the family itself. Needless to say, there was great commercial potential in divorce. The growing population of Americans thinking about divorce, going through divorce, or recovering from divorce represented a potential market to be exploited by providers of services in the legal, real estate, financial, and investigative professions. And since the "emotional divorce" was not over as quickly as the legal divorce, the need for professional therapeutic services in negotiating what was now a complex and potentially transformative process could extend long after the marriage was over.

As the market for therapeutic services expanded, so too did its penetration into the middle and lower echelons of society. Affluent middle-class Americans were more likely than less-well-off people to cite emotional growth or self-fulfillment as "reasons" for divorce and to seek private therapy during divorce, but lower-middle-class and working-class Americans increasingly found their way into therapists' offices. Indeed, perhaps more than any other single social force, divorce was responsible for democratizing private therapy. As one divorcing male laborer explained to a researcher, "I went through quite a bit of counseling, which the average person should go through. . . . If I got any friend that has a problem, I'll just say, 'Hey, go to counseling.' As a joke, but it's not a joke. I truly have faith in it. A person cannot work on his problems himself."[18]

The legal process of divorce created yet another expanding market for professional psychological services. Contentious child custody battles often brought therapists into the courtroom as expert witnesses to deliver their assessments of the competence of warring mothers and fathers and to offer evaluations of the children's emotional health. The Harvard child psychiatrist Robert Coles writes: "What a bonanza those [divorce] courts are for my ilk—we are the ones who get the patients, who are appointed mediators, who decide when the children should visit which parent: mediation in the name of something called 'mental health.' " According to Coles, one consequence of this alliance was that therapeutic opinion was recruited in support of divorce itself: "Now . . . my profession of psychoanalytic psychiatry is often summoned up to defend particular divorces, even the more general phenomenon of divorce, as a readily available and far from objectionable alternative to what is often called a 'bad marriage,' meaning, of course, one in which psychological pain is to be found."[19]

The Ideological Consensus

In the politically polarized debate over the nature and meaning of changes in family life, there was remarkably little dissensus over divorce. As it turned out, both conservatives and liberals could embrace expressive divorce and its claims. Both sides accepted the notion that divorce could generate individual psychological goods and benefits, albeit for different reasons.

Liberals were attracted by the psychological benefits as well as the political advantages expressive divorce seemed to hold for women. Liberals saw such traits as self-esteem, self-confidence, and self-determination as valuable assets for women. If divorce nurtured such traits and often required women to use them in the workforce, then divorce was fully compatible with the larger goal of economic independence for women. Moreover, as some strains of feminist thinking held, psychological inequality was one of the many forms of inequality between men and women. Women suffered from low self-esteem, a lack of assertiveness, a desire to please, and sometimes an excessive concern for the needs of others. Thus, if divorce promoted a greater self-confidence and self-awareness, it could reduce psychological inequalities between men and women. Freed from their psychological dependency on marriage, women would be more competent and able to "hold their own" against men in the workplace as well as in family life.

For their part, conservatives found the ideology of expressive divorce compatible with their philosophical commitment to a deregulated environment that left the individual free to pursue opportunities and maximize profits. And on practical grounds as well, conservatives embraced the idea of divorce as an individual prerogative to be freely exercised by adults, without interference by others. Leading conservative politicians had themselves exercised this prerogative, including 1996 presidential contenders Phil Gramm and Bob Dole and congressional firebrand Newt Gingrich.

Nevertheless, in relation to their respective traditions, the liberal embrace of expressive divorce is more striking than the conservative endorsement. Given the strong tendency within conservatism to celebrate market forces, often to the detriment of the family, it is not surprising that conservatives would adopt a conception of divorce shot through with marketplace values and reasoning. Twentieth-century American liberalism, on the other hand, has been vocal in both its concern for the welfare of children and its often skeptical view of the market. Indeed, the notion that there must be a boundary between the domestic domain and the commercial domain, the better to protect children from the corrupting values of the money world, was a defining tenet of liberalism, in general, and turn-of-the-century progressive feminism, in particular. That is why in the 1890s the editors of the progressive magazine *The Nation* saw the commerce in divorce as so threatening to the institution of marriage and the family. But by the late twentieth century many liberals and feminists were embracing a conception of divorce that disenfranchised children and gave the marketplace a gilt-edged invitation to burst into the domestic sphere and enter boldly through the front door.

Expressive divorce strained traditional liberal loyalties because it called attention to a growing fault line in the family between women and children. Throughout most of the nation's history, divorce was viewed as an event that split women and children from men and from the support and provision of the male breadwinner. However, it was assumed that women's and children's interests and fate in the family were shared, if not identical. By the late twentieth century, the cultural ideal of shared mother-child fates was challenged by a host of changes in women's lives, including increasing career and educational opportunities for women, mothers' growing work-force participation, a decline in number of children and thus the years of women's life devoted to child-rearing, and diminished focus on domesticity as a form of feminine achievement. All these changes expanded women's individual opportunities in the world outside of the family and placed increased strains on their family roles as wives and mothers. True, these strains more severely affected the husband-wife relationship than the mother-child bond; women continued to value their roles and identities as mothers and to carry the major responsibility for raising children. However, as historian Carl Degler has noted, the values underlying women's emancipation—independence, individualism, and self-expression—tend intrinsically to clash with the obligations imposed by family membership—solidarity, mutuality, and the subordination of maternal interests to the needs of children—and so have increasingly placed women and children as well "at odds." And the new conception of divorce, with its promise of psychological benefits and goods for women, has further reinforced those values.

Caught between defending the freedom of women to divorce and protecting the interests of children in the family, liberals chose to defend divorce as a freedom for women. From roughly the mid-1960s on, liberal opinion increasingly devoted itself to championing the rights and interests of single mothers and to condemning those who raised concerns about the impact of divorce on children as illiberal.

But the liberal retreat from representing the interests of children was only part of a much broader turn in opinion. The conception of divorce as a psychological entitlement for adults was, by its very nature, adversarial to children. It was nearly impossible to embrace the tenets of expressive divorce, on the one hand, and to serve the best interests of children, on the other hand.

CHAPTER FOUR

Divorce "for the Sake of the Children"

AFTER THE MID-1960S, Americans viewed divorces involving children more permissively, and more American divorces involved children. Although it is notoriously tricky to pin down the precise causal relationship between attitudes and behavior, what can be asserted with confidence is that attitudes toward divorce with children and actual divorces involving children were moving in the same direction at roughly the same time.

For most of the nation's history, concern for the well-being of children was a central reason for avoiding divorce. Most Americans believed that divorce imposed such severe and sometimes lasting hardships on children that it should be avoided except in marriages torn by violence or other severe abuses. Consequently, parents were enjoined to work out their differences (or at least conceal them) so that they could hold the marriage together "for the sake of the children."

This injunction was rooted in a tradition of thought about the social and moral bases of child nurture and well-being. It recognized marriage as society's chief institution for child-rearing and the most important source of social insurance for children. Marriage provided the basis for sustained investment and nurture by two parents; as important, it attached fathers to their biological children and fostered regular, sustained paternal support and sponsorship. Marriage also fostered a child's attachments to the larger social world. "Remember that a child's greatest need is security . . . ," a 1947 book on divorce admonishes. "Will he have that after divorce? What about the associations he has made, the friends he has, his neighborhood groups and clubs, his schoolmates?"[1]

The injunction that unhappily married parents should preserve the marriage for the sake of the children was also rooted in an ethical principle: the idea that parents have a duty and an obligation—to their children, to each other, and to the larger society—to place their children's needs above their own individual interests and even above their satisfactions with the spousal relationship. This ethical principle also imposed an obligation on parents in a troubled marriage to work diligently to resolve their differences, not simply to "save" the marriage but to improve it, for the children's sake. Implicitly it saw parents as the emotionally resilient and resourceful members of the family and children as the emotionally and economically vulnerable family members. It assumed that parents would be able to work out their problems in marriage more readily than children could manage the problems that came with divorce.

After the mid-1960s, this injunction lost support and credibility, both as a statement about the sources of child well-being and as a statement about the obligations of parents to children. One clear sign of its waning influence was the change in women's opinion. In 1962, on the threshold of the divorce revolution, researchers asked women whether they agreed or disagreed with the statement that "when there are children in the family parents should stay together even if they don't get along." Opinion was roughly divided, with 51 percent of the women disagreeing. By 1977, when researchers posed the question again to the same sample of women, 80 percent disagreed.[2] In the course of fifteen years this group of women had moved from divided opinion to an overwhelming consensus that unhappily married parents should not stay together for the children's sake.

Over an even earlier span of time, one of America's most popular advice-givers changed her mind on divorce with children as well. In 1957 Ann Landers defied readers to find "a single column in which I suggested divorce." By 1972, however, she was writing: "I no longer believe that marriage means forever no matter how lousy it is—or 'for the sake of the children' [italics mine]."[3]

Divorces involving children increased steadily after the mid-1960s.

The rate of children involved in divorce doubled between the early sixties and the late eighties. The absolute number of children thus affected grew accordingly; beginning in 1974 and continuing in each successive year for the next sixteen years, more than one million children annually saw their parents divorce. Historically, couples with children were less likely to divorce than couples without children, but this gap now began to narrow. By 1990 approximately 60 percent of American divorces involved children, a percentage exceeded only in Britain, where one or more children were involved in 66 percent of all divorces.[4]

The increase in divorce among couples with children profoundly changed the organization of children's family lives and the nature of parent-child relationships. Never before had so many American children had their families broken by divorce or had their lives divided between separate parental households. Since marriages dissolved, on average, around the seven-year mark, many children were quite young when their parents divorced. This meant that children would spend a substantial part of their childhood in a single- or cohabiting-parent household or in a stepfamily household. It also meant that such children were exposed to an increased risk of more than one family disruption during the course of childhood, since parents' partnerships after divorce were notably fragile and often fleeting.

Nothing in the history of American childhood rivaled the scale or speed of this change in children's families. In the space of little more than thirty years, divorce went from being a relatively rare childhood event, affecting only a small proportion of all American children, to a collective childhood experience, involving a near-majority of children. According to recent estimates, approximately 45 percent of children born to married parents are likely to experience parental divorce before age eighteen.[5] This statistic does not capture the full impact of divorce, however. Divorce commonly initiates a string of disruptive events in children's family lives, which may include one or more of the following: life in a single-parent household or cohabiting-parent household combined with partial residency or visits to a nonresidential parent's household; entry into a stepfamily household and possible membership in a second; dissolution of one or both cohabiting or stepfamily arrangements; and so on. Changes in family household arrangements often involve residential moves, which in turn lead to changes in schools, neighborhoods, and playmates. Consequently, divorce on such a scale unleashes a host of destabilizing forces into children's family lives. Indeed, if recent social history were written through the eyes of children, 1974 might be described as the Great Crash, a moment when divorce became the leading cause of broken families and unexpectedly plunged children into a trough of family instability, increased economic vulnerability, and traumatic loss.

Two Waves of Thinking

In the early years of the divorce revolution, no one knew how such a rapid and widespread increase of divorces would affect children. Much of the earlier research about children and divorce drew upon evidence gathered when the absolute number as well as the percentage of children whose parents divorced was small. The research also relied on unrepresentative samples of children and thus could not be taken as the basis for empirical generalizations about the current population of children of divorce. Moreover, these studies did not follow children over the years after their parents' divorces, so it was difficult to establish the trajectory of the divorce process over the course of childhood or to determine whether there were long-term negative effects of divorce. Finally, the research often relied on mothers' or other adults' reports and observations rather than on independently verifiable measures of children's well-being or children's own reports.

Ideological considerations limited investigations into the impact of divorce on children as well. In 1965, when then–Assistant Labor Secretary Daniel Patrick Moynihan identified family breakdown as the source of growing economic and social disadvantage among African-Americans in his report *The Negro Family: The Case for National Action*, liberal academics denounced him for blaming single mothers for such structural conditions as racism and poverty. After the furor subsided, few researchers wanted to go near such an explosive subject again. Sociological investigation of family structure languished for a decade—and a crucial decade at that. Between the mid-1960s and mid-1970s family breakdown among white American families began to move in the same direction as family disruption in African-American families. This suggested that the increase in single-mother families, though much more advanced among African-Americans, was not limited to black families but was a broad and pervasive family trend.

After the mid-1970s, thinking about the impact of divorce on children occurred in two separate waves. The first wave, covering roughly the next decade, preceded any large-scale empirical investigation. It mainly relied on speculative lines of argument. The second wave appeared after the mid-1980s. By this time a body of empirical evidence, gathered from well-designed, large-scale, and long-term studies, had emerged. These studies drew upon large, nationally representative samples of children in intact as well as divorced families and were controlled for such key variables as race, socioeconomic status, residence, and parents' ages and education. The second wave thus provided a more reliable assessment of the impact of divorce on the contemporary generation of children than did the first wave. It also offered a way of assessing the speculative claims made in the first wave of opinion.

Expressive Divorce for Kids

Several key lines of argument figured in the first wave of opinion. Though these arguments were not entirely consistent or compatible with one another, they coexisted within the speculative climate of opinion and enjoyed a rough parity.

One was a historical argument. On the basis of a reading of the large-scale and long-term demographic patterns in children's family lives, it suggested that divorce is the modern-day equivalent of parental death. Whereas children had once experienced family breakup as a consequence of parental death, now they were experiencing similar disruptions as a consequence of parental divorce. In short, the drop in mortality rates among American adults had given way to the rise in the "mortality" of American marriages. Though this was an accurate statement of demographic patterns, some took this pattern as compelling evidence that family disruption is an enduring and immutable pattern, a historical constant in the lives of children. Whether caused by death or divorce, marital dissolution as well as father-absence could be counted as one of the unavoidable risks of being a child. Therefore, the rising tide of divorce was not a sign of family decline, dysfunction, or disadvantage for children but simply a new cause of an old childhood condition.[6]

A second line of argument advanced the claim that divorce could benefit children in the same way that it benefited their parents. Kids too could gain psychological competencies and advantages from divorce. According to a representative 1974 book, *The Courage to Divorce*, "divorce can liberate children." Its authors, social workers Susan Gettleman and Janet Markowitz, emphasize the psychological goods and benefits of divorce for children. Because of the nature of their life experiences, the children of divorce have particular advantages and opportunities, including "greater insight and freedom as adults in deciding whether and when to marry" and, after divorce, exposure to new adults who help children "break away from excessive dependency on their biological parents."[7] Parents who decide to divorce should emphasize the shared psychological blessings of postdivorce family life in discussions with their children. The authors approvingly cite one mother's positive announcement of divorce: "Children, I have good news for all of us. There is going to be more happiness in this house from now on."[8]

The Courage to Divorce also claims that divorce will result in better relationships between nonresidential fathers and children, noting that divorced fathers can pay more attention to their children than unhappily married fathers. Compared with miserable married fathers, who often take extra jobs to get away from their wives, say the book's authors, divorced fathers have visitation privileges which provide "a number of undisturbed hours in which parent and child may be left alone with each other, to share thoughts, feelings and experiences."[9] As for the concern that father-absence is harmful to boys, it is exaggerated. "When fathers are not available, friends, relatives, teachers and counselors can provide ample opportunity for youngsters to model themselves after a like-sexed adult."[10]

The authors also argue that divorce no longer imposes severe economic loss and disadvantage on mothers and their children. On the contrary, marital dissolution can spur the career development and economic advancement of divorced mothers: "Divorce often impels a nonworking wife into gainful employment, while child-support payments (and often even alimony) continue. This may mean augmented income for the wife and children."

Gettleman and Markowitz see larger societal advantages as well in the march toward divorce: "[F]uture generations of women may not have to look forward to the humiliation of taking alms from men who do not love them and whom they do not love. . . . Men may be freed of what is often an onerous and unfair burden, and children, hopefully, will cease to be pawns in the parental struggle over money."[11]

Other popular divorce books offered similarly optimistic appraisals of the impact of divorce on children. Therapist Mel Krantzler, author of the 1973 best-selling *Creative Divorce: A New Opportunity for Personal Growth*, argued that family breakup may make children more sensitive and tolerant toward others. Out of the creative chaos of divorce can come "more cooperation and respect, more regard for differences as well as similarities, more opportunity for children to grow into the unique individuals they are capable of becoming."[12] According to another child expert, divorce provides "an ambiguous, expanded experience that moves kids to better adjustment in a society that is highly ambiguous and expanded."[13]

This line of argument suggested that the psychological benefits of divorce are not only direct but indirect. Divorce enhances maternal well-being, and given the close bonds between mothers and children and the likelihood that the mother will be the custodial parent, happier mothers will make for happier children. The crisis of divorce has "growth potential," a 1979 article in the *Journal of Divorce* notes, with benefits including "increased personal autonomy, a new sense of competence and control, *development of better relationships with children*, and the freedom and time to develop . . . interests [italics mine]."[14]

A third line of argument held that children are psychologically sturdy. They will be able to "bounce back" from the short-term difficulties of divorce, just as they recover rapidly from the sniffles or the flu. Moreover, many scholars claimed, divorced mothers usually remarried quickly, and their children then moved into stepfamilies, where they again enjoyed the advantages of a household with a second residential parent and an improved standard of living. Thus, for the majority of children who experienced divorce, the spell of time in single-mother households, and presumably the hardships that might accompany this sojourn, would be short-lived.

A fourth assertion was that the problems commonly attributed to divorce are actually due to socioeconomic differences in families with children. The inequities of class, race, and gender cause disadvantages for mothers and children and often contribute to a family's vulnerability to divorce. Thus, efforts to promote children's well-being by avoiding divorce are misplaced; a more effective approach is to eliminate the economic and social inequities that create disadvantage for single mothers and their children.[15]

Another argument made a similar kind of assertion about children's emotional and behavioral problems after divorce. People blamed "broken homes" for such problems as poor school performance, juvenile delinquency, and other forms of antisocial behavior. Yet, argued first-wave thinking, it was not divorce but rather marital strife and dysfunctional family relationships that caused children's most serious emotional problems. This led some to conclude that divorce would improve, rather than damage, children's family lives by eliminating the conflict, and thus the emotional stresses of living with mutually disaffected parents. Perhaps unwittingly, this argument contributed to a sharply dichotomized view of life before and life after divorce and thus encouraged a "happily ever after" vision of postdivorce life for children.

Singly or together, all these lines of argument provided little real insight into what was actually happening to children who were living through their parents' divorces in the 1970s and early 1980s. But that does not mean that the first wave of opinion had no influence. On the contrary, its influence was substantial. In a climate of opinion already increasingly permissive toward divorces involving children, first-wave thinking supplied what appeared to be an intellectually respectable rationale for such divorces.

Most influentially, this rationale established a new measure of child well-being: the individual marital satisfaction of each parent. In contrast with the earlier view which linked children's interests to their parents' marriage, the new view tied children's interests to the emotional well-being of each parent but particularly of the mother. Since divorce could improve the psychological status of one or both unhappy parents and create opportunities for a better family life in the future, then children's interests could be represented and served by divorce.

This rationale for divorce also offered a reprieve from the ethical imperative for parents to preserve the marriage for the children's sake. In their intimate and family relationships, parents' first responsibility was to themselves; if they sought their own satisfactions, then their children's happiness would follow—a form of reasoning that William J. Doherty describes as "psychological trickledown." Consequently, first-wave opinion stood on its head the traditional injunction to stay married for the sake of the children. Now, the argument went, children are better off if their unhappily married parents divorce.

This was a remarkable change in expert opinion not only because it overturned the long-standing belief in marriage as the source of children's basic security but also because it shifted the weight of expert opinion from protecting the interests of children to defending the rights and prerogatives of parents to pursue their own satisfactions. By equating children's well-being with the achievement of individual adult satisfactions, first-wave thinking could attend to the experience of adults, assuming that children's best interests would thereby be served. Since the psychological benefits of divorce would trickle down from parents to children, it was no longer necessary for the social and legal world to represent the interests of children in marriage as separate from those of their parents or to defend children against the self-interested actions or misconduct of parents in a troubled marriage. In essence, therefore, this new rationale for divorce excluded children as independent stakeholders in their parents' marriage.

This shift toward greater concern with parental satisfactions had one unexpected and perverse consequence. Once parents were relieved of the obligation to preserve their marriage for the children's sake, they were also relieved of the obligation to conduct their divorces with their children's best interests in mind. In the legal negotiations over the division of family assets and the arrangements for child custody, children's interests often came last. Parents locked in custody battles squabbled over "my time" and "your time" as if the only interests at stake were those represented by the warring parents and as if the main goal in the custody arrangements were to achieve an equitable distribution of time based on the competing claims of each parent. Children's needs were not represented, nor was it easy for family courts to make a fair and independent determination of what the children's needs and best interests were. Thus, children were essentially disenfranchised, not only as stakeholders in their parents' marriage but also as interested and potentially injured parties in their parents' divorces.

First-wave thinking also contributed to an increased interest in efforts at the therapeutic management of the psychosocial impact of divorce on children. In a reversal of earlier thinking about the relative psychological sturdiness of parents and children, it tended to be pessimistic about the capacity of adults to resolve their marital problems without resort to divorce and optimistic about children's capacity to overcome, or at least survive, the dislocations and loss caused by their parents' divorce. Adults were emotionally fragile and thus needed divorce, while children were emotionally resilient and thus could handle it. One consequence of this shift was the abandonment of serious efforts to pressure couples to work out their marital problems. After the 1970s the old enthusiasm for marriage preservation and counseling vanished. It was replaced by a new enthusiasm for therapeutic interventions designed to manage the damage of divorce for children and to nurture the individual characteristics that would make children more resilient and "divorce-proof."

This therapeutic orientation to children's "adjustment" to divorce evaded entirely the ethical dimension of family breakup. Children's pleas and hopes for reconciliation between their parents were treated as a problem for therapeutic management. The idea that children's passionate desire for a family household with both Mom and Dad might have independent standing or impose a moral claim on parents was never entertained. Instead children's persistent wishes for an intact family, like some children's wishes for a pony, were viewed as extravagant. As the advice manuals for divorcing parents consistently maintained, the responsible parents' task was to try, gently but firmly, to convince their children of the impossibility of reconciliation and of the finality of divorce.

Sobering Up

By the mid-1980s a fuller body of research, based on empirical studies, had emerged; these studies had been tracking large samples of children from both intact and divorced families over the course of a decade or more. Unlike earlier research that depended heavily on reports by adults to assess children's well-being, these studies gathered information through face-to-face or telephone interviews with children themselves and also used objective measures of behavior, such as school attendance, educational attainment, work-force attachment, and adolescent childbearing as the basis of comparing the well-being of children in intact and disrupted families. The National Survey of Children, directed by sociologists Frank Furstenberg, Jr., and Nicholas Zill, set out in 1976 to interview a nationally representative sample of approximately two thousand children, then ages seven through eleven, through their middle childhood and adolescence; it also conducted interviews with the children's parents and teachers. It surveyed its subjects again in 1981 and 1987, when the oldest of the youths had entered their twenties. Sociologists Sara McLanahan and Gary Sandefur expanded research knowledge even further with their 1994 study *Growing Up with Single Parents: What Hurts, What Helps.* Based on four nationally representative bodies of survey evidence that included a wealth of information on children and young adults, this study carefully examined how children from single-parent, including divorced single-parent, and stepparent families fared in their school, family, and social lives compared with children from married two-parent families. McLanahan and Sandefur's study represented an empirically grounded effort to shed light on several unresolved and hotly disputed questions. Was divorce's impact on children significant enough to warrant public concern and attention? Or should it be viewed as a private choice which had few negative consequences for children or the society? Were the damages caused by divorce economic and therefore reparable by increased income? Or was there something about the disruptions of divorce that created noneconomic forms of loss and disadvantage and thus might be reparable only by reduced levels of divorce? Were children "better off" living with two married parents, even if the parents didn't get along, or would they lead happier lives in a single-parent or stepfamily household?

The body of empirical evidence also provided a way of comparing outcomes for children in families with two married parents, single-parent families, and stepfamilies. Such a comparison was important because it furnished an objective way of assessing whether the fast-increasing post–nuclear family structures were simply alternative living arrangements with equal or better capacity to achieve good outcomes for children, or whether their capacity was compromised or diminished as a result of family disruption. Obviously, if the post–nuclear family arrangements were equally successful in promoting good outcomes for children, there was no reason for concern about their rapid spread.

In the 1980s, clinicians also began to publish results of their research on and treatment of the children of divorce. In 1989 clinical psychologist Judith Wallerstein and coauthor Sandra Blakeslee published the results of a fifteen-year study of 60 divorcing parents and their 131 children in their book *Second Chances: Men, Women, and Children a Decade After Divorce.* Their subjects were first interviewed in 1971, while they were going through divorce, and then again one, five, and ten years after the divorce, so that the study, which also included information collected at the fifteen-year mark, captured the experience of children in divorcing families over an extended span of time. In the early 1980s another group of child-serving professionals, the American Academy of Pediatrics, began to issue policy statements based on their growing body of clinical experience with the children of divorce.

Both Wallerstein/Blakeslee's and the American Academy of Pediatrics' clinical observations were noteworthy because they were based on the experience of middle-class children whose lives before divorce had been relatively untroubled economically and emotionally. Although some researchers disputed Wallerstein/Blakeslee's claim that their sample population did not have pathological family histories, they picked their subjects from a population of "white, middle-class married couples who had lived together continuously with children under one roof and where there was no severe social pathology, illiteracy or criminality" and presumably where there were few severe stresses caused by such other factors as poverty, racism, and recent immigration.[16] By selecting more advantaged families, Wallerstein and Blakeslee sought to eliminate some of the other factors contributing to family breakdown and to capture "in bold relief" the effects of divorce itself. Similarly, the clinical observations of America's baby doctors captured the divorce experience of a relatively healthy mainstream population. Unlike child psychiatrists and psychologists, private pediatricians tended to see and treat large numbers of physically and emotionally healthy, developmentally on-track children. Consequently, their clinical experience on divorce included the experience of a relatively advantaged group of children without severe pathology.

In general, these new studies offered a much more qualified and sober appraisal of divorce's impact on children. They suggested that divorce carries multiple risks and losses for children, including loss of income, loss of ties with father, loss of residential stability, and loss of other social resources. The evidence also presented a picture of a downward spiral in children's economic and family fortunes after divorce, with marital dissolution initiating a chain of disruptions and losses. Second-wave thinking also identified divorce as an important risk factor for school dropout, problem behaviors, lower educational and job achievement, and likelihood of teenage parenthood that could only partly be explained by income effects.

On several key points, moreover, these studies modified or completely overturned the speculative assertions of first-wave thinking.

First of all, the empirical evidence established that divorce was an important cause of economic disadvantage and not simply, as others had earlier argued, an effect. Divorce itself caused reductions in income and losses in household economies of scale. It also increased the risk of poverty and welfare dependency in families with children that were not poor or welfare-dependent before divorce. Mothers and children in families that were not poor before separation suffered an average decline in income after divorce of 50 percent.[17] According to 1993 figures, the poverty rate for children living with divorced mothers was 38 percent, compared with 11 percent for children in two-parent families.[18]

In their study McLanahan and Sandefur used empirical evidence to test the argument that families that break up are more disadvantaged to begin with. To do so, they selected a sample of African-

American and white children who, at age twelve, were living with both parents. Then, using data that reported on the status of the same children five years later, at age seventeen, they divided the teenagers into two groups: those whose parents had remained married and those whose parents had divorced or separated in the intervening five years. They compared the income of these children at age twelve and then again at seventeen. Their data showed three things: First, there was a difference in family income by race; second, there were income differences between black families who remained married and those who eventually separated or divorced; and third, regardless of race or income level, the dollar loss caused by divorce per se was substantial.

For example, white adolescents whose parents stayed together experienced an increase in median family income from $61,559 to $66,696 between ages twelve to seventeen. By contrast, white teenagers from families who broke up saw family income decline from a predivorce level of $62,367 to a postdivorce level of $36,662. Black teenagers whose parents remained married experienced an increase in median family income over the five-year period from $39,040 to $40,934. Black adolescents whose parents had separated or divorced by the time they were seventeen experienced a decline in their family income from $28,197 to $18,894. (Overall median family income is high because parents with teenagers are older and thus likely to be earning at higher levels than younger parents.)[19]

This analysis is revealing in several ways. First of all, it shows substantial differences in family income by race. Both groups of white families (stable and unstable) of twelve-year-olds earned more than either group (stable or unstable) of black families with twelve-year-old children. Given these differences, it is likely that the black married parents are more economically stressed and perhaps more vulnerable to divorce. Second, the stably married black parents of twelve-year-olds were earning roughly eleven thousand dollars a year more than the black parents of twelve-year-olds who eventually divorced or separated. This further strengthens the argument that economic stress is a factor in family disruption. (Interestingly, there is not a corresponding pattern of income difference between the white families who stay married and those who eventually divorce. Indeed, the white families who eventually divorce or separate are actually earning slightly more than those who remain married.) Nevertheless, a third point is also clear. Regardless of race, the adolescents whose parents broke up suffered a substantial income loss as a direct consequence of divorce while those whose parents stayed together experienced a gain in family income over the five-year period.

The economic losses directly connected with divorce obviously affected mothers, the residential parent in the vast majority of households formed after divorce, as well as their children. Consequently, there was no empirical basis for the idea that divorce gives mothers new opportunities for economic success, as the first wave of thinking suggested. Rather, it showed that the opposite was true. Though women might have to intensify their work-force participation, their greater attachment to work did not reliably lead to greater economic well-being and "growth" for single mothers and their children but left them running harder and falling behind.

The evidence also suggested that one could expect to see a pattern of economic divergence based on family structure in a society with high levels of divorces involving children. Children who grew up in families disrupted by divorce were more likely to be economically vulnerable and disadvantaged than children who grew up in families with two married parents.

The second-wave research overturned the idea that divorced mothers quickly remarried and that children thereby regained all the advantages of a two-parent married family. In fact, many mothers stayed single. After the 1970s, rates of remarriage began to decline, dropping 38 percent for divorced women between 1970 and 1990. Except for young divorced women ages twenty to twenty-four, divorced women were less likely to remarry than divorced men.[20] The time children would spend in a single-mother household was not brief but lasted, on average, six years. For African-American children it could extend even longer since the remarriage rate among black women is lower than among white women. Only 33 percent of African-American mothers had remarried within ten years of separation. Finally, although half of all children in single-mother families eventually lived with stepfathers, half of these new marriages were likely to end in divorce before the child turned eighteen. So remarriage did not reliably lead to a stable family life but often contributed to the pattern of family instability triggered by divorce.

Moreover, the evidence clearly pointed to a set of risks and problems associated with stepfamily life. Although children in stepfamilies enjoyed family incomes roughly equivalent to those in intact original two-parent households, they were two to three times more likely to suffer emotional and behavior problems and nearly twice as likely to have developmental or learning problems as children in intact families.[21] The McLanahan and Sandefur study also showed that children in stepfamilies were more likely to drop out of high school, to become unwed teenage mothers, and to be unable to hold steady jobs as young adults than children who grew up with both married parents.[22]

The second wave of research also pointed to several persistent and long-term consequences of family breakup. The impact of divorce could not be compared with a cold, which disappeared after a short time with no lasting effect. It was more like a serious chronic disease which could be managed but carried multiple and increased risks to overall well-being and which, for a significant minority of affected children, led to serious long-term difficulties. Moreover, a majority of children suffered damage to their relationship with their father.

The empirical evidence also provided a better way of assessing the claim that children's emotional problems are caused by marital strife rather than divorce. It clearly showed that children in families with warring parents did suffer from emotional difficulties before the divorce, compared with children in married families where the parents got along. At the same time it cast doubt on the first-wave argument that divorce reliably improves children's relationships with parents or brings a new reign of domestic peace and contentment. For example, for most children the damage to father-child relationships was not a result of living with unhappily married parents. It was a direct result of divorce and the departure of the father from the family household. If divorce relieved some stresses, it also contributed to new stresses and risks for children.

Similarly, the first-wave notion that marital dissolution reliably brings a cessation of family conflict was not borne out by the evidence. Divorce could provoke new hostilities; parental conflict often escalated during and after divorce, creating new kinds of deprivation and loss, even an increased threat of violence and abuse to children. Incidents of hitting, pushing, and stalking, along with kidnapping and assaults with a deadly weapon, occurred among parents in the aftermath of divorce. One study of divorced, mainly middle-class California parents revealed that three and a half years after separation most of the divorced parents were coping with their daily lives in ways that did not appear to indicate pathology or deep distress; despite persistent tensions, they were able to meet schedules permitting children to spend time in both households and thus were engaged in "cooperative" parenting. Indeed, the researchers characterized their portrait of divorced families as "fairly optimistic." Yet the study also shows that among these "fairly representative" families, there were "almost all the kinds of distressing events that regularly capture headlines. There were several cases of kidnappings; there were cruel stepparents; some parents had threatened each other with knives or guns; and some had been beaten by the former spouse and told us they went in fear of their lives; some had tried to get the former spouse arrested; in some cases, a parent's drunk driving had endangered the lives of children; there were families so disorganized that young children were being left essentially unsupervised and unprotected; some couples had had irreconcilable differences over their children's religious training."[23] This study points to two troubling features of middle-class divorce: First, it suggests that divorce elicits bad behavior, even among reasonably competent parents, and second, it offers evidence that children may be placed at risk by their divorcing parents' bad behavior.

On the crucial question of whether children are better off if their disaffected parents divorce or stay married, McLanahan and Sandefur's study provided guidance. If the conflict is high-level, persistent, and marked by physical violence or severe abuse, the researchers concluded, children may be better off if the parents separate. However, when it comes to the "softer" definitions of marital dissatisfaction—emotional estrangement, boredom, another romantic or sexual interest, changes in one spouse's priorities or values—the case was less open-and-shut. In these instances, McLanahan and Sandefur argue, "the child would probably be better off if the parents resolved their differences and the family remained together, even if the long-term rela-

tionship between the parents was less than perfect."[24] Since some estimates suggested that about 10 to 15 percent of marriages ending in divorce involve high-level conflict and violence, this left a substantial
percentage of troubled marriages involving children in the "softer" and
therefore potentially salvageable category.

The second-wave research also overturned the notion that death
and divorce represent similar kinds of loss for children. Parental death
is a far more severe and tragic form of loss for a child than divorce,
permanently severing the parent-child bond and forever disrupting a
primary human attachment. It also deprives a child of the presence
and protection of an adult who has a biological stake in, as well as an
emotional commitment to, the child's survival and well-being. However, the death of a parent is commonly recognized as a tragic loss and
brings an outpouring of assistance and sympathy as well as expressions
of solidarity and support. Relatives and friends offer sympathy and
help. Also, the resources of the marriage provide a basis for stability
even after a parent has died. For example, widowed mothers may be
the beneficiaries of private insurance, pensions, health insurance, even
mortgage insurance established during their marriage. Equally important, from the standpoint of the child's emotional well-being, the
widowed parent can share in the child's grief, maintain an idealized
image of the departed parent, and establish the continued presence of
the parent by drawing upon his or her memory. Thus, although the
child's loss is profound, the sense of connectedness to the parent is not
broken by death. Divorce, on the other hand, can disrupt a child's relationship with a living parent and often create unresolved feelings of
loss and grief that are not shared by the other parent. In a society permissive toward divorce, the child's experience of divorce is not viewed
unambiguously and thus does not elicit outpourings of sympathy and
support. Moreover, a living parent who remains remote or absent can
be a source of continued torment in a way that a parent who dies is
not. Finally, and most obviously, death is usually involuntary, while divorce is voluntary on the part of at least one parent, a distinction that is
not lost on children.

Professionals who worked closely with children also offered a
gloomier assessment of the impact of divorce on children. Judith
Wallerstein and Sandra Blakeslee's study rejected the idea that the vast

majority of children bounce back quickly from their parents' divorce. Five years after the divorce, more than a third of the children were experiencing moderate or severe depression. At ten years a significant number of the now-grown young men and women appeared to be troubled, drifting, and underachieving. At the fifteen-year mark, many of the thirtyish adults were struggling to establish secure love relationships of their own. In short, far from making a speedy recovery from their parents' divorce, a significant percentage of the young adults in the study were still suffering its effects. Cruelly, the experience of parental divorce damaged many young adults' ability to forge strong attachments of their own, in both their work and their family lives. The emotional difficulties associated with divorce lasted much longer and involved a higher percentage of children of divorce than the first wave of thinking claimed.

Several leading divorce researchers criticized the Wallerstein/Blakeslee study as exaggerating the extent and duration of the emotional difficulties caused by divorce. Moreover, they claimed that since their study lacked a control group—a population of children with similar characteristics from intact families—it was impossible to know whether these emotional difficulties were unique to children from divorce or perhaps part of some more pervasive generational pattern of change.[25] Maybe it was simply getting harder for all young people to find work and love in the 1980s.

Other clinical reports, however, seemed to support Wallerstein and Blakeslee's observations. One came from the nation's pediatricians, who, over the course of a little more than a decade, issued two policy statements on divorce. In 1983 the American Academy of Pediatrics described the clinical manifestations of the effects of divorce on children. The doctors' group cited irritability, separation anxiety, sleep problems, and regression in toilet training as common behaviors for children under three; while tantrums, combativeness, poor school performance, and hyperaggressiveness figured in the conduct problems of older children. Adolescents commonly manifested anger, antisocial behavior, and somatic complaints. Nonetheless, though not sanguine about divorce, the statement was not unduly pessimistic either. The academy emphasized that the problems were in most cases transitory, and that with proper and early intervention they could be resolved.

Thus, the 1983 policy statement stressed the importance of cognitive care and therapeutic outreach. The duty of the pediatrician was to help children understand the reasons for the divorce and to assist parents in finding outside support and help through social agencies, mental health centers, private psychologists, women's centers, and therapists.

In 1994, after another decade of clinical experience dealing with children of divorce, the academy issued a second policy statement. This time the pediatricians' group underscored the "considerable prevalence and morbidity of divorce" for children. Up to half of children were likely to manifest symptoms in the first year after their parents' divorce, the academy reported, with aggression in school-age boys and depression in early- and mid-adolescent girls the most troublesome. In contrast with its earlier view, the academy now stated that divorce-related problems persist: Children's "sense of loss is ongoing and may reemerge especially on holidays, birthdays, special school events, and when attempting to integrate multiple new family relationships."

The second policy statement not only detailed the impact of divorce on children's health but also pointed to the impact of high and sustained levels of divorce on the relationship between child health professionals and parents. Increasingly, pediatricians were being called upon as expert witnesses in contested child custody cases. Not only were the nation's baby doctors called upon to treat ear infections, administer DTP shots, and give camp physicals, but they were also expected to render opinions and to take sides in parental fights over access to medical information about the child and court battles over custody. The American Academy of Pediatrics urged its members to stay out of the divorce fray and, if necessary, to hire their own legal counsel.[26] This practical advice, delivered in the most dispassionate tones, nonetheless spoke volumes about the impact of divorce on other social relationships.

By the late 1980s popular books on divorce and single-parenthood had also backed away from their earlier optimism. Compared with the first generation of divorce books, this literature is more sober in its assessment of the effects of divorce on children. Unlike researchers, it is true, the popular writers still tout the advantages of divorce for children. Compared with children who grow up in two-parent families, they say, children in single-parent families show more flexibility in gender roles. They are more independent and competent in dealing with adversity. And children whose parents divorce have a heightened sense of possibility.[27] As one author explains, ending an unhappy marriage "opens children to the realization that a person is never totally locked into an unchanging and cheerless destiny."[28] In comparison with the earlier books, however, the optimism is less buoyant, the tone less confident. Children suffer from family breakup, these writers acknowledge, and, against all expectations, the children have retrograde longings for their fathers.

Shoshana Alexander's *In Praise of Single Parents* is a good example of second-generation advice literature. Alexander does not minimize or rationalize children's grief at the loss of their intact family. Indeed, she tells story after story of sad children, mired in the misery of divorce. There is the story of Danielle, whose parents split up when she was three and a half. Immediately after the divorce the little girl comforted herself by adopting the Holy Family as her own and engaging in nightly conversations with Jesus, Mary, and Joseph, who, in her imagination, hovered at the foot of her bed. But nine years later Danielle has not "gotten over" her parents' divorce. She still yearns for an intact family. She fills dozens of spiral-bound notebooks with her own stories of happy two-parent families. "I make up families," she says. "That's what keeps me alive." According to Alexander, Danielle's mother is stunned by the persistence of her daughter's grief and mourning. "Even though I have been so aware of the lack she has suffered, and I have so much wanted to address it . . . I am astonished that I have not been able to do that . . . she has obviously experienced tremendous fragmentation."[29]

Similarly, the literature gives a painful accounting of the distress caused by an unknown or vanished or inconstant father. Children began pestering mothers with the "daddy question" at an early age. Indeed, the testimonies of single mothers on the child's early consciousness of father absence are consistent with the research evidence on children's precocious awareness of fatherlessness.[30] "It just broke my heart each time Trevor would ask the question: Why don't I have a father who loves me?" one single mother lamented. Shoshana Alexander's son, Elias, at age three wants to know who made his daddy go away. "Did you make him go away?" he asks his mother. Then he raises his deeper concern: "Did I make him go away?"[31]

As the second-generation advice books acknowledged, mothers' and children's experiences after divorce were not identical. Children worried and wondered about a father's absence or lack of involvement in their lives. They wanted to know why their parents had to break up and why they could not get back together. Alexander observes: To answer such questions truthfully and appropriately can challenge us to our bones.[32]

Is Divorce a Problem for Children?

Taken together, the body of empirical evidence generated in the second wave presented a far bleaker picture of the impact of divorce on children than that held out earlier. The second wave called into question the first wave's leading idea—namely, that the happiness of individual parents is a reliable guide to the well-being of children. Indeed, what the later research revealed was a distinct pattern of divergence between children's well-being and divorced parents' level of satisfaction after the dissolution of marriage. As surveys consistently showed, one or both parents deemed their lives better after divorce. According to Wallerstein and Blakeslee's study, for example, 80 percent of divorced women and 50 percent of divorced men believed they were better off out of their marriages. By contrast, nothing in the evidence suggests that children experience equally high levels of satisfaction after divorce. To be sure, there are children who say that their parents' marriages were so desperately unhappy or conflictual that they were relieved when their parents parted. Yet not even the most optimistic interpretation of the evidence would permit the conclusion that 80 percent of children are better off because their parents' marriages ended. Particularly for children in stepfamilies, the evidence strongly disputes the "happily ever after" scenario. A 1990 survey of more than nine hundred children, ages ten to seventeen, found that children in stepfamilies were more likely than children in either intact or single-parent families to wish for more time with their mothers, to report frequently feeling "sad and blue," and to lack parental participation in school or homework activities.[33] Indeed, the weight of the evidence suggested that parental divorce, with its chain of disruptive events, is a significant source of disadvantage for children and an important and relatively recent factor contributing to the sharp divergence in school, employment, and economic-achievement outcomes between children in intact families and those in families disrupted by divorce. Furthermore, the research demonstrates that even advantaged children of middle-class, college-educated parents are not exempt from the risks associated with divorce. The chances that a white girl from an advantaged background will become a teen mother are five times as high, and the chances that a white child will drop out of high school are three times as high, if the parents do not live together.[34]

These findings also shed light on the question of the comparative capacities of families in varying structures to achieve good outcomes for children. The evidence clearly showed that growing up in an intact two-parent family is an important source of advantage for American children. Though far from perfect, the married-parent family offers children greater emotional and economic security and better future life prospects than its fast-growing alternatives: single-parent families or stepfamilies. This doesn't mean, of course, that all two-parent families are better for children than all single-parent families or stepfamilies. But at the very least, the later findings have substantially undercut the first-wave proposition that all family structures produce equivalent outcomes for children.

It is true that, even given this evidence, some leading researchers in the field have continued to warn against exaggerating the harmful effects of divorce. They argue that the statistical differences between middle-class children of divorce and middle-class children in married-parent households are often small, that children's responses to divorce are variable, and that only a minority of children suffer severe and long-term emotional damage from it.

However, many of the studies showed a doubling or tripling of the risks for children who experience parental divorce, hardly an insignificant difference. Further, one form of long-term damage experienced by a *majority* of such children is a disruption in their relationships with their fathers. Also, by focusing on the *percentage* of children who are likely to experience long-lasting damage, some researchers have obscured the more significant fact that there has been an increase in the absolute number of children exposed to parental divorce. If the absolute number of such children is small, obviously the minority who are likely to be severely damaged will also be small. Expressed another way, marital breakup in a society with low levels of divorce may be a serious problem for individual children but not for the society's children as a whole. However, when the absolute number of children experiencing divorce reaches a million a year, then the minority who suffer long-term difficulties becomes much larger and divorce takes on additional significance as a social problem.

Nonetheless, some in the research community remain reluctant to accept this point. This is significant because social scientists are among the chief arbiters of what constitutes a social problem. It is they who are called upon to define the size and scope of a problem and to identify the populations most at risk. Given this influential role, the state of social-scientific opinion on the impact of divorce on children is particularly revealing.

Some researchers have contended that divorce does not constitute a serious problem for children because it does not cause long-term damage in a majority of the children who experience it. But this sets an unusually demanding standard for social concern. If the same standard were applied in other contexts, we would have far fewer social problems to worry about. We would not have to worry about crime, for example, because the majority of its victims are not damaged over the long haul. We would not need to worry about short-term unemployment, nor would we have to fret over poverty, since the majority of Americans who experience a spell of poverty do not remain poor for a lifetime. In setting this uniquely high standard, therefore, these researchers would seem to be exhibiting more than scholarly caution; they are apparently reflecting a larger recession among family experts in concern for the well-being of children.

The effort by scholars to minimize the damage divorce does to children is noteworthy in another way. Since the beginning of the century, academic social scientists have played an important role in establishing empirical measures of child well-being, in identifying the hazards affecting the lives of children, and in gaining governmental support for the regular monitoring of child well-being. Overall, their attention to child welfare has contributed to a higher level of child-centeredness in public policy and greater awareness of childhood as a stage of life requiring strong social protections. However, on the issue of divorce and its effects on children, some scholars seem to have strayed from this tradition.

Clearly, ideological pressures have played a role in influencing social-scientific opinion. Many liberal academics fear that raising concerns about the hardships of divorce for children may play into the hands of the political right. "Family values" conservatives, they believe, are intent on driving women back into traditional homemaking roles and even dangerously abusive marriages, thus undermining women's considerable progress toward freedom from domestic misery and tyranny. In an exchange with Indiana Republican and (then) Representative Dan Coats, a member of the House Select Subcommittee on Children, Youth and Families, one leading divorce expert, sociologist Andrew Cherlin, reflected this political sensitivity. The way to deal with the problem of divorce, Cherlin argued, is not to rely on "moral exhortation" to "get women back in the home," but to accept it and deal with its practical consequences.[35] Apparently, Cherlin feared that conservatives would use evidence on the harmful effects of divorce as grounds for forcing women back into the kitchen, although how such a historic reversal in the trends in women's work-force participation could be accomplished remains unclear.

Other scholars acknowledge the empirical evidence on the negative impact of divorce on children, but argue that the short-term costs borne by children have been more than offset by the benefits won by their newly divorced mothers. For example, historian Stephanie Coontz writes:

> In the real world, there are tradeoffs in all decisions. Children's initial response to divorce is often negative although they do adjust if the parents do not continue battling afterward. But women, despite initial pain and income loss, tend almost immediately to feel that they benefit from divorce. A 1982 survey found that even one year after divorce a majority of women said they were happier and had more self-respect than they had in their marriages. The proportion rises with every passing year. What are the tradeoffs, even for the child, between short-term disruptions and long-term maternal misery?[36]

Coontz assumes a rosy scenario: a divorce that brings an end to parental strife. Unfortunately, many failed but low-conflict marriages can give rise to high-conflict divorces; parental strife often escalates after a marriage breaks up. What's more, the gains in reported maternal happiness after divorce do not reliably translate into similar increases in children's happiness. Nonetheless, Coontz's argument offers another illustration of the shift away from a concern for the plight of dependent children. It has been customary to distinguish between the interests of independent adults and dependent children, and to use this distinction to establish a higher obligation to look after the welfare of children. But on Coontz's utilitarian scale, children and adults are treated identically, and as regards their well-being are equally subjected to the calculus of "tradeoffs."

All this said, it is not scholarly opinion that has been truly decisive in shifting the focus away from children. There are stronger forces working against any public consensus that divorce poses a serious threat to the young. One is the steady entrenchment of divorce as a way of life. By the 1990s divorce had become as American as the Fourth of July. Indeed, it was hard to find an adult American under sixty-five who did not have personal experience of divorce, either directly as a participant or indirectly as a witness to divorce among family, friends, or coworkers. But it is not simply habituation to divorce that weakens concern for the well-being of children. It is also the sense of divorce as an adult entitlement that has to be protected against challenge, criticism, or infringement. The entire framework for thinking about divorce has come to be shaped by this sense of entitlement, so that expressions of concern about children are often angrily rejected as unfeeling attacks on divorced individuals. More to the point, it is impossible to criticize divorce as a trend affecting children without seeming to criticize or judge the divorced mother, who is doing the best she can under difficult circumstances. The culture of divorce recruits social support, compassion, and sympathy for the divorcing grown-ups and maintains a discreet silence about the plight of the children.

CHAPTER FIVE

The Children's
Story of Divorce

THERE HAS BEEN ONLY ONE sustained effort to chronicle and attend to children's experience of divorce, and that effort has been undertaken by the writers of children's books. Few scholars have paid close attention to the emergence of a children's literature devoted to divorce, much less credited it as an important source of evidence. Yet this literature provides a remarkable account of children's experience of divorce, a story radically at odds with the story told in the scores of books on divorce for adults.

Children's literature was innocent of the theme of divorce until the last third of the twentieth century. But as divorces with children became commonplace, as more and more American youngsters were summoned by their parents to hear a speech that began with some version of "Mommy and Daddy are so unhappy they cannot live together anymore," divorce started to invade the world of children's storybooks.

Divorce books for children began pouring from the nation's presses in the 1970s. The books came in all sizes and shapes and genres. There was a divorce book for every age group. For the youngest children there were picture books with divorcing dinosaurs and Muppet kids "worried about divorce." For preschool children there were workbooks and coloring books to help children express their feelings through drawing. For older children, there were divorce dictionaries and advice manuals offering information and counsel on how to deal with judges, therapists, and lawyers. For teenagers, there were divorce novels, suggesting *It's Not What You Expect* or, more hopefully, *It's Not the End of the World.*

At the same time, children's books on illegitimacy and parental abandonment began to appear. There was resurgent interest in stepparents as well. A new figure, the violent and sexually abusive stepfather, joined a more familiar character, the cruel and calculating stepmother, in the pages of these children's books. During the 1970s and 1980s the fascination with these dark themes grew. In 1977 a comprehensive bibliography listed more than two hundred pages' worth of children's books dealing with loss and separation. By 1989 the list had grown to more than five hundred pages.[1]

The inspiration for some of these books came from children themselves. During the late 1970s and early 1980s, while the experts were confidently predicting that children would benefit from the divorce experience, children themselves were furiously scribbling letters to their favorite authors, seeking information, advice, and solace about what was happening to their families.

"My parents are devvorst," one child writes to Beverly Cleary, the author of many popular children's books. "My dad is the kind of person who never wants to be around kids." In another letter, a girl confides: "I wish I could sue my parents for malpractice but I know I can't so I just try to forget what they do."[2]

Author Richard Peck wrote his 1991 novel *Unfinished Portrait of Jessica* after reading one young correspondent's account of her parents' breakup. She writes first of her father's departure and then of his eventual remarriage:

> The day he left, I had been listening to them argue. I guess my dad was stressed out and my mom was just a bitch. . . . I was crying and screaming, "Daddy, please don't go," when he walked out the door. I followed him out and clung to his leg until he got to the car. This was when he pried me off his leg, jumped in the car and sped off. He wouldn't even look me in the eye, and he didn't say goodbye. . . .

Her letter continues:

At nine is when I moved in with my dad. Everything was perfect until my dad met my stepmother. . . . She was the type of step-mother to be in Cinderella. She still is. . . . She's a psychologist, and therefore she feels like she can solve all the problems of the world. She and my father have a booklet on how to parent and everything. . . . Well, now they've more or less run me out of the house with their rules and booklets and insincerity. I'm not liv-ing with them now. . . . I've left my dad, just like he left me, but at least I said goodbye.[3]

For some unhappily married writers, the kids' interest in divorce coincided with their own. Judy Blume wrote a best-selling divorce novel for kids to "try to answer some of my children's questions about divorce, to let other kids know they were not alone and, perhaps, be-cause I was not happy in my marriage."[4] After her third marriage failed, Erica Jong wrote *Molly's Book of Divorce* to help her preschool daughter "deal with a life in which she is always leaving socks, under-pants, Teddy bears at another house." But, as Jong acknowledges, "I also wrote it for myself. It ends with a party in which the divorced spouses and their new partners all kiss and make up."[5]

A Literature of Loss

While liberation is the dominant theme in the adult literature on di-vorce, loss is the common theme that unites this large and various chil-dren's literature. Indeed, not since the Puritans invented a juvenile literature devoted to death has a children's literature been so preoccu-pied with themes of loss and bereavement. Most often, the pain of loss is caused by the absence or separation from the father, a theme re-flected again and again in the titles: *Daddy Doesn't Live Here Anymore; I Won't Go Without a Father; Where Is Daddy?; At Daddy's on Saturday; Daddy's New Baby; My Dad Lives in a Downtown Hotel; Who Will Lead Kiddush?; Will Dad Ever Move Back Home?*

In a smaller number of stories, it is the mother who is absent. More often, however, the mother is present but distracted and sad. The child grieves for the "old mother" who used to cook better meals, laugh more, and work less. Children mourn the loss of other beloved adults as well. In *Grandma Without Me*, a little boy is no longer able to celebrate Thanksgiving with his paternal grandmother. "I don't think Mommy wants to see Daddy and Grandma any more. She acts like they died."[6] In another story, a child suffers the loss of her father and then her mother's boyfriend. First there was Daddy. "Daddy divorced us when I was little. He never comes to see me." Then there was the boyfriend, Gary. "I wished Gary would stay with us forever and never go away like Daddy did." The child worries: Could Mommy be next? "Sometimes I'm scared that Mommy will leave me too."[7] Pets also go away in these stories, or become the focus of custody fights between the parents. In Anne Fine's *Alias Madame Doubtfire*, the kids stand mutely aside while their parents squabble over custody and care of the guinea pigs.

Loss is not a new theme in children's literature, of course. Countless children's stories deal with the death or loss of a parent. But in earlier children's books parental absence is fated, not chosen. A mother or father dies from illness or accident or goes away because of war or work. Moreover, in the classic tradition, children stand at a distance from the experience of loss. The burdens of grief are borne by the adults. As one example among many, consider Edith Nesbit's *The Railway Children*, a book published in 1906 and widely read ever since, in both Britain and America.

The Railway Children's father is taken from the house in the middle of the night by mysterious visitors. After his disappearance, the children and their mother are obliged to leave their city home and move to a modest cottage in the country where she struggles to make a living as a writer. She is no longer as available to them as she once was. Instead of reading to her children at teatime, she must withdraw from the family circle and spend "almost all day shut up in her upstairs room, writing, writing, writing." Over the household there hangs continually the mystery of the father's abrupt departure and absence.

But the three children—Peter, Phyllis, and Bobbie—are remarkably unscathed by these domestic upheavals. Such events remain matters of concern purely for adults. "Mother told them they were quite poor now, but this did not seem to be anything but a way of speaking. Grownup people, even mothers, often make remarks that don't seem to mean anything in particular, just for the sake of saying something, seemingly. There was always enough to eat and they wore the same kind of nice clothes they had always worn."

Even their father's disappearance, while disturbing, remains a problem for grown-ups. (Toward the end of the book, it is revealed that the father has been arrested and convicted—falsely—on a charge of espionage for the Russians [!], but his innocence is finally established and he is released.) Their mother conceals her sadness and refuses to give the children any information on the subject: "I want you not to ask me any questions about this trouble; and not to ask anybody else any questions."[8] Thus, in *The Railway Children* loss is something adults endure separately and privately. And because the grown-ups carry the burdens and privations associated with loss, the children are free to have adventures, to explore and engage the world.

By contrast, in the modern literature, it is children who are consumed with anxiety and grief. The little girl in *Two Homes to Live In* worries when her father is not on time: "Sometimes I had scary thoughts. One time when Daddy was late, I thought what if he doesn't come at all?"[9] Other times the child is not worried or sad but wistful: "Dad, I wish you lived in the apartment across the hall so I could see you every day."[10]

In Ken Rush's subliminal and haunting picture book *Friday's Journey*, the story centers on the loss of the intact family. As a boy and his father hop the subway for the regular weekend trip back to the dad's apartment, the subway itself becomes a memory train, triggering remembrances of earlier family outings. Like station stops, a single image of a trip shared with both parents flashes by on each page of the picture book: father and mother and son on a picnic together, father and mother and son visiting a museum, father and mother and son watching boats from a bench on the pier. On the last page father and son get off at the Spring Street stop and watch as the train disappears into the tunnel. The boy sees the faint image of his mother standing alone at the window in the last car. Like the subway itself, his feelings of sadness rattle underneath the surface pleasures of the weekend visitation with his dad.[11]

Not all the stories are so subtly evocative of children's feelings. In some, children express their explosive resentments. "Sometimes I feel sorry for my mother and other times I hate her!" says the girl in Judy

Blume's *It's Not the End of the World*.[12] In *I Wish I Had My Father* a boy who has never known his father dreads Father's Day. "I hate Father's Day and here it comes again. . . . I wish I had a father I could know."[13] In Maria Gripe's *The Night Daddy* a girl who has never known her father is sullenly defensive: "My mommy isn't married, and I'm just as glad. . . . I never cared for fathers much."[14] A book collectively written by young teens tells of other resentments: "[A] girl in our class sometimes feels like introducing her father's girlfriend as 'that asshole who sleeps over once in a while.' "[15]

In books for younger children, gently understanding parents deflect the angry outbursts, but in the teen fiction the parents reciprocate; as often as adolescents give vent to their resentments, their parents strike back. A fourteen-year-old boy who says his mother's "hobby" is marrying remarks: "Mother doesn't like me. She never has."[16] Another story recounts a conversation between a divorced mother and her son: "I was the one that was stuck with you . . . and you are quite a hateful child, Roger."[17]

The literary children of divorce suffer other forms of loss as well: The geography of household and neighborhood becomes more unstable as parents split up. Living in divided households, the children are on the move, constantly changing venues and schedules. The illustrations show children packing and unpacking, getting in and out of cars, coming and going, saying hello and good-bye. The suitcase is the only secure fixture of this peripatetic childhood.[18]

In what is probably the most common motif, the bedroom itself is lost. Divorce evicts children from their own bedrooms. Now they have two places to sleep or a shared sleeping space or a new bedroom. In departure from domestic tradition, the child's bedroom is no longer a fixed place. It is portable: a sleeping bag, a pullout couch, "two places to sleep."

Viewed in broad cultural terms, the loss of the child's bedroom as a fixed and dedicated space is an important development. Until the seventeenth century bedrooms were public and portable; houses had rooms with beds but not bedrooms. The idea of placing a stationary bed in a separate space was a social innovation. It provided a place of retreat from the public activities of the household and created a zone of privacy for the family, thus reinforcing the distinction between family members and nonfamily members—servants, guests, tradespeople, and others having contact with the household. At the same time the private bedroom segregated adults from children and contributed to the growing recognition of children as special and separate members of the household. Along with children's nurseries and classrooms, the child's bedroom began to appear in eighteenth-century English houses, ending the promiscuous mingling of children and servants and parents in a single bed and the casual jumbling together of youth that had once typified household sleeping arrangements. Increasingly, children were segregated by sex as well as by age, part of an effort to protect girls from sexual contact with brothers or other males in the household.

In *Children in the House* Karin Calvert tells us that nineteenth-century Americans were especially concerned with the child's bedroom as a protected and separate domain. By the middle of the century, experts were advising that even newborns, who had traditionally slept in a cradle at the mother's bedside, should be placed in another room. Bed-sharing was discouraged, even among siblings. One nineteenth-century physician grudgingly permitted "not more than two older children to share a bed, so long as they had sufficient room so that they would not touch each other."[19] But the ideal was a separate bedroom and an individual bed for each child.

The same protective impulse prompted reform of children's night-dresses. Earlier in the century, children commonly wore loose night-dresses and nightshirts to bed, but this sleepwear could hike up, leaving children's bodies exposed and unprotected. Dr. Denton's pajamas, first introduced around 1850, solved that problem by encasing the child in fabric from neck to toe. The new pajamas also included covering for the child's hands, which prevented thumb-sucking as well as masturbatory exploration.[20]

From the nineteenth century on, therefore, children's sleeping costumes and arrangements were designed to preserve children's sexual innocence. Practically as well as symbolically, the bedroom became a place secure from sexual knowledge or experience. All the familiar bedtime rituals—reading stories, saying prayers, and kissing good night—were now expected to take place in the child's bedroom rather than in that of the parents, with its erotic associations. But even beyond its significance as a place of safety and privacy, the child's bedroom is a sign and symbol of the growing child-centeredness in family and household arrangements.

In light of this tradition, it is significant that so many of these stories dwell obsessively on the bedroom as the place of loss and on the bedroom as a lost place. It is here that the child has early intimations that her family is about to fall apart. The bedroom is the place of first knowing, the place where the child's sleep is disrupted by the sounds of fighting. In the award-winning storybook *Where Is Daddy?*, Janey listens to "her mommy and daddy's voices going up and down, sometimes soft, sometimes shouty. The anger between them made a pain inside her, and she cried and cried."[21]

The bedroom is the place where children lose physical as well as emotional control. In one story, a little girl named Katie begins wetting the bed. Her mother consoles her: "You're sad, Katie. So am I. It's okay."[22]

Innocence is also lost when children must confront the evidence of parents' sexuality as well as their own confusions over love and sex. In *The Night Daddy*, one of the early children's novels about an unwed mother and her child, the erotic undercurrents are unmistakable. The mother hires a young man to care for her daughter while the mother works nights as a nurse. The girl is determined to resist the babysitter's friendly overtures. She bars her bedroom door and hangs out a sign: PRIVATE PROPERTY! DO NOT DISTURB! TRESPASSING FORBIDDEN! The young man, an aspiring writer, seduces her with nighttime snacks and bedtime stories until the fatherless child admits him to her bedroom and adopts him as her "night daddy." In turn, he invites her to his house. The relationship develops like a courtship, the pair drawing closer by sharing confidences and playing make-believe until they become intimates, as comfortable and familiar as an old married couple.[23]

The problem of parents' sexuality is explicitly addressed in the advice literature for older children. Judy Blume's popular *Letters to Judy* devotes a chapter to "Confronting Your Parents' Sexuality." A twelve-year-old girl writes: "I feel weird . . . finding my mother in bed with someone who she's not even married to. And I feel yucky knowing that he has his pants off too."[24] Child psychiatrist Richard Gardner tells boys that some mothers want their sons to behave like husbands:

"Such a mother may hold hands with her son and kiss him a lot. She may even want him to sleep in the same bed she does. . . . It's a very bad idea for a boy to do all these things with his mother."[25] Thus, the bedroom motif hints at a larger transformation in the climate of the post-divorce household, from warm and affectionate to overheated and eroticized.

Finally, and importantly, the preoccupation with bedrooms tells us that this literature is concerned with interiors. Classic children's literature occupied spacious physical and imaginative terrain. Until the 1970s the children in books were out-of-doors children; their landscape was the backyard or the neighborhood or the railway yard or the great Mississippi or the South Seas or the Milky Way. Psychologically the child's direction was outward as well. A child left the household to explore the larger world, to move beyond the family circle. The adventures might be child-sized, but the direction was from the family to the larger world. Personal growth and character development involved the conquest of egocentricity, and a child's maturity came about through ever-widening sociability.[26]

By contrast, the landscape of the divorce literature is an interior landscape. The geography is that of the house or apartment. In a large number of these stories, the child's entire world has shrunk to the size of a small bedroom. All the action unfolds in close domestic quarters. But the inwardness of this literature is not only spatial but also psychological. This literature is confined and limited to the workings of the child's inner world; the dramatic interest no longer revolves around the child's efforts to master the social world outside the family but instead focuses on the conquest of the confusing feelings unleashed by family breakup. This may explain why there is so much diary-writing and journal-keeping in these stories and why, in comparison with popular children's books of the 1960s, even the very best of these divorce books feels claustrophobic. Indeed, it is in the work of a beloved and gifted writer of children's books that one sees most vividly how themes of family breakup alter the social and psychological landscape of children's literature.

The Survivor Child

In 1984 Beverly Cleary won the Newbery Medal, America's most prestigious prize in children's literature, for her book *Dear Mr. Henshaw*.[27] The award was notable in two respects. Though two earlier Cleary books had been named Newbery Honor books, this was the first of her twenty-seven books to win the Newbery Medal. It was also a first in the history of the Newbery awards. After twenty-two years of handing out literary prizes for books featuring historical heroes and talking animals, the Newbery committee gave its top award to a children's book on divorce.

Dear Mr. Henshaw is the story of a boy named Leigh Botts who moves to a new town and a new school after his parents get divorced. Leigh is lonely and unhappy, and his mother, who works for a catering service, has to be away from the house for long hours. Most of all, Leigh misses and dreams about his father, a long-distance trucker. The boy keeps a map of the United States nearby so that he can trace his father's cross-country travels. Unfortunately, his father is not nearly so curious about his son. No matter how many times Leigh asks him to stay in touch, his father disappoints. He promises to call, but the phone doesn't ring. He promises to write, but the letters don't arrive. He promises to send the child-support check, but the check is often late.

Leigh begins a correspondence with his favorite author, Boyd Henshaw. Mr. Henshaw is no father substitute (he is busy, far away, and properly formal), but he does encourage Leigh to write back and to answer a set of questions about himself and his family. At first, Leigh considers this assignment a pain in the neck, but gradually he begins to describe, and then come to terms with, his grief and resentment over the loss of his father.

As he begins to acknowledge and confront his feelings, he stops mailing the letters altogether and instead uses the "Dear Mr. Henshaw" letters as a personal journal. The letters now begin: "Dear Mr. Pretend Henshaw." This moment marks the beginning of Leigh's acceptance of his loss. Leigh no longer needs an epistolary father. By facing up to the emotional facts of his situation, he finds a way to come to terms with his sadness about the divorce.

Accepting the Newbery Medal, Cleary spoke of the challenge of writing a book about divorce. The idea for *Dear Mr. Henshaw* had come in 1982, after several boys had written to ask for a "book about a boy whose parents are divorced."²⁸ *Runaway Ralph*, an earlier Cleary book about a dog named Ralph, prompted letters on vanishing fathers. "I had a father named Ralph once, but he ran away," confided one child. A boy writes: "Ralph wants to run away. That is how I feel about my father. My father gets me mad. I want to get custody of my mother, but I am not sure. My mother is better."²⁹ Yet Cleary's trademark was humor; her books were filled with funny adventures. As she described it, the challenge was to write about the feelings of a lonely boy without falling into the depressing genre of the teen problem novel.³⁰

To judge from the critical as well as the reader response, Cleary met the test. Critics praised her light but truthful presentation of the experience of divorce. "Divorce is presented as a wrenching experience for everyone involved," one reviewer comments, "but it is also clear that the problems can be surmounted." Although a few adult readers expressed reservations about giving it to children because "it wasn't funny and because Leigh's parents were not reconciled at the end," children found humor as well as comfort in the book. Their lives, they wrote, were very much like Leigh's.

Yet *Dear Mr. Henshaw* represented a departure for this popular children's author. Her earlier stories chronicle the everyday adventures and misadventures of ordinary children growing up in small-town Oregon. Cleary could take a simple problem—how to get a stray dog home on a bus—and turn it into an adventure of daring, determination, and invention. (As we learn in the book *Henry Huggins*, you get the dog home by wrapping it up in brown paper and string, paying ten cents like any other law-abiding passenger, and taking a seat beside a fat man at the back of the bus. Then you hope for the best.)³¹

All of Cleary's earlier characters—Henry Huggins, Ramona, Beezus, Ellen Tebbits, and Otis Spofford—belong to the tradition of "resourceful children" in American literature. Historian Bernard

Wishy tells us that the resourceful child first appeared in the late nineteenth century; Huck Finn is the prototype for all such children. Resourceful children are not part of the adult world, nor does the adult world disrupt their world, except to elicit from them evasion and manipulation.[32]

Interestingly, Cleary had written an earlier book about a boy who was being raised by a working single mother, but Otis Spofford, the title character in her 1963 novel, belonged to the "resourceful child" tradition. In contrast with Leigh Botts, Otis is blissfully unaware of his mother's inner life; his father (presumably dead) is never mentioned. Indeed, Otis's nontraditional family is as unremarkable and stable as the traditional families in Cleary books. His interests and adventures revolve around pulling pranks and bending rules; his deepest anxieties center on how to get out of trouble with his teacher and explain away (or cover up) his latest bit of mischief. And Otis's mother, like most parents in earlier Cleary stories, remains as reliable as a Timex watch and about as fascinating.[33]

Leigh Botts shares some of the qualities of Otis Spofford and other earlier Cleary characters. Despite his above-average problems, he is an average kid—a "medium boy," as he calls himself. His ordinariness is a strength. He can roll with the punches because this is the lot of an ordinary boy. He is emotionally sturdy as well. Leigh is caught up in his parents' problems but not captive to them. Like Henry Huggins, he has his own boyish pursuits, like rigging a lunch-box burglar alarm to capture a lunch-box thief.

Despite these similarities, however, Leigh does not fit in with Henry Huggins and his carefree crowd. Leigh Botts is unable to separate himself from the pressures and problems of the adult world. Neither is he able to escape or ignore his parents' domestic discord or his father's faithlessness. He must somehow engage the adult world on adult terms. He is not a resourceful child but a new kind of character: a survivor child.

For these reasons *Dear Mr. Henshaw* never rises to the level of earlier Cleary novels. It lacks the antic adventure and the utter nonsense of the earlier books. There are no belly laughs in *Dear Mr. Henshaw*, just wan smiles. We root for Leigh, but we can't sit back and relish his adventures. He is a child we must keep an eye on, not because he might pull a stunt but because he might fall apart.

Bibliotherapy for Children

Unlike *Dear Mr. Henshaw*, much of the divorce literature churned out over the past twenty-five years has little literary merit. It is designed with the explicitly therapeutic purpose of helping children "feel better" about their parents' divorce and of helping parents explain their divorces to children.

Bibliotherapy was first used in the 1960s to deal with mentally ill patients, but by the 1970s the custodians of children's literature—librarians, teachers, and parents—had begun to use it for mentally healthy children who had family troubles. Bibliotherapy offered a popular and inexpensive way to deal with the grief and loss caused by family breakup and related problems. Well-to-do parents could turn to private therapists and Prozac to manage their children's distress, but for parents who could not come up with one hundred dollars per session for private therapy and for teachers in financially strapped schools and day care centers, therapeutically correct books on divorce provided one way of healing the hurt.

According to librarian Joanne Bernstein, who has edited the leading bibliography of children's loss literature, the purpose of bibliotherapy is to help children discharge repressed emotions, develop insights into their own behavior, and build a sense of solidarity with other children who have suffered similar loss. Thus, a pervasive message of many books is that family breakup is both common and normal. "Do you know how many people separate and get divorced every year?" asks a children's book entitled *Why Are We Getting a Divorce?* "Millions and millions and millions . . . If there was ever a school for the kids of divorced or separated parents, it would have to be the biggest school in the world."[34]

One of the goals of bibliotherapy is to help children understand the reasons for their parents' divorce. Without some clear explanations, child psychiatrist and author Richard Gardner warns, children will turn into "little spies on their parents" or become angry and insurrectionary, sabotaging what little domestic tranquillity remains in the household. Indeed, the clinical evidence supports this view. The news of parents' decision to divorce can trigger angry, aggressive behavior in some children. It is not too fanciful to see these behavioral responses in exactly the terms Gardner describes—as a kind of protest activity, a way for children to register their strenuous objections to divorce.

For no matter how troubled family life may have been, the official declaration of divorce brings finality and closure to family life as the child has known it. It is no longer possible for children to deny the evidence of their parents' troubles or to cling to the illusion that life with Mom and Dad can continue in the old way. For some children, the "night my dad left" or the "day my parents told us they were getting divorced" forever changes the timetable of personal history.[35] Writing of the Johnstown Flood, which devastated a Pennsylvania community, sociologist Kai Erikson suggests that this disaster represented a kind of historical "end-time" for its residents. Even two years later "it was a common occurrence for survivors to give vital statistics about themselves as to the date of the flood, as if that were the last day on which they had measured their existence in that way, as if that were the last day they knew themselves to be living at all."[36] For children, divorce represents a similar kind of end-time.

Consequently, the books try to offer a statement of the "just causes" for divorce. On the crucial question of why Mommy and Daddy are getting a divorce, virtually all the children's divorce books adhere to the same script: Mommy and Daddy are unhappy with each other. Centrally important to this account is a history of dissension. How do we know Mommy and Daddy are unhappy? They fight a lot. Parents who fight a lot cannot live together. That is why mothers and fathers get a divorce. As children know, fighting is bad, but happily, divorce will bring an end to the fighting. Once parents divorce, children will be able to grow up in a peaceful home with a happy parent.

When it comes to "vanished fathers," the answer to the child's "why?" is handled more ambiguously. Most books try to establish the premise of a loving but incompetent and immature parent. In *Do I Have a Daddy?* the little boy asks his mother, "Why did my daddy go away?" His mother explains: "[C]aring for a baby is a big job. Your daddy wasn't ready for that."[37] Child psychologist Lee Salk emphasizes parental unhappiness as a cause for abandonment: "Daddy (or Mommy) believed that he simply couldn't find happiness in our family and had to go someplace else to make a different life. . . . I know you miss him and wonder how he is, where he's living, and what he's doing. . . . you're probably angry too that he did this without letting us know." Nonetheless, experts bluntly say, there is something wrong with fathers who do not stay in touch with their children. As Dr. Salk explains: "It's selfish and not very nice but I guess he felt he couldn't explain it to us."[38] According to Richard Gardner, children should stop looking for love from such a negligent father and seek it instead from substitute fathers, including scoutmasters, coaches, counselors, or youth club leaders.

While the books for young children properly offer simple explanations for divorce and father-loss, focusing on themes of parental conflict and unhappiness, the literature for older children admits a wider range of causes. *What Teens Should Know About Divorce in the Family*, a pamphlet found in a junior high school guidance office, lists the following reasons for "why divorce happens": lack of communication, alcohol or drug abuse, family violence, growth in new directions, conflicts, and "a couple's relationship changes." The divorce novels for teenagers are less neutral: Parents break up with each other because they are weak, irresponsible, unfaithful, abusive, addicted, violent, or insane. They abandon their children because they don't care. "My father split the scene with some broad when I was five. He has never bothered to get in touch with me."[39]

Nonetheless, the books say, kids in divorced families need not feel that they have more problems than some children in intact families. Gardner tells his little readers: "Don't think that every child whose parents are still married is better off than you are. Many of them are worse off."[40] Similarly, children who have little or no contact with their fathers will feel better knowing that their experience is not unusual. The young boy in *My Dad Lives in a Downtown Hotel* finds comfort in his friendship with Pepe, another boy who lives apart from his father. "[L]ots of kids got no dad living in the house," Pepe confides. "There's even a boy on my block who doesn't even know who his dad is!"[41] The wayward father is a stock character in teen novels as well; when the father in the novel *Unfinished Portrait of Jessica* drops in after a long and unexplained absence, his daughter observes: "I didn't have to explain this sudden Dad. Half the school were without dads or with part-time dads or with dads who come and go."[42]

Like the adult literature, the therapeutic children's literature tries to accentuate the positive aspects of divorce. "You start to see your mother and father as individual people rather than parents," one book promises, "and they will start to see you as a person as well as their child. . . . It's like finding two new friends whom you know you're going to like for a long time."[43] Some books promise that divorce will add new people and more enriching experiences to children's lives. "You have an edge on kids who've never been through what you have, because you've experienced different lifestyles," one advice book notes.[44] Books also tell children that their fury and distress will diminish over time. They must look to the future with its promise of a happier life.

Regulating the Loss Experience

More than any other body of writing on divorce, this literature reflects a deep solicitude for children and a desire to ease their fears and suffering. Yet as a popular tool for dealing with children's distress the bibliotherapeutic approach has some obvious limitations. Its effort to offer "reasons" for divorce proves weak and unconvincing. "We love you but not each other" is a hard idea for children, who are united to both parents, to understand and accept. Indeed, it shakes a child's egocentric notion that "Mom and Dad love each other because they love me." Even more difficult for adults to get across to children is the thought that "your daddy loved you once but maybe not anymore." Why would a father cease to love a child? Did the child disappoint his father or make him angry? How can a child make a dad angry when the dad has never been around? But perhaps the most difficult idea for children to comprehend is that parents, the most powerful figures in children's lives, may be helpless to sustain the one adult relationship that matters most to a child. What may make it an especially hard notion to grasp is that, presumably in an effort to spare children the harder and uglier truths, some of the stories make the parents' marital troubles sound fixable. According to one children's divorce book, parents leave their marriage because "the couple can't agree on how to spend money or whether to go out or stay home on the weekends," or maybe they split up because "the man is spending his time with other people and doesn't hug his wife and praise her the way she hoped he would."[45] But since parents constantly urge children to patch up their differences with playmates and to stop their fighting with siblings, the children may wonder why parents can't do the same with each other.

There is also a problem with the effort to get children to seek comfort in their solidarity with other children of divorce. The idea that books can provide solace for children in difficult circumstances is well founded and well established. In a 1940 edition of *A Parents' Guide to Children's Reading*, for example, the National Book Committee observed that good books could help children overcome the sense of isolation and difference caused by physical ungainliness, ostracism, handicap, racism, and broken families. However, earlier thinking about the therapeutic value of literature assumed that children had the imaginative capacity to identify with an ideal; books helped children deal with their troubles by shaping a child's aspirations.[46] Thus, the committee suggested, handicapped children might warm to stories about animals that have overcome handicaps, like *The Blind Colt* by Glen Rounds. A timid child might respond to the story of an Indian who overcomes his fright. Children in broken homes might be comforted by the very pleasant family life in Edward Eager's *Half Magic*.[47] By contrast, contemporary bibliotherapy assumes that children will be helped, not by appealing to their aspirations and hopes, but by offering them a group identity as victims of family breakup and father-loss. But this approach probably has limited efficacy at best; there is no evidence that children are less anguished by divorce because other children are also experiencing that anguish. Indeed, like the victims of divorce themselves, the comforts of victimhood are small.

After consulting this helping literature, one is left with the uneasy feeling that these books may be more therapeutic for adults than for children. No one can criticize the effort to provide parents and other concerned adults with the language and an occasion for talking about difficult subjects like divorce. Yet talking about divorce in a "rational and supportive" way may suit parents better than children. In the final analysis, reasons may not be what children are after.

More fundamentally, the rise of a therapeutic children's literature is yet another revealing sign of the tendency in a culture of divorce to treat children's symptoms of unhappiness rather than to deal with its cause, to regulate children's distress rather than to prevent it. Angry children are disruptive presences, as any parent or teacher will testify. They disturb the peace and cause various kinds of mayhem. Consequently, when a society turns to books to treat the growing number of angry and bereaved children in its midst, it is using literature not just as a teaching or helping tool but also as a regulatory tool, a way to make unruly children more tractable and grief-stricken children more manageable.

A Literature of Dissent

Nevertheless, the children's books on divorce are enormously useful in another way. They can be read as a commentary and critique of divorce itself, as viewed from the corner of the culture reserved for children. Unlike the adult literature on divorce, this literature offers clear testimony to the confusions, dislocations, and hardships caused by divorce. There are no promises of personal transformation through divorce, no claims for the annealing powers of love, no optimistic forecasts about grief as the source of growth. The dominant themes are anger, fear, sadness, and loss.

Cast against the companion adult literature, the children's stories are also less upbeat about the economic consequences of divorce. These books do not see expressive possibilities in having less money. "The idea of not having enough money can be very frightening," *The Kids' Guide to Divorce* plainly states. "Being poor is an awful thought."[48] Leigh Botts worries about the economic viability of the catering business where his mother works: "I thought of Mom squirting deviled crab into hundreds of little cream puff shells and making billions of tiny sandwiches for golfers to gulp and wondering if Catering by Katy would be able to pay her enough to make the rent."[49] Just as some of the books encourage children to look for their own father substitutes, others encourage children to take economic initiative: "One thing you can do is investigate ways to be financially independent to some extent. If you're under sixteen, you'll probably have to be quite creative to find a job, but you can still find a way."[50] Even very young children can ease the economic strain if they follow the advice in *Dinosaurs Divorce*: "Living with one parent almost always means there will be less money. Be prepared to give up some things."[51]

Children's literature also offers a harsh and unflinching view of divorced parents and of parent-child relationships after divorce. In its children's books, each generation encodes a "public" or consensual understanding of the claims of adults on children and the claims of children on parents and the larger society.[52] Critic Anne Scott MacLeod describes the governing consensus in the mid-twentieth century as follows: "Children and parents existed within a system of mutual respect, love and responsibility which was bounded on every side by a pervasive though rarely articulated code of duty. Responsibility took its place among the unspoken dictates of duty: that parents took care of children was assumed without discussion."[53]

However, MacLeod notes, the parent-child relationship did not assume equality and certainly not emotional equality. "Adults managed things, solved problems, guided and taught children. They were responsible for making life work and one way or another, they always did." Moreover, parents protected children from certain forms of knowledge deemed harmful to innocence, particularly knowledge of spousal conflict and adult sexuality. Children, on the other hand, had a reciprocal set of obligations: to be "affectionate, responsible, and within reasonable limits, good."[54]

Divorce literature in particular, and much of recent juvenile literature in general, have reversed the old rules. Commenting on this pattern, MacLeod observes that "the traditional hierarchy of parents and children has been dismantled along with, emphatically, the system of mutual respect and affection. . . ."[55] Parents are no longer the rule-givers but, rather, the rule-breakers. It is up to the children to improvise a set of rules. Moreover, parents are incapable of solving problems, especially the problems that arise within family life. Problem-solving too is thus left to the children. Consequently, MacLeod writes, children are exposed to aspects of adult life that once were considered unsuitable, and adults are exposed to the scrutiny of children who see them in so diminished and incompetent a state that they command no authority or obedience.[56]

In the predivorce literature, parents also stand as representatives of a stable social order. Indeed, it is this stable world that serves as the social backdrop for children's subversion of the established order. For example, Astrid Lindgren's beloved Pippi Longstocking books are based on the premise of how wonderful life would be if a child could live alone without parents. Nine-year-old Pippi lives in a house with a horse and a monkey: "She had no mother and no father, and that was of course very nice because there was no one to tell her to go to bed just when she was having the most fun, and no one who could make her take cod liver oil when she much preferred caramel candy." But Pippi's social world is populated with reliable adults and obedient children. Next door to her live a father and mother and two charming children named Tommy and Annika. "They were good, well brought up, and obedient children. Tommy would never think of biting his nails, and he always did exactly what his mother told him to do. Annika never fussed when she didn't get her way, and she always looked pretty in her well-ironed cotton dresses." Tommy and Annika and all the grown-ups uphold the rules so that Pippi, with her carrot-colored hair and her wild ways, can subvert them.

In the divorce literature, however, children inhabit a shifting and uncertain social world. Grown-ups are undependable and incompetent, and—a theme that recurs insistently—fathers are especially untrustworthy. Living in unstable families with unreliable parents, the literary children of divorce have been robbed of their traditional prerogatives to push against and even subvert the rules and boundaries. Rascality now belongs to the grown-ups, depriving children's literature of much of its high spirits, humor, and spunk.

The erosion of the traditional consensus also weakens the sense of obligation to conceal domestic conflict and troubles "for the sake of the children." According to the new rules, children must do more than put up with their parents' unhappiness and marital discord; they must also invest in their parents' future happiness. A new imperative pervades the literature, even the read-aloud books intended for the very young; in essence it says: Understand how unhappy your parents are, and do what you can to help them feel better. "Try to forget how sad you are and remember how sad they are," advises one author. "Why don't you see if you can cheer them up instead of waiting for them to cheer you up?"[57] Another book for young readers, *Good Answers to*

Tough Questions About Divorce, shows a cartoon mother hugging her child, with the word-balloon saying: "I feel bad because this divorce has been so hard on you." To which the good little cartoon boy responds: "That's ok, Mom. I can understand why both you and Dad needed to do what you did."[58]

Indeed, many obligations traditionally associated with parents are now assigned to children. Experts remind children that their parents are simply going through a stage: Be patient and understanding. *Dinosaurs Divorce*, a picture book for preschoolers, suggests: "Parents may need you to take care of yourself more." Children must become the steadying presences in families torn apart by parental anger and grief. In one divorce novel the reversal of roles is made fully explicit—a son consoles his crying mother by reading her a story and then tucking her into bed.

A century ago Henry James anticipated this reversal of familial obligations in his novel *What Maisie Knew*, a portrait of a five-year-old child caught "like a shuttle-cock" between divorcing parents and implicated in their romantic games and sexual dalliances. Like his contemporary Edith Wharton, James was fascinated with the impact of divorce on children; in *What Maisie Knew*, he recounts the entire history of a vulgar divorce from the child's point of view. Indeed, we see these divorcing parents exactly as little Maisie sees them; we look up at them as if we too stood only three feet tall. Her father is teeth; her mother "all kisses, ribbons, eyes, arms, strange sounds, sweet smells." But looking up to these adults, as James makes clear, is exactly what we cannot do. They are utterly unlovely and unlovable, shallow, self-centered, and committed to their daughter only insofar as they can use her to get back at each other. Through Maisie, her parents "sealed a compact to deal venomously with each other. They felt indeed more married than ever, inasmuch as what marriage had mainly suggested to them was the unbroken opportunity to quarrel." But even as Maisie's knowledge of her parents' untrustworthiness grows, she continues to love these awful people. Her devotion to such childish adults, who cannot even pursue romance on a grand scale but can only play little games, is parental. The more inconstant her parents' attentions, the more steadfast her love.

In *Maisie* James pursues the themes of innocence and experience, seeing and knowing, that absorbed him throughout his literary career. He portrays Maisie as utterly incorruptible; despite her growing knowledge of her parents' lies and ruses and deviousness, she remains morally untainted. Indeed, her moral vision deepens with each shocking revelation, each breach of trust and confidence.

In real life, however, a child like Maisie is psychologically quite improbable. The drearier empirical record shows that bad behavior from adults does not elicit good behavior from children. Indeed, the opposite is more likely true. Adult misconduct and incompetence do not strengthen children's character but ultimately weaken and corrupt it.

Recent memoirs from young adult survivors of divorce testify eloquently to this point. In a 1994 essay, Generation Xer Elizabeth Wurtzel writes: "We did not learn about bitterness and hatred on the streets (the supposed source of all terror)—we learned from watching our parents try to kill each other. We didn't learn to break promises and (marriage) vows from big bad bullies at school—we learned from watching our parents deny every word they once said to each other."[59] When Wurtzel's memoir, *Prozac Nation*, came out, critics were not generous. Reviewers accused her of self-absorption and self-pity and urged her to "grow up." But the paradox is that while divorce may call for more grown-up behavior on the part of children, it does not lead to maturity. Rather, it reinforces and enlarges egocentricity. That may be why the memoir is so fitting a literary form for young adults barely out of their teens and still nursing the emotional aches and pains of divorce.

CHAPTER SIX

More Perfect Unions?

LIKE THE LITERARY CHILDREN of divorce, American children saw their family relationships change dramatically as a consequence of divorce. As divorce became a common family event, it moved outside the jurisdiction of a "marriage system" and established its own institutional rule over parent-child relationships.

More important, the shift from a family system in which marriage governed family relationships to one in which divorce dictated the arrangements between ex-spouses and their children led to an ideological shift. A new ideology arose to challenge the ideology associated with nuclear family life and to propose another way of thinking about the nature of family attachments and obligations in a world where spousal bonds were fragile and marriage and parenthood were coming apart.

The End of "Broken" Families

Divorce gave rise to a host of living arrangements for families with children that did not fit the dominant nuclear family model. In the early years of the divorce revolution these post–nuclear family households were defined according to their relationship to marriage. Single-parent families were "broken" because the marriage bond had been broken.

Correspondingly, it was assumed, such "broken" families could be repaired through marriage. Contemporary opinion regarded the single-mother household as transitional, and single-motherhood itself as a temporary and undesirable status, to be remedied as quickly as possible through marriage or remarriage. Younger mothers, especially, were viewed as eager candidates for the bonds of wedlock. The assumption was that single mothers, like all single women, were single-mindedly waiting for wedding bells.

Stepfamilies were also defined by marriage, though in a more culturally favorable way. Because they were formed through marriage, stepfamilies were often portrayed as indistinguishable from intact married-parent families. The popular 1970s television show *The Brady Bunch* introduced a stepparent family into the family sitcom world ruled by Ozzie and Harriet Nelson and Ward and June Cleaver. Though this big family united two sets of children through their widowed parents' remarriage, the Brady Bunch did not look or act very different from the small and intact Cleaver family. This blended bunch seemed nuclear to the core. (Interestingly, Generation Xers, the children of the divorce revolution, love *The Brady Bunch*, possibly because it combines postnuclear family structure and nuclear family culture.)

Even during the 1970s, as the divorce rate soared, scholarly opinion continued to assume the centrality of marriage. Researchers frequently pointed to remarriage rates as evidence for the notion that the high rate of divorce, though it reflected individual marital breakdown, does not undermine the nuclear family or the institution of marriage. In 1976, for example, family policy analyst Mary Jo Bane wrote an influential book, *Here to Stay*, which argues that high levels of family disruption are changing but not destroying the nuclear family. This optimistic view persisted into the 1980s. In 1986 historian Tamara Hareven told a congressional subcommittee that "divorce today in a way reflects a choice people make of replacing a poor marriage by a better marriage—a marriage that works."[1] However personally distressful, divorce is thus part of a social "reaffirmation of family life." Moreover, Hareven noted, divorce gave children in tension-ridden families a shot at joining a well-functioning stepfamily.

But demographic trends were increasingly at odds with this view. There was a steady weakening of the relationship between marriage and parenthood. More children were living in family households with a never-married mother or unmarried cohabiting parents. Never-married mothers were less likely than divorced or widowed mothers ever to marry. Rates of remarriage declined after the 1970s, confounding expectations that divorce would inevitably lead to new and better marriages. Apparently women's romantic, economic, and social interests in marriage or remarriage were eroding. Even more directly, the small but significant trend of "single mothers by choice" challenged established ideas about single mothers' desire for marriage. Since this form of single motherhood was elected, rather than fated, it was hard to sustain the view of single motherhood as accidental or undesirable when a growing number of women remained wedded to single motherhood as a chosen status.

Cultural as well as demographic trends called for a rethinking of the old assumptions. The new valuation of divorce and single motherhood as sources of personal freedom and social progress required a new valuation of the post-nuclear family as well. If these families were created as the result of positive change, then they could hardly be viewed as "broken," structurally deficient, or deviant. Instead they might better be described as fully realized structures that were alternatives to, or even improvements on, the nuclear family. Consequently, the first step in redefining the fast-growing post-nuclear family was to assign an independent status and identity to its diverse structures.

The second step was to develop a new ideology of family life that fitted the new structural arrangements of the family. The nuclear family was defined not only by the structural features of the family household—namely, a family organized around a married couple and their children—but also by a distinctive set of ideas about love, marriage, and parenthood. Two ideals were closely associated with the modern nuclear family. One was the ideal of child-centeredness, with parents making heavy investments of time and money in their children and lavishing affection upon them. The other was the ideal of affectionate and long-lasting marriage. Nuclear family ideology linked lasting marriage with affectionate child nurture. The marriage relationship was the source of the social and emotional capital that was routinely invested in children.

However, as more and more Americans left marriage and raised children "on their own" or across family households, this ideology faced a cultural challenge. The established organization of the family around a married couple now competed with the new family structures created through divorce or nonmarriage. The weakening of marriage as the central institution of family life and particularly as the institution governing child-rearing called for a cultural reconfiguration of parent-child relationships in families where parents were not married to each other but continued to hold responsibilities for raising their children. Specifically, the challenge was to preserve the ideal of child-centeredness while forsaking the legal and institutional bonds of marriage and the cultural norm of marital permanence. But if marriage did not govern parent-child relationships, what did? If the spousal bond was not the wellspring of parental love and commitment, what was?

The shaping of a new cultural identity for the post-nuclear family transformed the very definition of "family" itself. The traditional definition of "family" as formed through marriage, blood, and adoption gave way to a new definition that emphasized the quality and content of affectionate bonds over bonds of blood or marriage. The emergence of this new way of thinking about family attachments and obligations was historic, for it overturned notions about family bonds and kinship ties that had governed thinking about family for nearly two hundred years.

To appreciate the scope and significance of this ideational shift, it is necessary first to consider the features of the modern nuclear family, the model that has shaped notions about love, marriage, and parenthood for most of the nation's history and, for better or worse, has engraved its iconic images on the American imagination.

A Short History of the Nuclear Family

The contemporary view of the nuclear family is mired in ideological claims and counterclaims and heavily influenced by the images of television family sitcoms. Consequently, many Americans have a mistaken and confused notion of the origins and definition of what historians call the modern nuclear family. According to one popular conception, the modern nuclear family first emerged in the 1950s as the result of suburbanization and a repressive postwar cultural campaign for family "togetherness"; according to another popular view, the nuclear model arose a century earlier as the result of urbanization and industrialization.[2] In either case, both popular "stories" suggest that the organization of the family around the married couple and their biological children represented a decline from an earlier American tradition of extended families, close kinship bonds, generational solidarity, and communal patterns of child-rearing. Too, popular belief confuses the nuclear family structure—married parents with their biological or adopted children—with the "separate spheres" domestic ideology, which took shape among middle-class families in the nineteenth century. The "separate spheres" doctrine divided the work of family into male breadwinning and female child-rearing, established women's sovereignty in the home and men's sovereignty in the work force, and ordained a gendered division between paid employment and unpaid domestic labor.

In the last decades of the twentieth century, with dramatic increases in women's work-force participation, the "separate spheres" ideology has lost influence, especially among younger Americans, and has been largely replaced with a "shared spheres" ideal of work and family responsibilities. But many families who embrace this more egalitarian ideal are nuclear families. Thus, contrary to what many popular accounts suggest, the discrediting of the 1950s Ozzie and Harriet model of breadwinning husband and homemaking wife does not mean the bankruptcy of the married-parent family. The two-earner married-parent family is still nuclear in its structure, and its shift to a "shared spheres" model is a testament to the nuclear family's capacity to respond to the socioeconomic and cultural changes of late-twentieth-century life.

The history of the modern nuclear family has been meticulously detailed in the several works of the historian Lawrence Stone, and his scholarship helps correct several popular misconceptions. First, the nuclear family is not a recent historical invention but emerged among the upper social echelons in northern Europe in the eighteenth century and spread gradually, fitfully, and unevenly within and across these Western societies over the course of more than a century and a half. In Britain the nuclear family first appeared among the upper middle class and gentry and from them spread both up and down the social ladder.

Because of common intellectual traditions and early patterns of northern European migration and settlement, the nuclear family established itself as the dominant family form in the new American Republic sometime between 1780 and 1820.[3] Instead, therefore, of appearing first in the 1950s with postwar economic expansion and suburbanization, or in the 1850s with the economic shift from an agrarian to an industrial economy, it emerged before the Industrial Revolution as part of a distinctive set of social, economic, and intellectual changes in Britain and other northern European societies.

Second, the extended-family household, with grandparents, parents, and assorted aunts, uncles, and cousins living under one roof, has not been a historically significant, much less dominant, household structure in American society for at least the past century.[4] Moreover, if Americans want to live in extended-family households, the opportunities to do so have steadily increased with increasing life expectancy, declining marriage and remarriage rates, and declining fertility. But in this century the multigenerational family household has become increasingly rare. Even among black and Hispanic families, in which children are more likely to share a residence with a grandparent as well as with parents, only a minority of children—27 percent Hispanic and 23 percent black, compared with 11 percent non-Hispanic white—live in extended-family households.[5] Indeed, the fact that the extended family is so uncommon may be one reason why Americans continue to romanticize such arrangements.

Third, the modern nuclear family was rooted in a set of ideas that took shape in eighteenth-century Western thought and placed new valuation on the individual as an independent social actor, possessed of the right and freedom to pursue happiness. "This 'pursuit of happiness,' which included both spiritual and physical pleasure of the individual, was more than just an eighteenth century elitist fad which somehow found its way into the American Declaration of Independence," writes Lawrence Stone. "Jefferson knew very well what he was doing. He was adopting a widespread and powerful notion of eighteenth century philosophy which was essential to the rise of affective individualism, namely 'the desire to live happily.' "[6]

It is hard to overstate the importance of this affective ideal as a dominant and pervasive force in shaping American family relationships. Within family life "affective individualism" contributed to more egalitarianism in family relationships, a higher level of parental nurture and investment in children, a more affectionate climate in family life. It also established a cultural ideal of child-centeredness. By the mid-nineteenth century, writes historian Robert Griswold, "men and women from all social classes conceived of family relations in affective terms, placed a premium on emotional fulfillment in the family, considered women's opinions and contributions worthy of respect and consideration, emphasized male kindness and accommodation, and assumed that children were special members of the household in need of love and affection."[7]

Consequently, the popular view of the modern nuclear family as an illiberal institution, harboring forces of patriarchalism and authoritarianism and hostile to the interests of women, ignores its historical origins in the eighteenth-century liberal tradition and overlooks the evidence that this family structure sprang from the same philosophical soil as the Republic itself.

Affective individualism had perhaps its greatest influence on the marital partnership itself. One clear sign of its impact was the shift from marriages arranged by parents to marriages contracted between a man and woman who freely chose each other on the basis of mutual sympathies, affections, and interests. In the early seventeenth century the selection of a spouse was dictated by considerations of property, power, and politics and was controlled by parents, though the marriageable children could exercise a veto over the decision after spending a few hours in the company of their prospective partners. From the mid-seventeenth century on, in both England and America, there was a steady shift toward the independent election of a marriage partner, with a reversal of the traditional role that parents played in the selection process. By the late eighteenth century, marriageable children had gained the right to select their prospective partners, while it was parents who possessed veto power over choices they considered unsuitable.[8]

Writing in the 1830s, Alexis de Tocqueville saw the free choice of a spouse as a distinctive feature of American family life, making for greater regularity and morality in marriage. In comparison with Old World societies, where forced or clandestine marriages persisted,

American society was remarkably free of such abuses: "[W]hen each [individual] chooses his companion for himself without an external interference or even prompting, it is usually nothing but similar tastes and thoughts that bring a man and a woman together, and these similarities hold and keep them by each other's side."[9]

Affective individualism influenced marriage in a second important way. It led to a more affectionate, exclusive, and emotionally expressive marital ideal, a spousal relationship based on romantic and sexual attraction and secured by the enduring bonds of friendship and mutual regard. Emotional exclusivity and intimacy were part of the new ideal. As the norm of affectionate marriage spread, the honeymoon gradually changed from a rowdy public celebration among relatives and friends to the modern ritual devoted to mutual sexual and emotional exploration.[10] The bridal suites at Pocono resorts are shrines to the achievement of this modern ideal.

The notion that conjugal unions should be founded in friendship and mutual affection established a new moral basis for marriage as well. Marriages based on ruthless calculation or reckless passion no longer fitted the new ideal. Only a partnership based on love constituted a truly virtuous union. Love had a particular meaning here; neither sexual passion nor romantic love provided adequate foundation for a marital union. Only rational love, the affections disciplined by reason and judgment and tendered in a spirit of mutual regard, met this new standard.

That marriages could resemble friendships constituted one of the more daring cultural notions of the time. Even more radical was the proposition that marriage should be *enduringly* affectionate, that spousal bonds must remain loving bonds over the course of a lifetime. As the most brilliant exponent of this marital ideal, Jane Austen clearly distinguishes between long marriages and true marriages; in *Pride and Prejudice*, her portrait of five marriages that variously succeed, falter, or fail in achieving the ideal of rational love, the longest marriage, the partnership between Mr. and Mrs. Bennett, is a durable relationship but one devoid of spiritual attraction or intellectual interest. We learn that Mr. Bennett chose his wife for her physical beauty, but her beauty has faded, and the comely bride has turned into a silly wife who must be petted, indulged, and endured. Even the shared duties and mutual interests of parenthood do not compensate for the dullness of the senior Bennetts' marriage.

Of course, the cultural ideals of the nuclear family did not always fit the reality of nuclear family life. The historical record shows that the model of affectionate marriage was frequently violated: Conflict and dissension blighted many marriages; violence and hatred erupted in others; bitter disappointment marked still others. Nonetheless, the point is that these behaviors represented abuses, violations, or departures from the cultural norm of affectionate marriage, not expressions of it.

Marriage and Kinship

In the modern nuclear family, marriage is the institution defining kinship ties, including the reciprocal set of obligations between parent and child. As anthropologist David Schneider has observed in a classic 1968 study, marriage is both fact and metaphor in the American kinship system.[11] As social fact it is the institutional mechanism linking a man and woman to their biological children. Marriage establishes the social and geographic identity of the family; it is through marriage that a child claims support and affection from one identified father and one mother living together in a common household. Marriage also establishes the economic bases of the family; it provides the institutional mechanism for transferring resources from the older to the younger generation, for recruiting help from relatives, and especially for attaching fathers to their biological children and securing sustained and regular paternal investment in their offspring.

As cultural metaphor, marriage locates the source of parental love in conjugal love. It is through the marital union that sexual love is transformed into generative love and passion is transformed into altruism. Moreover, marriage particularizes love by tying it to a family household shared by a couple and their children and to the emotional and social resources of that household.

Of course, in the American kinship system the parent-child bond is based on blood as well as marriage, and these biological bonds represent a second and reinforcing source of parental love and obligation. Unlike the affections, which have no substance and thus can be alienated or transferred, blood is a "biogenetic fact"; it is "either there or it is not, and if it is there, it cannot be altered or terminated."[12] Blood ties are permanent and inalienable, and the cultural norm in the nuclear family is that parent-child relationships are double-stitched and bound—through both marriage and blood, with love as the central cultural symbol linking the two.

The marriage and blood bonds constitute the source of what Schneider calls "diffuse and binding solidarity," "diffuse" because these ties are not linked to the performance of a narrow and specific behavior and "solidarity" because these parent-child bonds rest on mutual trust and permanence. However, it is permanence that distinguishes parent-child ties from other important social bonds. For example, friendship requires diffuse solidarity as well; the cultural definition of "friend" does not specify all the things one must do in this relationship. On the other hand, as Schneider explains, friendship includes the freedom to evaluate performance and to terminate the relationship if performance disappoints or fails. In his words, "friends are relatives who can be ditched if necessary, and relatives are friends who are with you through thick and thin . . . whether they do their job properly or not."[13] Robert Frost captured the essence of family solidarity when, in *The Death of the Hired Man*, he defined "home" as "the place where, when you have to go there, / They have to take you in."

Like all kinship systems, the American system represents an ingenious ordering of family relationships. Its particular genius is that it accords adults an extraordinary freedom and choice in their family arrangements. Moreover, it pays homage to an ideal of love that combines sexual and romantic love with friendship. Affectionate marriage does not admit cold or empty unions, nor does it approve arrangements designed to advance the interests of the larger kin group or to satisfy mere social convention. Even in recent decades this ideal has changed little; Americans still bestow their highest praise on a spouse who is not only lover but also "best friend."

At the same time the central and defining feature of the modern nuclear family—marriage based on voluntary affections—presents several problems. First, it is vulnerable to disruption and thus inherently unstable. Affections waver, fade, or die, and ties based on affections can weaken or dissolve. It is not accidental that the diffusion of the norm of affectionate marriage in the eighteenth century was accompanied by rising levels of marital dissatisfaction and breakdown.[14]

Moreover, at the same time that affectionate marriage fosters high parental investments in the couple's children, it also provides a shaky institutional foundation for child-rearing. In families organized around a large kin group, marital dissolution need not disrupt the familial sources of children's nurture or security because other relatives can assume responsibility for child-rearing. But in the modern nuclear family, organized around the married-couple household, children depend on the stability and durability of their parents' marriage in order to draw upon and benefit from the emotional and economic resources generated by the family. Consequently, with the rise of the modern nuclear family, marital dissolution, whether caused by death or divorce, became a central threat to the welfare of children and to the public weal. The popular view that the breakup of the family household constituted a tragedy for children reflected the cultural understanding of the central importance of marriage as children's most basic form of social insurance.

Finally, in this·system of family relationships there is an underlying tension between the contingency of marital bonds and the permanence of parent-child bonds. The cultural understanding is that a parent can divorce a spouse, should the marriage become unbearable, but that a parent can never divorce a child. The spousal bond, based in voluntary affections, is dissoluble while the parent-child bond, created through spousal love, is indissoluble. Yet because marriage plays so central a role in defining parent-child relationships, its dissolution makes parental bonds, especially father-child bonds, harder to sustain outside marriage and common residence with children.

The problematic character of the modern ideal of marriage is even more obvious when cast against the backdrop of human history. The very idea that voluntary ties of affection can serve as a reliable basis for permanent attachments and binding obligation seems foolhardy. It defies much of the inherited experience and wisdom about the essential and natural bases of human bonds in the ties of blood and common ancestry. It ignores property and status as sources of power and mutual interest. Moreover, it poses a problem of permanence: How can children achieve a stable and secure family life, with sustained and high levels of parental nurture and investment, in a system in which the marriage bond is so fragile and vulnerable to disruption?

The Norm of Marital Permanence

The nuclear family model tried to solve this problem with the cultural norm of marital permanence. According to David Schneider, this norm may be defined as follows: "A spouse is for better or worse, for the long run, and the quality of the loyalty (or love) is enduring without qualification of time or place or context."[15] Marital permanence preserved freedom of individual choice in the selection of a marriage partner but required that this free choice could be exercised only once. Under these cultural terms, one-time choice turned into a lifelong commitment, with a clear set of binding duties and obligations between the spouses as well as between the married parents and their children.

The norm of permanence helped stabilize the shaky foundation of marriages based on affective individualism. It also created the cultural condition for generous and long-term investments in the marriage. An assumption of permanence encouraged spouses to invest in the relationship, without fear that such emotional and material investments could be lost with the dissolution of the marriage. Over time spousal investments generated emotional and social capital that could be drawn upon in the rearing and sponsoring of their children and, later, in mutual help and caregiving as they themselves aged. (When the divorce revolution overturned the norm of permanence, it consigned a large number of older women, divorced after many years of marriage, to the status of economic refugees; at age forty-five or fifty-five or sixty-five, these divorced women found themselves in the category of "displaced homemakers," having lost a lifetime's investment in what they thought would be a safe venture.)

Still, the notion of marriage as a once-and-for-all choice was not entirely satisfactory because such a choice violated the notion of choice itself. Much of twentieth-century thought on marriage struggled with the contradictions implicit in the norm of permanence. Until the era of expressive divorce, marriage counselors stressed the dynamic character of marriage and the responsibility of spouses to adjust to changes over the course of the marriage. The idea of a dynamic and flexible relationship within the fixed boundaries of marital commitment helped reconcile the opposing notions of choice and commitment and served to anchor the renegade affections in a sturdier institutional framework. As we have seen, experts also distinguished between foolish "courtship" love and mature married love, blaming marital unhappiness on individuals' failure to make a successful transition from immature to mature love. "The files of any family case work agency or any divorce court," writes one marriage counselor, "are crowded with cases which demonstrate that the basic immaturity of the man or woman, and their unreadiness for the demands of marriage, are the fundamental factors in their marital troubles."[16]

At the same time, the marriage experts maintained an abiding faith in love as the only authentic basis for marriage. A loveless marriage held together out of fear of the stigma of divorce or out of sheer dependency was fraudulent. As a result, they insisted, sometimes obsessively, on the renewal of romantic love in marriage. It was predictable that many couples would become disaffected and disgruntled over the course of a marriage, but, with help from the experts and the local florist, they could rekindle their love again and again.

One of the most compelling statements of this cultural ideal can be found in *The Best Years of Our Lives*, the 1946 William Wyler film that portrays the reentry of three returning GIs into domestic and marital life. Homer, youngest of the three, has had his hands amputated and must regain confidence in his own manhood before he can marry his childhood sweetheart. Fred must face the disappointment and failure of his hasty wartime marriage to a party girl. But it is Al, a steady family man, who occupies the dramatic center of the movie. Al must settle down to his desk job as a GI loan specialist at his bank after engaging in the unsettling but exhilarating business of war. Most important, he must reestablish and renew his romance with his wife, Milly. The measure of Al's domestic constancy is the constancy of his feelings for Milly. Yet mature married love, no less than youthful romantic love, has to be reawakened and renewed.

At a key moment in the movie Al and Milly's daughter, Peggy, announces that she has fallen in love with Fred and intends to break up his marriage. When her parents object, Peggy lashes out: "You've forgotten what it's like to be in love. Everything was so perfect for you. . . . You've never had trouble of any kind."

Milly, played by a radiant Myrna Loy, doesn't lecture her rebellious daughter but turns instead to her husband, Al, and muses aloud: "How many times have I told you that I hated you and believed it? How many times have you said you were sick and tired of me—that we were all washed up? How many times have we had to fall in love all over again?"

"Falling in love all over again" represented the cultural solution to marital dissatisfaction. Love feelings could be regenerated and renewed within marriage. According to this proposition, it is falling out of love, rather than falling in love, that is the fleeting and transitory event. Disaffection can be chased away by rekindled affection, just as a black cloud can be washed away by a hard rain.

Finally, the norm of marital permanence recognized children as the primary stakeholders in their parents' marriage. The notion of "staying together" for the sake of the children grew out of this widely shared understanding. Implicitly the "staying together" notion also required parents to conceal their difficulties and conflicts from the children and generally to keep adult troubles out of the children's view, because marital conflict threatened to destroy spousal love and thus weaken the bases of parental attachment and affection. The obligation to preserve the marriage reflected the deeper understanding that marital stability and child well-being were culturally linked.

"As Long as We Both Shall Like"

As marriage began to erode as the central institution governing family relationships, so too did the norm of marital permanence. A small but revealing sign of the change came with the popular trend toward self-written marriage vows. In some ceremonies, the traditional pledge to marry for "as long as we both shall live" was replaced with the more limited promise to marry for "as long as we both shall love," which in many cases meant "as long as I feel happy and satisfied with the arrangement." At least one sourcebook on marriage vows suggests an even more contingent pledge: to marry for "as long as we both shall like." In his divorce book J. Randall Nichols, an ordained minister and teacher at the Princeton Theological Seminary, provides a more so-phisticated rationale for the limited and contingent marriage vow: "The marriage vow is sign, seal, and vehicle of self-investment; it is not a 'promise' that even could be kept on the same order of promising to do this or that; it is a commitment to work in relationship."[17]

No-fault divorce law offers even more compelling evidence of the abandonment of the norm of marital permanence. As legal scholar Donald S. Moir notes, no-fault divorce carries the message that "the marriage covenant is freely and unilaterally terminable, that the welfare of children is subservient to the personal fulfillment of adults, that a parent's affective relationship with his or her children may be terminated at any time without cause at the will of the other parent."[18]

But the decline of the norm of marital permanence was only part of a larger change in the way Americans began to think about family bonds. As more Americans exited marriage, a new ideology arose to challenge the established connection between marriage and parenthood and to propose a new set of understandings about the sources of binding attachments in families in which both biological parents do not raise and care for their children in the same household.

The ideology of post–nuclear family life shares some common features with its cultural precursor. Like the ideology of nuclear family life, it places affectionate choice at the center of family relationships. It too asserts the voluntary nature of the ties that bind. But it departs from the nuclear family ideology in several crucial ways. First, it rejects marriage as the central institution of family life. Under its terms, marriage continues to exist but only as an intimate relationship. It loses its status as the institution governing childbearing and childrearing and is demoted to the status of another love connection, subject to the same kind of valuations and measures of satisfaction as living together. A *New Yorker* cartoon nicely captures the essence of the new view. "I'm not talking about a permanent commitment," a suitor smoothly assures his prospective mate, "I'm talking about marriage."

Second, the post–nuclear family ideology—what I call the Love Family ideology—abandons the norm of permanence in marriage and other intimate partnerships in favor of a norm of unfettered choice. Individuals are free to pursue their love interests and choose their love partners outside the institutional confines of marriage. Because unfettered choice implies frequent change, this model of family relationships is marked by dynamism; turnover in family membership is one of its distinguishing features, as college textbooks on marriage and the family often point out. One typical textbook notes: "Whether your choices involve a philosophy of life, a career, or selecting a mate, most of them are revocable. *Although the emotional or financial price is higher for certain choices than for others (for example, backing out of the role of spouse is somewhat less difficult than backing out of the role of parent), you can change your mind* [italics mine]."[19]

Moreover, as the language of choice implies, family relationships can be cast in the familiar terms of marketplace relationships, in which individuals maximize their psychological capital by moving through a series of intimate relationships. A given relationship can form, unfold over a period of time, and probably then dissolve. Perhaps one or more of these dissolutions will involve legal divorce, but virtually every dissolution necessarily involves an emotional divorce. If just one emotional divorce can, according to the canon of expressive divorce, enhance self-knowledge and growth, how much more may the individual gain through a succession of such growthful experiences?

Thus, although it upholds the idea of "glorious voluntarism" in establishing family bonds, the new ideology sets aside the other two defining features of the nuclear family ideology: its institutional basis in marriage and its defining norm, marital permanence. More to the point, it rejects the notion that strong spousal bonds are important to parent-child bonds or that marriage is central to the security and well-being of children.

Instead the Love Family ideology proposes a new definition of what constitutes a family. A family is defined not by blood, marriage, or adoption but by bonds of voluntary affection. While nuclear family ideology affirmed love as the foundation of intimate partnership, it anchored that commitment within the institution of marriage. By contrast, the Love Family ideology liberates sexual, companionate, and parental love from its institutional and cultural moorings in marriage. Love alone dictates the arrangements and content of family life.

In parent-child relationships as well as in adult partnerships, the Love Family ideology emphasizes the qualitative and expressive, rather than the instrumental side, of love bonds. Emotional disclosure and exploration, physical and verbal demonstrations of affection, and an openness and frankness about sexuality are valued as the crucial measures of family warmth, intimacy, and solidarity rather than such instrumental measures as securing a good income, paying the bills, and living in a nice house.

In the post-nuclear family the affectional climate of the household rather than its structural organization determines family well-being. What matters most is not what a family looks like on the outside but how it feels on the inside. Similarly, the family conditions fostering child well-being cannot be identified with a particular family structure and especially not the traditional nuclear family structure. It is the quality and warmth of the affectional bonds between children and adults that are the crucial determinant of children's happiness and well-being.

Finally, the love bonds between parent and child (or any caregiver and child) are idealized as ungendered love. According to the Love Family ideology, there is no mother love or father love—simply love. However, since most children share households with their mothers, this notion favors the love bonds between biological mother and child. A father's love becomes unnecessary in a Love Family regime because it can be entirely compensated for from other sources. Thus, the fatherless household is not deficient in any essential way, nor is father absence problematic.

As the literature on single motherhood makes clear, the void left by an absent father can be filled with a compelling love story. If the single mother genuinely cared for her child's father, she can tell the child he was conceived in love, even if the love did not last. One mother plans to tell her son "how much love his father and I shared that summer. It was glorious and I think I will actually say to Corrin that he is a love child, created through this extraordinary experience with his father."[20] This affirmative story helps children with their attitudes toward men and maleness. If you speak of the child's father with a "loving light" in your eyes, another writer notes, your daughter will grow up with positive feelings about men and your son will feel good about his masculinity.[21]

On the other hand, if the mother's relationship was fleeting or disappointing, it may be harder to stick to a convincing love child story.

Nonetheless, mothers must try to find some "positives" to pass on to their offspring even if they are ambivalent about their children's fathers. In her memoir of single-motherhood, Anne Lamott writes of her son's father: "He is very tall and nice-looking, although his character is a bit of a problem, in that he doesn't seem to have a great deal of it. . . ."[22] Still, her son did inherit his father's straight hair. "Gene-wise," Lamott concedes, "I could have done a lot worse."[23]

For the mother inseminated by an anonymous donor, there are greater obstacles to constructing a satisfying story. A full paternity story may threaten the mother's own choice for independent maternity. Indeed, a child's need for a father undermines the very act of intentional motherhood by asking the child's mother to identify the father and thus invite contact with a man who is otherwise unsuitable or unwanted. However much the child may want this connection, the mother must reject it. One recommended approach is to focus on the biological father's altruism rather than his identity: A mother might tell her child that "your father was a nice man who wanted to help me become your mother." Still, if the mother wishes to remain free of social and legal entanglements with the biological father, the facts of her child's paternity must remain sketchy. Therapist and author Jane Mattes's counsel is to disclose only the father's first name and place of last residence. This will give the child enough biographical information for a short father story, as in this condensed version: "My father's name is Dave. . . . He's in Vermont."[24] Sometimes, however, a single mother may choose to keep her child innocent of even the most rudimentary knowledge of the father and simply, in the words of one such woman, "keep the story open and alive."[25] Whatever the circumstances of conception, mothers are encouraged to empathize with the desire for knowledge of the absent father and to offer support to children as they "seek their own healing."[26]

Needless to say, the unregulated commerce in sperm represents the ultimate invasion of marketplace values into family relationships. In ethical terms, moreover, the instrumental use of men's bodies to gratify women's desires for solo motherhood raises the same concerns that women have rightfully raised about men's exploitative use of women's bodies to satisfy their desires. Too, there is an ethical problem in intentional solo motherhood with an anonymous donor because it places a mother's wish to be independent of the biological father above the child's need to have knowledge of and contact with the father.

Another ideological claim made on behalf of the post-nuclear family is that it enjoys more permeable boundaries than the nuclear family. Marriage is an exclusive arrangement that closes out others; its very privacy and exclusivity—often symbolized by the one-family house with the white picket fence—often conceal terrible pathologies. As the writers of one college textbook on the family observe, "nuclear families may engage in small scale nuclear warfare. Although they fit the structural norm on the outside, they may be hiding extensive conflict, alcoholism, incest, abuse and hatred beneath the surface. . . ."[27] By contrast, the post-nuclear family includes both related and nonrelated members who are united not by bonds of blood or marriage but by mutual interests and affections.

Finally, the Love Family ideology posits a new idea of kinship. "No longer are biology and the law the only ways to make a family," one writer notes. "Increasingly family membership is based on choice and shared experiences. . . . In an age of divorce, you choose your 'relatives,' who may include a friend or lover as well as a mother or brother."[28] Thus, unrelated others—coaches, teachers, baby-sitters, Big Brothers, friends, parents' boyfriends or girlfriends, and other "fictive kin"—can be considered members of a family. "Through babysitting coops and support groups," writes Shoshana Alexander, "we find family."[29]

In a "special report" on the New American Family for *Parenting* magazine, novelist Barbara Kingsolver weaves together the tenets and the vision of this new cultural model of the family.[30] According to Kingsolver, the nuclear family was "born" in the booming postwar forties and fifties, when "couples raised children far from their extended family." Isolated from kin and uprooted from community, this family structure quickly failed. "The neat family model constructed for the baby boom," Kingsolver writes, "is gradually returning to the grand lumpy shape that human families have tended toward since they first took root. We're social animals, deeply fond of companionship, and children love best to run in packs." If the "grand lumpy" family is the normal family configuration, then the "tidy and symmetrical" nuclear family, which concealed so many pathologies, represents the deviant form.

Far from being isolated and fractured, these new family structures encourage a broader set of social relationships and a richer network of kin. Kingsolver's daughter has "three sets of doting grandparents," for example. Because post–nuclear families include more people, including nonrelated others, they promote sociability and tolerance. In contrast with the small, private nuclear family, the operatic Love Family—with its large and protean dimensions, its boisterous and clanging presence—reflects the "thriving, parti-colored world" of a multicultural society.

The diverse arrangements of post–nuclear family life also multiply the potential sources of help and nurture and inspire a new spirit of voluntarism and social cooperation. To illustrate her point, Kingsolver retells the old children's story of "stone soup": A pair of starving soldiers in a war-ravaged land invite a bunch of villagers to partake in a delicious stone soup. They begin the preparations by casting a stone into a pot of water. Unbidden, the villagers in turn toss in a carrot or an onion or a potato from their meager stores, and the whole assemblage feasts on a rich and hearty "stone soup." "Every family is a big empty pot," sums up Kingsolver, "save for what gets thrown in. Every one turns out differently. Generosity, a resolve to turn bad luck into good, and respect for variety—not suspicion and name-calling—this is what it takes to nourish a nation of children. If your soup contains a rock or two of hard times, it can still be a heck of a bouillabaisse."[31]

Parenting magazine's romantic celebration of post-nuclear families is hardly an isolated or eccentric expression of this new way of thinking about family relationships. In the world of family magazines the idea that a family is defined by its affections rather than by its structure has become widely diffused. Staid *Good Housekeeping* magazine launched an advertising campaign based on Love Family notions in the early 1990s. One of its spreads features a single mother, her two children, and her boyfriend's four children who spend the weekends. The advertisement reads: "The new traditionalist family. Its structure may be changing but its strength is not." In its 1992 Collector's Edition on the American Family, *Life* magazine editorializes along the same lines: "The truth is, what a family looks like—Ozzie and Harriet or Full

House—is less important than what it feels like."[32] As one midwesterner argued on the editorial pages of the *Cleveland Plain Dealer*, a "family is a feeling."[33]

The idea that a family is defined by love feelings is not limited to popular magazines; it has become pervasive in American thinking about family relationships. According to a survey conducted in the late 1980s, 74 percent of Americans believe that a family is a "group of people who love and care for one another" while only 22 percent think a family is a group of people related by blood, marriage, or adoption.[34]

Even lexicographers are moving away from the traditional definition of "family" as formed through ties of blood, marriage, and adoption. In 1992, for example, the *American Heritage Dictionary* dropped the words "blood, marriage or adoption" from its definition and instead described a family as "Two or more people who share goals or values, have long-term commitments to one another, and reside usually in the same dwelling place."[35]

The textbook definition of "family" has been revised along similar lines. According to one representative college text, "a family can be a group of people who simply define themselves as family based on feelings of love, respect, commitment and responsibility to and identification with one another."[36] Books for younger children adopt a nearly identical definition; in *What Kind of Family Do You Have?*, the glossary describes a family as "a group of people who care about each other and share their lives together."[37]

Survey research indicates support for a Love Family model as well. For example, a growing number of Americans reject the notion that marriage is a prerequisite for parenthood. Over the course of a decade Roper surveys show a pattern of growing support among white women for "single motherhood by choice." In 1974 women disagreed by more than two to one with the statement that "there is no reason why single women shouldn't have children and raise them if they want to"; by 1985, the last time the question was asked, slightly more women agreed than disagreed. Male opinion shifted similarly over the same time period.[38] A 1993 survey commissioned by the conservative Family Research Council shows that a majority of Americans support the idea that a "woman should be able to have a child out of wedlock without anyone passing judgment."[39]

More consequentially, Love Family ideology is winning over younger Americans. Teenagers have seized upon the idea that a family is a love feeling with the same enthusiasm that they have latched on to other culturally significant ideas. Across the socioeconomic spectrum, from inner-city teenagers to middle-class college students, young women say that they will have a child "on their own" if the right man does not come along. According to the same Family Research Council survey, 70 percent of young adult Americans, ages eighteen to thirty-four, believe that a woman has the right to bear a child outside marriage, compared with only 29 percent of Americans ages fifty-five or older.

Juvenile literature and especially fiction for adolescent girls enthusiastically endorse the notion that a family is a "love feeling." A growing number of magazine stories and popular novels for teenage girls center on the quest of finding your true "love family" rather than the more traditional adolescent task of enduring your biological or adoptive family. In *Looking for Home*, a teen novel endorsed by the American Library Association, seventeen-year-old Daphne Blake runs away from her own unhappy family when she discovers she is pregnant. She finds a job as a waitress in a homey restaurant run by a retired surgeon who introduces himself as T. Peter Perry: "Ex-M.D. Ex-husband. Ex-member of the rat race." T. Peter has not been a good father to his own children, but he is loving and paternal with Daphne. Another very good person is his chef, a college student named Junior Lee, who was abandoned by both his parents but raised by a loving aunt. He offers Daphne this big-brotherly counsel: "I didn't have a father at home, and it's not a requirement . . . all a child has to have is somebody to love them." A third adult who completes the circle is an artist named Mattie who invites Daphne to live with her in her beautifully appointed Victorian house. Mattie's only living relative, her sister, dies just as Daphne's baby is about to be born—fortunately creating room in the woman's heart for Daphne and her baby.

Supported by caring adults, Daphne chooses to keep her baby rather than give it up for adoption. Happily, Daphne is not faced with the difficulties of solo mothering. Mattie, T. Peter, and Junior pledge to raise the child with her. "Love doesn't have an artificial limit of time or distance or place, or even of blood," Daphne discovers. "It goes on as long as everyone involved is willing to do whatever it takes to keep it going."[40]

The Republic of the Love Family

There are compelling reasons why the Love Family ideology has become so widely diffused and popularly embraced. First of all, it appeals to democratic sympathies. The novelist Carol Shields captures the essence of its great appeal when she writes: "Almost everyone gets to say it—I love you. And to hear it said to them. Love is, after all, a republic, not a kingdom."[41] The Love Family is inclusive, opening its membership to all but the lone individual and making room for same-sex as well as opposite-sex parents, single and cohabiting parents as well as married parents. Secondly, Love Family thinking takes the optimistic view that love is a readily available and inexhaustible resource, flowing from diverse sources and ready to be tapped by families with children. Thirdly, it grants single parenthood equivalent social and moral status with married parenthood and thus recognizes the sacrifice, hard work, and steadfast commitment of many single mothers and fathers. Finally, it reflects the American commitment to tolerance, a guiding principle in a nation based on ethnic, religious, and racial diversity.

Most appealingly, Love Family ideology is cast in the politically resonant language and imagery of the American experiment itself. To a remarkable degree, in both structure and content, the story of post–nuclear family life parallels the oldest of all American stories: the story of the nation's origin and founding. In the post–nuclear family story, as in the story of the nation's founding, the dramatic interest revolves around one defining event: the dissolution of affectionate bonds that have grown empty and cold and the formation of a new and "more perfect union" based on ties of mutual interest and affection.

The resemblance between the new family ideology and political ideology is more than rhetorical. It reflects what political philosopher William Galston calls "the unfolding logic of authoritative, deeply American moral-political principles" in the realm of intimate and family life. These principles include the founding ideals of the Republic: equality, independence, freedom of expression, and the pursuit of happiness. The penetration of such ideals into family relationships is a phenomenon Galston calls the "regime effect."[42]

The regime effect has played and continues to play a particularly important role in establishing the philosophical basis for the steady expansion of women's rights and freedoms within the family. During this century the logic of the regime unfolded in the direction of establishing the rights and freedoms for women in marriage and in the dissolution of marriage. It also gave impetus to a critique of the separate spheres division of work within the family and called for a new, more equitable set of arrangements in childrearing and breadwinning. It contributed to a more egalitarian conception of the marriage partnership, one that more closely approaches women's emotional needs for intimacy.

In all these ways, therefore, the Love Family ideology embodies the most deeply shared American beliefs and aspirations. It seems to set forth a better ideology than the nuclear family ideology it is steadily displacing, one more faithful to the spirit of the democratic experiment itself. What it offers is a "big tent" approach to the family, with all the attractions of the big tent: open admission, a place for everyone, and easy access to the exits.

The problem with this new ideology, however, is that it does not offer a compelling set of ideas about how to maintain permanence and stability in children's family lives at a time when adult intimate relationships have become so fragile and easily terminable. Through the institution of marriage and the norm of marital permanence, the ideology of the modern nuclear family sought to reconcile, however imperfectly and unstably, the competing tendencies in family life between individual interests and family solidarity, between emotional satisfaction and binding obligations, between seeking sexual and romantic fulfillment and meeting children's needs for a stable family life. Love Family ideology rejects marriage as the defining institution of family life and as the source of parental love and investment in children, but it fails to come up with a competing proposition about how to maintain durable parent-child bonds and high levels of child well-being in a society in which the model of adult intimate relationships increasingly resembles the nonbinding relationships and short-term transactions of the marketplace.

CHAPTER SEVEN

Coming Apart

IF FAMILIES WERE MADE UP only of adults, the Love Family ideology might offer a plausible model for organizing family relationships. But the model falls short when it comes to children. As family members children cannot act as unfettered individuals pursuing self-interests. By virtue of their biological and developmental immaturity, children are needy and dependent. They are not free to choose their parents or to forge their own intimate bonds. Children cannot participate as full members in the regime; they are not able to vote for the family members of their choice, nor are they competent to negotiate the terms of their family life according to their own interests and needs. They must depend on parents and on the larger social world to represent and serve their interests as well. In brief, children place claims on adults that cannot be fully comprehended by the political terms of the regime.

Nor can parent-child relationships be described in marketplace terms. In the short term, at least, children do not "give back" returns on parental time and investment. If parents are looking for such immediate paybacks, they are sure to be disappointed. Indeed, by marketplace measures, lavish investments of parental time and money represent a squandering of resources, particularly since American parents say they do not expect their children to support them as they grow old and infirm.

Similarly, because it requires the subordination of self-interest to the needs of the dependent other, the parent-child relationship is not compatible with the ethical principles of expressive individualism. The parental role carries an obligation to sacrifice one's own interests and defer or even limit satisfactions in pursuit of children's well-being, and this makes it a role that runs contrary to the expressive ethic.

But most fundamentally, the Love Family ideology fails to provide an accurate account of the durability and quality of parent-child bonds in the post-nuclear family. The empirical evidence does not indicate that such families promote better or stronger parent-child bonds, higher-quality parenting, more sources of support from nonrelated others, or a warmer affectional climate in the family household. Rather, the widespread shift from nuclear to post-nuclear family life has dramatically eroded the economic, psychological, and geographic bases for high-quality parental nurture and investment in children, weakened the durability, quality, and solidarity of parent-child bonds, and altered the emotional climate in the household. In a society of post-nuclear families and a regime governed by Love Family ideology, patterns of child-rearing have steadily moved from "high investment, warm affect" to "diminished investment, distorted affect."

Weakened Father-Child Bonds

If there were a national index of committed fatherhood, the father-hood index would be falling so fast it would constitute the social equivalent of an economic crash. The exodus of fathers from families, and especially the disengagement of fathers from their biological children, is so widespread that it has become a demographic feature of American family life and a common experience of American childhood, which may explain why so many recent Disney family movies feature children in search of a dad.

By every measure—durability, quality, and solidarity—the father-child bond is weakened by the widespread shift from the nuclear to the post-nuclear family. One large survey that looked at the divorced father–child relationship at three separate points in time revealed two reciprocally related features: the steady emotional and financial disengagement of fathers from their children and the persistent feelings of estrangement and resentment reported by their children. By the third wave of this survey, two-thirds of young adults in disrupted families reported poor relationships with fathers, compared with the still quite high 29 percent from married-parent families.[1]

Among the several consequences of broken father-child bonds, the easiest to measure and quantify is the widespread decline in fathers' economic sponsorship of children. Although the family has steadily shed its economic functions, it remains the primary social institution for transferring dollar resources between generations. Historically the main beneficiaries of these familial transfers have been children, and the most prominent group of donors has been adult men. But with the decline of marriage and the departure of fathers from children's households, the family and incentive structure for male investment in children has been profoundly damaged.

The financial contribution of fathers falls off dramatically when parents part. Fathers who have never been married to their children's mothers are the least likely to provide regular financial support to their children, partly because they have not been identified and paternal identification is the essential first step to securing legal child support, and partly because they tend to be younger and poorer than divorced fathers. About 40 percent of children who are eligible for child support do not have a legal child support award at all.[2] As for children whose fathers' responsibilities for support have been legally established, a quarter receive nothing and less than a third receive the full amount owed.[3]

Even when nonresidential fathers faithfully meet their child support obligations, their contributions lag far behind the contributions of married fathers who live with their children. Nonresidential fathers (mainly divorced) who reliably meet child support obligations contribute an average of three thousand dollars a year to their children, while married fathers obviously contribute a much higher proportion of their earnings to the family's maintenance and care. (According to 1990 figures, the median male wage is thirty thousand dollars. Although this is a pretax figure, the male wage may be taken as a rough proxy for the median paternal income available for investment in children.)[4]

The failure to provide adequate financial support is only one form of paternal disinvestment in biological children. With the loss of a common residence with their children comes a loss of routine contact and involvement in the child's life. Indeed, while paternal money investments can be transmitted by "off-site" as well as "on-site" fathers, paternal time investments require regular father-child contact. In married-family households such paternal time investments are parceled out in the daily business of driving children to school, drilling on multiplication tables, reading bedtime stories, giving baths, or coaching soccer games. By participating in the everyday events of a child's life, keeping track of the small victories and setbacks, fathers are able to connect with their children.

When fathers and children live in separate households during part or all of the year, these routine exchanges are not as frequent or as easy. Thus, the loss of a household brings a decline in father-child contacts and a loss of paternal time investments. According to the National Survey of Children, close to half of all children had not seen their nonresidential parent (overwhelmingly the father) in the past year, and only one in six had weekly contact or better.[5] As time goes on, a child's contact with his or her father becomes increasingly infrequent. Ten years after a marriage breaks up, nearly two-thirds of the children report not having seen their fathers for a year.[6] Residential distance further reduces the likelihood that fathers will be involved in their children's lives.

The departure of the father from a child's household is often the first step in a downward spiral in the relationship, by which the father becomes steadily more distant from the child, and the child's access to the father's love, support, and sustained involvement progressively weaker. Social psychologist Robert S. Weiss describes the specific stages of this downward spiral: Separate residency diminishes contact; diminished contact reduces opportunities for routine sponsorship; diminished opportunities for sponsorship weaken the incentive for involvement; weakened incentive reduces a sense of binding obligation. The result is emotional disengagement and a loss of commitment. Weiss writes: "Without a relationship to the children, affectionate awareness diminishes, as does the sense of kinship obligation. Nor is there a basis for a sense of companionship. The parent's life is reorganized, with parental concerns no longer of central importance or, possibly, with feelings of concern for the parent's own children replaced by less pressing feelings of obligation for a new partner's children."[7]

As Weiss suggests, the nonresidential father's disengagement from his children is often influenced by his relationship with a new partner. Men who enter new family households with children, often as a result of remarriage or cohabitation, frequently shift their support and sponsorship to the "new" children, either stepchildren or children born as a result of the new relationships or marriages.

A father's troubled relationship with an ex-spouse can also work against regular contact with the children. If hostilities with an ex-wife continue after divorce, and particularly if the mother tries to subvert the father's relationship to his children, then the father may also withdraw from his children's lives. Evidence points to postdivorce parental conflict, rather than the grievances existing before the breakup, as the strongest factor in paternal disengagement. Fathers who are blocked from regular contact with their children, as a result of either punitive visitation arrangements or mothers' efforts to interfere with fathers' visitation, are also less likely to pay regular child support. In 1990, 76 percent of fathers who had no contact with their children never paid child support, compared with 57 percent of fathers who saw their children monthly.[8] Some evidence suggests that the loss of any semblance of a working parental partnership, rather than indifference to the child, contributes to paternal disengagement from the child.

Of course, none of this excuses paternal abandonment of children. Failure to provide for children represents irresponsibility of the most unforgivable kind, deserving of the full force of social and legal sanctions available to punish such willfully negligent behavior. Yet when paternal irresponsibility becomes a mass phenomenon, it is also necessary to inquire into the institutional and structural sources of such widespread misbehavior. The evidence strongly suggests that the mass disengagement of fathers from their children is driven by the erosion of a social ecology that supports strong paternal obligation, and particularly the erosion of marriage as the primary social institution for child-rearing. Because marriage provides the basis for a working parental alliance and ensures the father's coresidency with the child, it is the best guarantor of frequency of contact, regular involvement, and sustained paternal investment.

The deep structural reasons for paternal disengagement matter little to children, however. They see the father's absence as evidence that their father does not love or care about them. Not surprisingly, when asked to name the "adults you look up to and admire," only 20 percent of children in single-parent families named their fathers, as compared with 52 percent of children in two-parent families.[9] Yet lack of contact with the father, even lack of respect for their father, does not mean that children's longings for him disappear. "Most children do not give up on their biological fathers," Judith Wallerstein and Sandra Blakeslee observe in their multiyear study of middle-class children of divorce, "even if they are ne'er-do-wells who have abandoned them without a backward glance." But even for children who see their fathers, there is often a profound sense of loss. Wallerstein and Blakeslee note, "Most of the young people regularly visit their father, yet most feel they have lost them."[10]

Father-loss narrows and darkens children's horizons. Deprived of a father's sponsorship, many children lose confidence in themselves and their futures. Children from middle-class divorced families have lower expectations for college and future employment than their counterparts in intact families. This is not surprising, since many teenagers know that the child support payments will end at the very time they finish high school; according to one study, only one in ten high schoolers from divorced families was confident that he or she would have the money for college tuition.[11] Many who do attend college have to drop out periodically or carry several part-time jobs as full-time students. Thus, with respect to this crucial predictor of future economic success, the middle-class children who grow up in married-parent households are likely to enjoy advantages over children whose parents are divorced, remarried, or never married.

The damaged father-child relationship may make it more difficult for sons to stay on the same occupational rungs as their fathers, much less climb higher. One study which looked at occupational patterns among men in both disrupted and intact families found that men from disrupted-family backgrounds are more likely to have a lower occupational standing than their fathers, even after income effects are taken into account, than men who grew up in households with married parents. This was true for both black and white men. The researchers concluded that "the experience of family disruption during childhood substantially increases men's odds of ending up in the lowest occupational stratum as opposed to the highest."[12]

Finally and more broadly, in a society where father-child bonds are weakened or severed by widespread family breakup, fatherhood loses its status as a voluntary relationship. Increasingly, fatherhood in a post-nuclear family regime is a status defined and governed not by cultural values or social norms but by legal norms. This is not good news for children; fathers' contributions of income and time become more meager and grudging as they become less voluntary.[13] Even fathers who reliably pay child support often fail to volunteer assistance beyond their legally established obligations.

In contrast with a system in which married-fatherhood and voluntary paternal support are the norm, a system of single-fatherhood and legally regulated obligations requires increasingly coercive and intrusive measures to gain even incremental improvement in support. Indeed, fathers who live with their children usually work hard to increase their income and their family's standard of living; nonresidential fathers, on the other hand, tend to lose their incentive to put more money in their children's household. Some may actually reduce their workloads or refuse opportunities for better jobs, either out of resentment at the postdivorce arrangements or out of a sense that their extra earnings would not result in more time or better relationships with their children. Thus far, stricter legal control and enforcement of paternal obligations have not been very successful in putting more money in children's family households; during the 1980s intensified federal, state, and local government efforts to boost child support payments increased the percentage of women receiving payments by less than 3 percent. Moreover, these extremely modest gains benefited children in more advantaged families—those with college-educated and stably employed mothers—rather than those with mothers who had attended or finished high school.[14]

This pattern of weak attachment and help-giving does not improve when the children are adults. Divorced fathers are far less likely than never-divorced fathers to see children on a regular basis, to have an adult child living in the household, or to consider an adult child a likely source of help in time of need. Reciprocally, adult children of divorce are less likely to help their aging fathers than adults who grew up in intact families.[15]

Since a sense of family obligation is rooted in childhood experience, as sociologists Alice and Peter Rossi have observed, widespread paternal disengagement or abandonment may lead to an erosion of the felt sense of obligation. The Rossis write: "It seems likely that the broken home experience lowers obligation to one of the parents, no doubt the noncustodial parent. The fact that one parent, typically the father, left the family, may also project the notion to a child that men have lower commitments to their children, a powerful lesson that may have the long-term effect of lowering the child's sense of obligation to parents and to children."[16]

Stressed Mother-Child Bonds

Although the mother-child bond remains the most durable and primary of all human attachments, it is not undamaged by divorce or nonmarriage. Mothers may believe that getting out of an unhappy marriage will make them better mothers, but for many mothers, say Wallerstein and Blakeslee, that may be wishful thinking. "In only a few families did the mother-child relationship in the postdivorce family surpass the quality of the relationship in the failing marriage . . . at the ten-year mark, over a third of the good mother-child relationships have deteriorated, with mothers emotionally or physically less available to their children."[17]

Maternal competence declines in the immediate aftermath of marital breakup. Caught up in the legal and emotional turmoil of divorce, mothers become distracted and sometimes depressed. Some mothers plunge into new self-improvement activities or romances to boost their sagging spirits and self-esteem; others take on a second job or increase their working hours. They may be less emotionally and physically available to their children, and as a result, family life may become disorganized, even chaotic. The physical appearance of the house may deteriorate; realtors observe that "divorce houses" are susceptible to sharp drops in market value because they fall into disrepair.

Since single mothers must fill two roles instead of one, they have less time for children.[18] By their own reports, divorced mothers are less likely to read to their children, share meals with them, and supervise their school activities than married mothers. Compared with married mothers, single mothers exercise less control and have fewer rules, about bedtimes, television watching, homework, and household chores.[19] The decline in time spent with the child is not simply due to the loss of a second adult, however. Parents in stepfamilies are even less likely than single parents to report involvement in children's school or afterschool activities. A 1990 survey of American children conducted by the National Commission on Children shows that children in stepfamilies are more likely than children in intact and single-parent families to wish for more time with their mother. Distressed and lonely mothers may also turn to their children as friends, confidants, and allies, placing unfair and inappropriate emotional burdens on them.

If there are no further family disruptions, mothers usually reestablish more stable and dependable relationships with their children. But for a significant minority of children, the mother-child bond suffers long-term damage. According to one study of young adults from both intact and divorced families, 30 percent of young adults from disrupted families report that they have poor relationships with their mothers, compared with 16 percent from intact families.[20]

In divorced families, the mother-child bond is strained in other ways as well. To begin with, the children and the mother are likely to have very different attitudes toward the children's father. In good marriages a wife's affectionate regard for her husband is communicated to the children in both small and large ways. But once the marital bond is severed, a mother seldom communicates such positive feelings. Some divorced mothers openly express their hostility toward the father or attempt to draw children into their emotional corner; others are cool or silent about the absent parent. Children's love for their father often becomes a lonely and even secret love which they learn to keep hidden out of fear of exciting the mother's anger and resentment. They may find it especially difficult to speak of their confused yearnings and unrequited love for a father who has dropped out of their lives because the very fact of father-absence supports the mother's (and other relatives') view that the father is a bum.

Moreover, mothers raising children in households where the biological father is absent may also be involved in their own romantic and sexual pursuits, depriving children of time and consistent attention. If a single mother had a new partner to whom she was not married, one study found, the children spent less time with her than if she was remarried or romantically uninvolved.[21]

Of course, many divorced mothers have no sexual partners, and some conduct their love lives discreetly, away from the children. Nonetheless, a growing number of single and cohabiting mothers and fathers bring lovers into the children's households. Because these relationships are new, single and cohabiting parents are likely to be caught up in the passionate contagions and noisy eruptions of the early stages of sexual intimacy. Compared with the affectional environment in households with married parents, who have usually settled into a more sedate sex life, the climate in these post–nuclear family households may be overheated and eroticized.

Through her example a dating or cohabiting mother may influence her own daughters' attitudes toward sexual behavior. According to sociologist Arland Thornton, daughters of both divorced and remarried mothers have more permissive views of sex outside of marriage (and of divorce itself) than daughters whose mothers remained in intact marriages.[22] This may explain why economically advantaged teenage girls in single-mother and mother-stepfather households are at much higher risk for early sexual activity, and unwed teen pregnancy and motherhood, than their peers in married-parent households. The risks of sexual abuse and early sexual initiation are also considerably higher in post–nuclear family households than in intact families. Young girls are more likely to be abused by their mother's boyfriend or new husband than by their biological father.

The solidarity of mother-child bonds can also be threatened by the mother's new love interests. In rare and shocking instances, like the Susan Smith case, mothers actually kill their children in order to free themselves for a new romance. More commonly, mothers are caught between the needs of the children and the desires of a lover, and in this clash of interests the lover may be put first. "All the pulls single parents can feel between their children and an intimate relationship," writes one single mother, "can meet symbolically in the bedroom."[23] Yet despite the strong evidence of increased risk of sexual abuse to girls in households with live-in boyfriends or other unrelated adult male residents, there has been notably little public attention to the problem of boyfriends living in the children's household and no experts publicly warning single mothers against leaving children alone with boyfriends. The reason, one suspects, is that such cautions might be read as an infringement on the mother's love pursuits.

Perhaps the strongest evidence of the divided love interests of mother and child comes when the mother remarries. Indeed, it is remarriage that poses the greatest challenge to the idea that a happy mother makes for happy children. For remarried mothers, the new marriage brings great happiness and satisfactions as well as respite from the burdens of single-parenthood. But children, especially girls, rarely share these ecstatic feelings; while boys often respond positively to a new male presence in the household, girls who have established close ties to their mother in a single-parent household see the stepfather as a rival and intruder. Stepfathers also pose a sexual risk to children, especially stepdaughters. They are more likely than biological fathers to commit acts of sexual abuse, and are less likely to protect daughters from other male predators. According to a Canadian study, children in stepfamilies are forty times as likely to suffer physical or sexual abuse as children in intact families.[24]

Decline in High-Quality Parenting

Researchers have noted that there is a kind of natural system of checks and balances when a mother and father raise a child in a shared household. Of course, extremely divergent approaches and opinions with respect to child-rearing can provoke conflict, but when parents agree on common goals while bringing different emphases, sympathies, and competencies to bear in the shared task of raising children, the complementarity usually serves children well. For example, a permissive father and a strict mother can mutually balance and buffer their respective relationships with the child. A second parent in the household can also take over when one parent is incapacitated by disabling emotional or physical illness, or when one parent is simply less competent. Clearly, two parents also provide a stronger economic safety net.[25] Importantly, too, both married biological parents have a shared history and body of knowledge about the child dating from infancy, which encourages strong bonds of trust and cooperation.

If the parental partnership falls apart, however, these complementary differences may turn into sources of persistent conflict, mistrust, and competition. In the most intensely conflictual postdivorce relationships, the courts must resolve disputes. More commonly, the parents simply learn to avoid each other. One study, which followed divorced parents and their children for three years after separation, found that talking and exchanging information about the children fell off during that period. Some parents had stopped speaking to each other altogether and instead used answering machines, teachers, babysitters, or others to carry messages—messages, moreover, that were usually limited to matters of scheduling or logistics.[26] But although such an avoidance strategy may help defuse tension and hostility between the parents, it necessarily lowers the quality of parenting. Each parent loses access to important information about the children's behavior, and miscommunication, confusion, and misjudgment are likely to increase, especially if parents rely on the children themselves to carry messages back and forth.

When the child's father is not present, maternal authority and discipline can be compromised. In both divorced and intact families, studies show, children comply more readily with fathers' than with mothers' demands. Mothers are better able to control teenage sons when they can invoke the support and authority of the father, but even in disciplining much younger children, a father's authority is important. One study showed that mothers were more effective in controlling two-year-olds when the father was present. Although many mothers exercise steely discipline and can call their children to order with a mere narrowing of the eyes or tightening of the lips, other mothers turn mushy and permissive when the father is not around.

If a mother's disciplinary authority is compromised by the absence of the child's father, his competence as a nurturer is even less reliable without her supervisory presence. Typically, mothers teach fathers how to care for small children, and in intact families fathers commonly defer to the mothers' judgments about child care. Single fathers who must care for infants and young children away from the mother's supervision may be clumsy and inept in performing the necessary tasks. If they return the children to their mother's household with diaper rash, dirty noses, and fresh scrapes, such fathers are immediately under suspicion for irresponsibility, neglect, or, even worse, abuse.

Indeed, fathering outside of the marriage partnership marks off entirely new cultural terrain, and the boundaries between physical caretaking and sexual abuse, innocent tussling and exploitative fondling, have become blurry and ill defined. How does a father handle the intimate tasks of bathing, diapering, and toileting small children in a setting unsupervised and unregulated by the mother, particularly when the mother expresses little confidence in his competence or conscientiousness in this domain? How should a mother interpret a toddler's reports of what Daddy did to her private parts? It is little wonder that affectionate fatherhood outside of marriage has become legally perilous for divorced fathers, as the rising number of child abuse charges associated with child custody litigation suggests. The problematic nature of nurturant fatherhood outside marriage may also help explain the current explosion of television docudramas and news stories featuring, in one critic's words, "fathers panting after their young."[27]

Arranged Parenthood

Although the arranged marriage has never figured significantly in American family life, arranged parenthood is a defining feature of post–nuclear family relationships. The very language describing parent-child relationships reflects the growing emphasis on legal regulation and control: mandatory paternal identification, custody, visitation, child support orders, mandatory mediation. A divorce workbook for young children offers instruction on "legal stuff." "What do you think a courtroom looks like?" it asks. "Draw a picture here."[28]

The court's supervisory presence intrudes into the small, discretionary everyday matters that define the very conduct of private domestic life. Family courts rule on children's participation in religious holidays, birthdays, and special family occasions like weddings or reunions. They may be called upon to resolve conflicts over parents' participation in PTA meetings and school recitals; the mailing of report cards and medical reports; their choice of dentists, pediatricians, and psychologists; even their decisions about music lessons or sports camp or religious education.

In high-conflict divorces, for example, some experts now recommend the adoption of a "parenting plan" that spells out respective rights and responsibilities, leaving almost no area of parent-child contact unregulated or undefined. One model plan spells out the rules for the purchase of snowsuits. "Each year, both Michael and David will need to be provided with appropriate winter clothing, which is to include a parka, snow pants, and winter boots. The father shall purchase these items for Michael and the mother shall purchase these items for David by September 1 prior to the winter season for which they will be needed."[29]

This highly contractual approach to parental rights and responsibilities is certainly not the norm. Nevertheless, it offers a revealing glimpse of how divorce erodes the independent and voluntary basis of parent-child relationships. Even more revealingly, this parenting plan suggests how child-centeredness weakens when the focus of attention shifts to the quarreling between divorced parents. Consider, for example, what this "parenting contract" says about the matter of children's toys:

> Toys will be considered as belonging to the parent who either purchased them or received them as gifts. If the children wish to take toys out of the home to which they belong, they may do so with the exception of bicycles, videos, computer games, and anything considered expensive or fragile by the parent who purchased or received that item. If a toy has left the home to which it belongs, the party may request it back by communicating with the other party in either verbal or written form. The party receiving such a request for the return of a toy must comply.... Any dispute as to the ownership of the previously purchased item or newly purchased item will be resolved only through a joint meeting with both parties present and the parenting coordinator.[30]

The idea that toys belong to parents first and then to the household is a startling notion, one that runs contrary to the psychological meaning of toys. Children's toys are more than mere playthings; for young children, they are also first possessions and therefore objects of egocentric attachment. Teaching children to share their toys is a way to teach children to share themselves, to trust objects deeply invested with their own selves to the disposition and care of others. Consequently, it is not a minor matter when children's toys are redefined as objects that parents own and squabble over.

Through court-ordered visitation arrangements, divorce restructures the way parents and children spend time together. Visiting is not something fathers do alone; children too become "visitors," subject to the same constraints and rigors of scheduling. The visitation schedule proposed in the parenting plan for four-year-old Michael and eighteen-month-old David goes as follows: Both boys go to their father's house on Friday evening; David returns to his mother's place two hours later. Michael stays overnight until Sunday and then returns to his mother's house. Michael also spends Tuesday evenings from five-thirty to eight-thirty with his father while little David has solo visits with his father for two hours on Thursday evenings. Although this schedule tries to accommodate developmental needs and differences of these brothers, it hardly fits the daily rhythms and routines that best suit small children. For older children, the obligations of visitation often conflict with school, sports, or weekend social activities, forcing kids to choose between time with parents and time with friends. If teenagers want to spend a weekend with friends rather than with their nonresidential parent, they run the risk of angering or hurting that parent or of feeling disloyal for preferring time with friends, even though it is perfectly normal for adolescents to prefer the company of friends over parents.

In *The Great Good Place*, a study of the ecology of neighborhood hangouts, writer Ray Oldenburg observes that organizing and scheduling are powerful tools, skillfully plied by the managing classes. Adult Americans seek escape from such organized time in their family and associational lives. Indeed, one of the central features of a strong civil society is the freedom of individuals to arrange private domestic time according to their own inclinations and preferences. But postdivorce arrangements allow no such freedom for children, whose healthy development requires unhurried and unorganized time; indeed, visitation inevitably swaps the superior unhurried time for inferior organized time, structured to fit parents' own work and household schedules.

Distorted Affect

Since the early nineteenth century the model for parent-child relationships has been one of warmth, mutual affection, and high levels of parental nurture. Following in this tradition, the Love Family model aspires toward parent-child relationships that are warmer and more nurturant, more expressive and open than those in the nuclear family. Yet the structural and institutional arrangements of the post–nuclear family work against the achievement of this ideal. The climate in the post–nuclear family household tends toward extremes; it can at different times be either hot or cold, but it may never be comfortably and consistently warm.

Affectionate parent-child relationships include both the expressive and the instrumental side of love. As the many studies of infant attachment suggest, demonstrations of warm, loving feelings—conveyed through both talking and touch—are centrally important in the very earliest stages of forming primary parent-child bonds. Moreover, although parents' verbal and physical displays of affection change as the child grows older, from cuddling an infant to praising a teenager, these expressive elements remain vital to affectionate child nurture.

Equally important are the instrumental expressions of love, the performance of tasks and investment of resources in the service of nurturing and sponsoring a child to independent adulthood. Instrumental love takes myriad forms, from providing food and housing to washing clothes to supervising schoolwork to scraping and saving to pay for college tuition. Both fathers and mothers engage in both forms of love, although in different ways. (For example, doting mothers almost never greet their sons with handshakes; doting fathers often do.) Of course, the two sides of parental love are most often fused; a parent cheering up a sick child with a hug and a bowl of chicken soup is expressing both forms of love.

The instrumental and expressive sides of parental love become un-stuck in a post–nuclear family world of divided households and arranged parenting. Because fathers do not live with their children, they cannot invest their time in the small and ordinary daily exchanges of help and advice. Their instrumental contribution may dwindle to the electronic or postal transmission of money or to nothing at all. Nonresidential fathers who seek emotional closeness across the barriers of distance and divided households must look for opportu-nities to express their love in noninstrumental ways, to maximize their emotional presence in children's lives while they are physically distant.

The marketplace has stepped in with products and services de-signed to foster expressive love bonds across households and miles. New communications technology helps children and fathers stay in touch; E-mail, faxes, even beepers, keep love alive. Old-fashioned tech-nologies are also used to transmit messages of love. Hallmark now of-fers "To Kids with Love," a special line of relationship cards inscribed with "thinking of you" messages for adults to send to the "special kid" in their lives.

One card shows a forlorn cat holding a picture of a kitten. Its block-lettered message reads: "I wish you were here—it's hard to hug a picture of you."

Another reads: "I'm sorry I'm not always there when you need me but I hope you know I'm just a phone call away."

Most of the "thinking of you" messages are ambiguously worded to encompass a variety of adult-child relationships and a range of cir-cumstances that might keep grown-ups and kids apart. At the same time, it is clear from the high emotional pitch of these cards that they are designed for single parents who are temporarily or permanently living apart from their children. How else to explain the intensity of feeling in this message?

Sometimes I miss you very much
When I can't be with you
And that is when I play a game
And here is what I do—
I picture what you're doing

Where you are and who is there
And send a special kiss and hug to you right through the
air!

Not all the messages are ambiguous, however. Some are expressly designed for parents who live apart from their children. One card features an airplane's-eye-view of a tiny grown-up and a child flying a kite. "Just because I don't live with you anymore doesn't mean I love you any less," it reads. "I sure do miss you."

Hallmark also sells cards for children to send to faraway fathers. There are plaintive Father's Day cards: "I miss you more than ever, Daddy, now that it's Father's Day, and even though I'm too far away to hug you with my arms, I just want you to know I'll be hugging you in my heart!"

Some Father's Day cards are designed for the important guy in a child's life. "Even though you're not my dad," says a smiley little bear, ". . . you're sure good at doing dad stuff! Thanks! Happy Father's Day."

One reason this sentimental commerce is so popular is that the cards serve as keepsakes as well. In this respect they enjoy a competitive advantage over phone calls or beepers. While experts encourage non-residential parents to stay in touch over the phone, any parent knows that children can be maddeningly monosyllabic over the phone. And children can't hang on to a voice once the connection is broken, whereas a card gives a child a permanent keepsake.

What is immediately striking about these cards is that they are cast in the language of romantic love. Their messages speak of the pain and suffering of parting, and then of the anticipation of the next meeting. In the meantime fathers and children yearn for each other. They linger over the photographs and memories of happy times spent together and promise to do it again sometime soon. Like young lovers, they ride the roller coaster of emotions, from despair to ecstasy and back again.

The Hallmark people have a good ear. With eerie accuracy, the cards echo the sentiments of absent fathers recorded in the social-scientific literature. As one father told a researcher, "I feel I am constantly searching for my children, I think I see their faces in other children's faces. It's a desperate kind of yearning." Like a rebuffed lover, another father said: "I'll go on pining forever."[31]

Yet this passionate suffering and yearning are not reliably translated into the more tangible currency of involvement and support. For faraway fathers, this distant courtship of children carries its own brisk efficiencies; instead of being there, fathers fling wispy heart hugs into the mail. Indeed, the Hallmark cards illustrate a larger cultural shift from instrumental forms of paternal obligation—paying the light bill, working two jobs, teaching Sunday school—to more expressive forms like dropping a Hallmark card into the mail.

Over time, cheap sentiment may come to represent commitment itself. The larger cultural message behind the "To Kids with Love" cards is that what children need is not a family life shared with father but occasional expressions of paternal love and caring.

During a segment of a recent Oprah Winfrey show devoted to children's pain and grief over their absent fathers, Oprah brought a "deadbeat dad" face-to-face with the daughter he had abandoned. As the father, a man named Tim Laws, guiltily confronted his teary daughter, Oprah chastised him: "Why haven't you been able to write a postcard, send a note, pick up the phone? I think that's really—that's basically it. You can go out right now and get them [*sic*] Hallmark cards—have a whole stack of them, you know? If we just agreed to maybe five times a year, she could hear from you and then you set the dates so she'd know on such and such a date? Or if you can't commit to five, do three...."

Jumping to Oprah's aid, the guest therapist chimed in: "It takes so little to keep in contact with your child. You think you have to write volumes of letters. It's like Oprah said, just a postcard. Just buying a card and sending it every couple of weeks. 'I'm thinking of you. I love you. Dad.' That's all you have to do."[32]

No one can criticize Oprah for her kindhearted attempt to coax or shame dads into staying in touch with their children, even at such a minimal level. But as a model of fatherhood the "five-cards-a-year" dad falls far short of what Americans increasingly believe is the ideal of good fatherhood: the involved, hands-on, emotionally expressive, and nurturing father. Indeed, in a post–nuclear family world the cultural model for fatherhood moves away from the ideal of involved fatherhood toward a safely reduced and remote paper fatherhood, symbolized by three documents: the birth certificate, the child support check, and the sentimental greeting card.

At the same time that divorced fathers are reducing their instrumental contributions and boosting their expressive exchanges, divorced mothers find their capacities strained and overloaded by increased demands on both the instrumental and expressive sides.

On the mother's side, the cultural tilt is toward the more traditionally maternal dimension of the parent-child relationship—the expressive rather than instrumental aspect of love bonds. Indeed, the Love Family ideology is a deeply feminized ideology. Its emphasis on expressive love as the defining measure of family strength and solidarity favors dispositions and competencies typically identified with maternity. Yet, perversely, post-nuclear family life can reduce the time and energy available for mothering, as well as the level of maternal supervision, by increasing the burdens of breadwinning. Although post-nuclear family life overloads mothers with instrumental tasks, its ideology fastens on the unlimited capacity of mothers to shower their children with love, setting up an impossible ideal for single mothers. And, poignantly, much of the advice literature on divorce embraces the economic adversity associated with single-motherhood in the name of increased individual freedom and choice.

Diminished Kinship Ties

One of the claims made on behalf of the post–nuclear family is that it provides a more diverse and emotionally rich set of relationships for children than does the traditional nuclear family. If the mother or father or both biological parents remarry, the child will have more relatives and thus access to more resources. Moreover, unlike the nuclear family bound to relatives through marriage and blood, the post-nuclear family creates new opportunities to build families based on ties of mutual interest and affection. According to a recent article in *The New York Times*, the growing numbers of children in single-parent families may find "natural" allies among the growing numbers of single, childless adults; "paraparents" may replace absent biological parents.[33] Experts also maintain that resourceful children often recruit surrogate parents; these "recruiter" children learn to "save themselves." Too, there are adults who volunteer their help, either informally or through such organizations as Big Brothers and Big Sisters.

Finally, there are parents' friends, other children's parents, neighbors, and godparents.

It is certainly true that the post-nuclear family household is more likely than the nuclear family household to have unrelated adults moving in and out. Baby-sitters or housekeepers, sometimes with their own children in tow, may join the family. The sexual partners of single parents may cohabit or may routinely spend overnights or weekends in the children's household. It is also true that remarriage brings more relatives into a child's life. When one or both parents remarry, children acquire stepparents, stepsiblings, and half siblings as well as new sets of grandparents, aunts, and uncles.

But this churning in household and family membership does not reliably translate into lasting ties between unrelated adults and children. Because cohabiting and stepfamily households are more likely to dissolve than married-parent households, the new relatives may drop out of a child's life as fast as they drop in. Actor Tom Hanks remembers how his father's remarriage to a woman with five children plunged him into a family life with strangers: "Suddenly it was like— bang, zoom!—there were eight kids around. I remember in school we had to draw a picture of our house and family and I ran out of places to put people, I put them on the roof. When he and she split up, I never saw those people again."[34] Moreover, unless stepparents adopt their stepchildren, there is no legal responsibility to care for them. Children, in any event, identify their biological parents as their "real" parents even when they are not in their lives.

The idea that a greater number of adults can provide more attention than two married parents is not borne out by the evidence. Dividing time among three or four parents rather than two is not likely to be as advantageous to the child as the time spent with two parents who live together in the same household. Similarly, recent research indicates that the quality of parenting is lower in multigenerational families than in single-mother families. According to McLanahan and Sandefur, the "average child raised in a stepfamily or by a mother and grandmother is doing less well than a child raised in a married two parent family."[35] Particularly unfounded is the notion that children can recruit their own surrogate parents, especially "parafathers." There is not a shred of evidence to support the optimistic idea that there are enough committed father substitutes to replace all the fathers missing in action from children's households, nor is there any reason to believe that young children have the capacity to recruit their own surrogate fathers. The concept of the recruiter child is like the concept of the poster child; it favors children with exceptionally engaging and highly marketable personalities.

Marriage brings together two families and, through those families, potentially two separate streams of support and help for the couple and their children. But when a marriage breaks up or never forms in the first place, the child's access to both sides of the family is often weakened, curtailed, or entirely missing. Of course, some fortunate children do acquire several sets of doting grandparents through remarriages, and some paternal grandparents remain close to their grandchildren, even after the children's parents have divorced and entered new relationships. But overall, children in divorced families are less likely to enjoy the help and support of both sides of the family than children of similar socioeconomic backgrounds in nuclear families.

Divorce or unwed motherhood may boost the levels of assistance from parents and other family members, but the help exchanges of money, child care, and housing usually come from the residential parent's—usually the mother's—side of the family. One study found that 59 percent of divorced white mothers and 39 percent of divorced black mothers receive money from kin outside their households.[36] However, fewer than half of all white single-parent families participated in kin networks. The same study challenged the popular idea that black single-mother families receive strong support from kin. Although black two-parent families were much more likely than white two-parent families to participate in a kin network, black single-parent families received less help from kin than either black two-parent families or white single-parent families.[37]

Moreover, in a nation that leads the advanced Western world in divorce and unwed teenage childbearing, intergenerational help exchanges may grow more infrequent or inadequate as the trends of family breakup become more entrenched. Multigenerational mother-child households are disproportionately poor and welfare-dependent, so their capacity for economic help-giving is extremely limited. More advantaged families do reach out to provide money, child care, and other forms of assistance to their divorced offspring, particularly their daughters. Indeed, the baby boom generation is unusually fortunate because its parents have been able to retire at age sixty-five, often fairly comfortably. Compared with their children, moreover, the postwar generation had much lower levels of divorce. Thus, divorced baby boomers may benefit from their parents' long-lasting marriages by drawing upon the social and emotional capital generated by these unions over forty or fifty years. However, Generation Xers, the children of the divorce revolution, may not be able to count on a similar lifeboat from their parents.

Weaker Social Bonds

Children's well-being does not depend on the parents or relatives alone but also on stable relationships formed with other adults and institutions. Even a newborn has a social identity; through its membership in a family household, it is geographically bound to a physical locale and linked to the neighbors, family friends, child-serving professionals—from doctors to teachers to clergy—who live in the same neighborhood and community.

Unlike family bonds, a child's social bonds are not fully established in the first years of life. Social bonds are the product of a shared history, and they form gradually over time. Moreover, compared with family attachments, they are often casual and episodic. Their benefits are small and cumulative. Ideally, therefore, in order to form solid and trustworthy relationships and to benefit from the social goods—information, attention, and help—generated by these relationships, children must have some measure of stability in their residential and household arrangements. Children who live in the same place in a stable family household are more likely to benefit from this social capital than children whose residences change and whose family lives are split across households, neighborhoods, and even schools.

Because family disruption destabilizes children's family lives, it weakens children's opportunities to form strong social bonds. The breakup of a marriage often means the loss of the family residence. Children leave the family house and move to another, often more modest place. In community-property states, where assets acquired during the marriage are often split evenly between the two parents, the court usually orders the sale of the house, one among many legal practices that ignore the interests of children.[38] Many of the postdivorce living arrangements are temporary, so children in disrupted families often face more than one residential change. Sara McLanahan and Gary Sandefur's research shows that children who live with both parents enjoy the most residential stability, whereas children in stepfamilies experience the least; children from single-parent families fall in between, although their moves are most likely to be caused by eviction or other stressful experiences.

If divorce caused only a single residential move, children might not be significantly affected. After all, moving from one house to another is a well-established American family tradition. But divorce commonly leads to further disruptions. A growing proportion of children in disrupted families will be caught in a revolving door of changing family households, moving from intact to single-parent to cohabiting to stepparent families. Half of the children whose families are disrupted by divorce will also experience a second disruption before they reach age eighteen.[39]

Moreover, because children of divorced parents are members of more than one household, they must divide their family lives between separate and sometimes distant residences. As a direct consequence of divorce, therefore, American children have become more migratory. As parents settle into their own places, children move between family households. On weekends, during summer vacations, and over school holidays, children shuttle back and forth between dad's house and mom's place.[40] A growing number of children have joined the ranks of frequent fliers, creating a special market niche in the airline industry and a special set of industry regulations for the "unaccompanied child." In airports one catches a glimpse of such children, with their brightly colored backpacks and their special airline escorts, but the larger segment of the migratory population remains less visible, traveling back and forth in automobiles, buses, or subway trains.

Historically, there is nothing new about children moving around by themselves. In eighteenth-century England apprenticeship and domestic service caused high levels of residential mobility among children. One scholar estimates that three out of every four males between the ages of fifteen and nineteen left their homes to go into service; two out of every three children of both sexes left their home parish, to be replaced by children from another, nearby parish.[41] Moreover, unaccompanied children made transatlantic voyages to the New World.

Nonetheless, the mobility of American children today is distinctive in several ways. It is new for children to move around as a routine condition of family membership, as a necessary part of sustaining a relationship with both parents. Increasingly, children must travel between households and across miles simply to have regular contact with a father.

It is also new for children to travel great distances as part of their regular family lives. In contrast with the apprenticed children, who usually remained within half a day's walking distance of their homes, today's children must often cover distances of many hundreds of miles.[42] Because the country is so large, American children are much more likely than their European counterparts to live more than a thousand miles from their nonresidential parent. Finally, in comparison with earlier patterns of child migration, some children are very young when they begin shuttling between households. Airlines allow children to travel unaccompanied at the age of five or six, but even infants are transported between households in cars or taxis, with frozen breast milk and ear infection medication tucked into their diaper bags.

If all this seems a matter of little consequence, it is because we see this growing instability in family living arrangements from an adult perspective. Although mobility is not an unmixed blessing for adults, sometimes making for loneliness, isolation, and even depression, it typically carries a positive meaning. Moving is commonly identified with self-improvement, career opportunity, and fresh starts. For children, frequent moves do not hold the same sense of possibility and opportunity. On the contrary, in a highly mobile society, where a driver's license is as important a passport to freedom as the right to vote, children are the last American provincials, bound to a family household and the local geography of the neighborhood. Thus, the mobility associated with family breakup imposes a double burden on children. At the same time that divorce disrupts children's primary family attachments, it also threatens to fragment their social identities.

As McLanahan and Sandefur argue, transiency affects children's social embeddedness. Children who move frequently are less likely to form stable and lasting bonds to other adults in the community or to other children. They may be less attached to schools, the most important institution in many children's lives, after the family and the church. They are less likely to have ready access to the body of "local knowledge" about schools and about community and afterschool activities. McLanahan and Sandefur also observe that divorce may reduce social contacts even when the family does not move, since family friendships also may be shattered.

Because dependable and long-term relationships confer a sense of worth—"I am a good and worthwhile person because I am reliably loved by another"—the diminished opportunities to form such durable ties have far-reaching emotional and social consequences. Lack of strong family and social bonds is a common denominator in the backgrounds of many juvenile delinquents. It is also associated with other risky behaviors, such as early sexual initiation, unwed adolescent childbearing, and dropping out of school. Shallow or inferior ties may also explain why children in stepfamilies, who have higher incomes and may live in more affluent communities than children in single-parent families, suffer similar rates of high school dropout and adolescent childbearing.

In brief, though life after divorce may present a rich and stimulating set of new experiences and challenges for adults, it does not have the same impact on children. Children are conservative creatures. They like things to stay the same. Troublingly, divorce makes change the only sure thing in children's family lives.

Diverging Paths

One of the central claims made on behalf of the post-nuclear family is that love determines child well-being, rather than the mere presence of married parents or the structural organization of the family. This notion recognizes a fundamental truth. Parental love is tenacious. It suffers much and endures much. Across time and cultures, parents have maintained enduring ties to children in the face of disruptions and separations caused by illness, war, poverty, famine, and disaster. Parental love is also heroic. Many parents make extraordinary sacrifices and endure tremendous personal hardships in order to provide a secure and loving home for their children. Consequently, parental love can and often does transcend the structural arrangements of family life.

Nonetheless, the evidence suggests overall that the structural organization of the family around a married couple and their biological or adopted children is more successful at forging strong parent-child bonds and promoting high levels of affectionate child nurture than the fast-growing alternatives: single-parent, cohabiting-parent, or step-parent families. That is not only because families with two parents enjoy greater earning capacity than single-parent families or because there are two adults rather than one in each family household but also because married parents are better able to combine the instrumental and affective sides of child nurture, to establish durable parent-child bonds, and to form stable families that are better able to recruit other sources of social and emotional capital. Consequently, the structural and affective bases of child-rearing are not unrelated but deeply and closely intertwined.

Indeed, despite its embrace of many of our most widely shared and deeply held notions about the individual's freedom to choose a partner based on mutual attraction and affection, the Love Family ideology undermines the very ideals it seeks to promote. Its ideal of families bonded through love feelings alone does not result in more loving families. In a culture where sexual and romantic love is fully liberated from the institution of marriage, with its reciprocal and binding duties, love is not enough to sustain strong bonds with both parents. This is not conjecture but an empirically founded observation.

Disappointingly too, a more sexually open and expressive Love Family does not make the affectional climate in the household warmer so much as it eroticizes the environment. Though the household may be filled with the sights and sounds of love, these passions leave children in the cold. For a child whose father has disappeared and whose mother is in the throes of a new romance, the affectional climate of the postdivorce household can be both hot and cold, but not comfortably warm.

When children must be raised across family households, high-quality parenting is far more difficult. The parental partnership is lost or damaged, and only a minority of parents in divided households are able to maintain the levels of cooperation, information sharing, and involvement that are typically present in stable two-parent households. When only one parent is engaged in child-rearing, the strains and stresses diminish time, supervision, and involvement in the children's school life. Other caring adults may provide some additional help, but even grandmother-mother households do not match two-parent households in the level of their supervision and control. The affective bonds between stepparent and child are extremely fragile and often nonexistent. A large percentage of children do not even consider stepparents part of their families, according to the National Survey of Children. The NSC asked children, "When you think of your family, who specifically do you include?" Only 10 percent of the children failed to mention a biological parent, but a third left out a stepparent. Apparently the sense of weak attachment is mutual. When parents were asked the same question, only 1 percent failed to mention a biological child, while 15 percent left out a stepchild. In the same study stepparents with both natural children and stepchildren said it was harder for them to love their stepchildren than their biological children.[43]

With the currently high levels of family disruption, therefore, child-rearing patterns are diverging by family structure. Intact families are pursuing a "high-investment" child-rearing strategy while disrupted families have diminished capacity to invest in their children. It is important to emphasize the word "capacity." Most parents strive to give their children every advantage they can, no matter what the structural arrangements of the family may be. However, the nuclear family structure has a greater capacity to generate the time, money, and supervision that are required for raising children in an increasingly complex and demanding economy and society. Indeed, because families with children are smaller and because parents are older and better educated than in the past, many married-parent nuclear families can focus all their resources and attention on one or two children, often investing lavishly in their children's upbringing. The nuclear family model has not ceased to be a viable form of family organization in a postindustrial society. On the contrary, it may be even more essential now than in the past, because child-rearing in a postindustrial society has become increasingly demanding of parental money and time. Since

American parents bear the principal responsibility for the education or training of their children after high school, and since post–high school education—either college or technical school—is the key to future job and career success, any trend that weakens the family's structural capacity to sponsor young people during this crucial stage of life also weakens the children's chances for economic success. College financial aid offices do try to pry tuition from both parents in divorced families, but tuition support, like child support, tends to become more grudging and meager when it is coerced rather than volunteered. For these reasons, growing up in an intact family will continue to be a source of advantage for children and will be one key predictor of success in a postindustrial economy.

Love Family arguments place individual choice at the center of family relationships. But notions of voluntarism and choice collapse under the weight of too much choice. The greater opportunity to elect a partner not once but two or three times results not in stronger family attachments but in weaker and more fragile love connections. The loss of permanence in adult relationships is not entirely undesirable, according to much popular thinking. The ability to shape and reshape intimate relationships—to have a second chance and a better shot at happiness—is a source of hope, optimism, and possibility. When nothing is forever, anything can happen, if not today, then maybe tomorrow or next year. Love is a lottery, and your winning number might come up next time. But this approach to adult relationships undermines the bases not only of children's security but of their freedom. As adults enjoy more freedom in the pursuit of a satisfying intimate life, children's family lives become increasingly subject to arrangement, regulation, and control. Children's relationships to parents and grandparents, their contacts with their nonresidential parents, their schedules and routines, even their vacations and "fun," are governed by distant and faceless forces. What's more, as adult behavior in sexual and marital relationships becomes less subject to social regulation, there is a growing effort to manage therapeutically the conduct of children distressed by their parents' divorce. A culture of divorce soothes children with antidepressants, consoles them with storybooks on divorce, and watches over their lives from family court.

CHAPTER EIGHT

Dismantling
the Divorce Culture

AT SUCH HIGH and sustained levels, divorce is not simply a legal mechanism for dissolving marriages but a social and cultural force that opportunistically reproduces itself everywhere. A high-divorce society is a society marked by growing division and separation in its social arrangements, a society of single mothers and vanished fathers, of divided households and split parenting, of fractured parent-child bonds and fragmented families, of broken links between marriage and parenthood.

The shift from a family world governed by the institution of marriage to one ruled by divorce has brought a steady weakening of primary human relationships and bonds. Men's and women's relationships are becoming more fleeting and unreliable. Children are losing their ties to their fathers. Even a mother's love is not forever, as the growing number of throwaway kids suggests.

Divorce is not the only force that has contributed to weaker family ties and more fragile families, but it has been the most important in shaping a new cultural disposition about the meaning of family breakup. Divorce has been damaging not only because it has contributed to the widespread trend toward family fragmentation and the paternal abandonment of children but also because it has won influential adherents in the society who defend family breakup as necessary for individual psychological growth and freedom.

When the divorce revolution began, no one could have predicted where it would lead, how it would change the shape and content of family relationships, or whether it would deliver on its promises of improving marriage and family life, especially for women. Thirty years later we have acquired a substantial body of social learning experience and empirical evidence on the impact of divorce on men and women, on children, and on the larger society. And this body of evidence tells us that the cultural case for divorce has been based on misleading claims, false promises, and bankrupt ideas.

Less Equality, More Inequality

One of the claims made for divorce was that with greater freedom to dissolve marriage, women would gain greater equality and independence in their family lives. Yet the evidence suggests that widespread divorce has generated new forms of inequality for women and children. It has contributed to greater economic insecurity and poverty among women and children, and it has been a principal generator of unequal opportunities and outcomes for children. Indeed, it is hard to think of any recent economic force that has been as brutally efficient as divorce in transforming middle-class haves into have-nots. In a high-divorce society—even if the wage gap continues to narrow, jobs continue to be plentiful, and child-support enforcement continues to be more efficiently and aggressively pursued—women are still likely to lose ground in their efforts to achieve economic equality.

Nor can it be said that widespread divorce has moved us closer to the social goal of greater gender equality. In a society marked by high and sustained levels of divorce, women not only bear double responsibilities for breadwinning and child-rearing but bear them alone. Thus, the achievement of a fair and equitable distribution of these tasks between men and women becomes ever more elusive. Moreover, in a high-divorce society the goal of involved, hands-on, nurturant fatherhood becomes more difficult to attain. Even for the most committed and determined divorced fathers, nonresidential fatherhood is a struggle. For those less heroic and resolute, solo fatherhood becomes close to impossible. Sadly, when extraordinary heroism is required, more men fail at fatherhood.

Less Freedom, More Coercion

Perhaps the most alluring and most powerfully sponsored claim for divorce has been its promise of greater personal freedom. One popular book promises women "the joy of handling your own money, learning to cope as a single mother, and the freedom to manage your time as you see fit."[1] Another proclaims that "there is joy in emancipating oneself." Yet in ways not fully anticipated, divorced women's freedoms and opportunities are often quite limited. Single mothers in particular may find it difficult to achieve a satisfying blend of work and family life, and to "be all that they can be." Society's principal cheerleaders for expressive divorce have been its most economically advantaged and well-educated women, but only their message, and not their privilege, has been transmitted to their working-class "sisters."

Divorce frees many men from the daily tasks of home and family life, and many men free themselves from the responsibilities of providing for their children. However, divorced fathers are not truly liberated. Their opportunities to share in the daily lives of their children and to enjoy the free and easy exchanges that come with daily life are lost. As they lose their franchise as fathers, many men also lose a central reason for working hard and participating in the life of the community. Divorced men also lose access to women's emotional and social intelligence in building and sustaining relationships. Men's social as well as family ties attenuate after divorce. They are less embedded in a network of relationships with kin and community, and less connected or committed to others. Although it is too soon to tell, fathers who abandon their children may be abandoned by their adult children when they become old, needy, and dependent, leaving elderly men to the care and custody of strangers.

In a culture of divorce, children are the most "unfree." Divorce abrogates children's right to be reasonably free from adult cares and woes, to enjoy the association of both parents on a daily basis, to remain innocent of social services and therapy, and to spend family time in ways that are not dictated by the courts.

More broadly, the divorce culture limits the family's freedom to conduct its own relationships without intrusion or coercion. The

American family is founded on the principle of glorious voluntarism. The freedom to choose our love relationships without interference from outside parties or interests remains one of our most enduring "family values."[2] However, the freedom to choose is not unfettered freedom. Through marriage the individual becomes committed to a set of duties and obligations, not only to the spouse but to children, relatives, and the larger society. These obligations are voluntarily made and kept. There is no constabulary to patrol family households and to enforce the proper conduct of daily family life. There is no legal oversight of children's homework or bedtimes, no government authority dictating how much time parents should spend reading to their children or how much money they should invest in sneakers or music lessons.

However, in a culture captive to an expressive ethos of divorce, the family becomes less able or willing to govern itself. Parental commitments outside of marriage become increasingly involuntary and subject to regulation. The obligation of fathers to provide for their children, an obligation freely accepted and (generally) faithfully honored by married fathers, becomes the focus of state supervision and enforcement. Parent-child relationships, once conducted without legal oversight, are governed by court-established visitation and custody arrangements. Paternity itself—the voluntary recording of a father's name on a birth certificate, an occasion once celebrated with cigars and champagne—becomes a matter of court-ordered and state-reimbursed blood tests. Adoption, the voluntary system of reassigning children to families, loses ground to a system of reshuffling children from biological parents to foster or residential care and back again. In brief, divorce and single parenthood invite, indeed often require more active supervision and regulation of family relationships by the state.

Even though the state can require certain forms of parental support, mainly for the economic upkeep of children, it can do so at only minimal levels. The state cannot force divorced fathers to take higher-paying jobs or work extra shifts for their children's sake. It cannot require divorced parents to set aside their anger and hostility and to assist each other in rearing their children. Consequently, compared with a system in which parents share a common household and voluntarily invest in their children, a family system characterized by a legally arranged and supervised parenthood is almost by definition one in which the levels of parental investment in children are likely to be low and somewhat fitful, even if the regulatory controls are steadily improved and tightened. Thus, Americans are moving away from a high-investment child-rearing strategy at exactly the time when the requirements of a postindustrial economy require even higher-level and longer-term parental and societal investments in children.

Less Altruism, More Individualism

Another claim made for divorce is that disrupted families with diminished capacity to provide for their children will be able to recruit support from kindly strangers. There is a liberal version of this claim, and a conservative version. Liberals look to the kindly taxpayers and the public sector as a source of support while conservatives find their kindly strangers in the voluntary sector. Liberals suspect that the conservative faith in an invigorated voluntary sector is an excuse for cutting taxes while conservatives suggest that the liberal faith in a generous public sector is a rationale for big government. Nonetheless, both sides seek to tap sources of altruism outside the family itself.

What neither side acknowledges is that the extreme individualism sanctioned by expressive divorce weakens the social basis for altruism. When family relationships are governed by marketplace notions of individual self-interest, both the spirit of kindness and the supply lines of kindly strangers begin to shrink. How many Big Brothers and goodhearted Cub Scout leaders can be found to replace all the missing fathers? How many single men and women will voluntarily enlist in the ranks of "paraparents" to help stressed-out single mothers? How many more foster parents will step forward? How many grandparents are waiting in the wings? Will a deadbeat dad who has abandoned three children of his own suddenly step forward to help the children of another deadbeat?

In brief, Americans cannot sustain a vigorous voluntary sector or a generous public sector if the voluntary basis of family obligation erodes and if a radically individualistic ethic pervades thinking about family relationships. To be sure, many Americans are morally motivated to help needy children, while others are philosophically committed to public spending on children that is at least as generous as public spending on the elderly. So there will always be a community responsive to the needs of children. But in a culture of family breakup, it becomes increasingly difficult to make the arguments and win the support for public sacrifice for children. If parents are entitled to put their own psychological needs and interests first, why should others feel obliged to volunteer their resources and help? If fathers can reduce their financial contributions to their own flesh and blood, why should others be compelled to make up the difference? If families are not making hard sacrifices for their children's sake, why should corporations?

If the divorce culture continues, both parental and social altruism will decline. The kindness of strangers will be replaced by the coldness of the trustee. Indeed, as some conservatives acknowledge, the end of the welfare state may bring about the rise of the custodial state. A depleted voluntary sector may have to depend on an expanding "involuntary sector," made up of such institutions as prisons, orphanages, and residential homes. In the twenty-first century "commitment" may revert to its most literal and pejorative meaning: involuntary confinement to an institution.

Consequently, for all the efforts to liberate individuals from the psychological bondage of family ties, to achieve greater affective and expressive satisfactions in family life, to create warmer and closer partnerships, Americans find themselves in the grips of a cooling trend in relationships, a harsher climate of regulation and control, and a chillier and more inhospitable environment for children.

A Society of the Uncommitted

How many divorces over how many years can a nation sustain without serious damage to its social fabric? There is no precise way to answer that question, but it does not require sophisticated statistical projections to make the argument that Americans have already experienced too much divorce over the past twenty-five years and that the current trends cannot be sustained for another twenty-five years without profound loss and damage to children, families, and the society. If we do not act with deliberate speed to reduce divorces involving children, we will surely become a nation with a diminished capacity to sponsor the next generation into successful lives as citizens, workers, and family members. More alarmingly, we will lose the capacity to foster strong and lasting bonds between fathers and children, between older and younger generations, and between children and the larger society. A sense of permanence and trust will continue to erode, and with it, the commitment to invest in others. Self-investment will be the safer and saner bet.

For the past three decades American children have attended the school of divorce and learned its lessons. The main lesson is that families break up, relationships end, and love is not forever. One psychiatrist, studying the attitudes of young adults toward "committed relationships," noted that they displayed a "comparison shopper's mentality" which introduces the kind of calculation and guardedness that works against commitment and even against the ability to fall in love. As one young adult from a divorced family explained: "My own opinion is that if a man and a woman get along for five or ten years, that is as much as can be expected. People change and they stop sharing. It is much more sensible to plan on a series of relationships—perhaps three or four."[3] This view is widespread among younger Americans; it suggests that divorce not only erodes the social bases of commitment but also extinguishes the very idea of lasting commitment.

Dismantling the Divorce Culture

Divorce is necessary in a society that believes in the ideal of affectionate marriage, and particularly in a society that seeks to protect women from brutality and violence in marriage. But it is not necessary to do away with divorce altogether in order to dismantle the divorce culture. Rather, the goal should be to change the way we think about the meaning and purpose of divorce, especially divorces involving children. Just as the environmental movement required a new consciousness about how an individual's private decision to buy a car affected the natural world, so too a movement to dismantle the divorce culture must create a stronger awareness of how an individual's personal decision to divorce affects the family and social world.

For parents, divorce is not a solo act but one that has enormous consequences for children. A mounting body of evidence from diverse and multiple sources shows that divorce has been a primary generator of new forms of inequality, disadvantage, and loss for American children. It has spawned a generation of angry and bereaved children who have a harder time learning, staying in school, and achieving at high levels. High and sustained levels of divorce have also raided children's piggy banks, depriving them of the full resources that they might have had growing up in an intact family. In middle- and upper-middle-class families the process of getting a divorce has also diverted family resources away from children toward the professional service sector, where an entire industry has sprung up to harvest the fruits of family discord.

Finally, divorce is never merely an individual lifestyle choice without larger consequences for the society. Divorce has contributed to welfare dependency and given rise to an entire public bureaucracy devoted to managing and regulating the parental tasks and obligations of raising children. It has imposed a new set of burdens and responsibilities on the schools, contributed to the tide of fatherless juveniles filling the courts and jails, and increased the risks of unwed teen parenthood.

Once we acknowledge that divorce is a family and social event involving other stakeholders and imposing costs on others, then we can begin to think and talk about high levels of divorces involving children as a social problem that must be addressed rather than as an expression of individual freedom that cannot be infringed. This will engender activism rather than passivity in the face of what some now say are irresistible and unstoppable trends. It was just such activism in the face of what seemed to be unstoppable trends toward environmental despoliation that inspired the effort for cleaner water and air.

A second and complementary step toward dismantling the culture of divorce is to repeal the language and ethic of expressive divorce and treat divorce as a morally as well as socially consequential event. The ethic of expressive divorce recognizes the rights and needs of the liberated self, but has nothing to say about the responsibilities of the obligated self. It has no language for talking about the special obligations of parents to children or about the social trust invested in marriages with children. Even after thirty years of sustained high levels of divorce, we are still reluctant to speak about the moral obligations involved in divorces with children for fear of "blaming" and thus psychologically burdening adults. Yet the truth is that divorce involves a radical redistribution of hardship, from adults to children, and therefore cannot be viewed as a morally neutral act.

Changing the way we think and talk about divorce will have several likely consequences. First, if children are treated as key stakeholders in their parents' marriage and as those most at risk in the dissolution of the marriage, then parents, clergy, therapists, judges, and policymakers will be more likely to attend to the claims and interests of children. Second, if divorce is regarded as a central source of disadvantage and father-loss for children, there may be a stronger effort at educating the public about the risks of divorce to children. Third, if marriages with children are considered a kind of special trust, there will be greater societal effort aimed at preventing the dissolution of such marriages. Not all marriages can or should be saved "for the sake of the children," but clearly, of the six out of ten divorces that involve children, some are salvageable. Yet the effort to strengthen and preserve marriage has been all but abandoned in recent years, either as a commitment by parents unhappy in their marriages or as a goal for family professionals. For example, among the hundreds of workshops offered at the annual conventions of the leading professional organization of family therapists, the American Association for Marriage and Family Therapy, marriage rarely appears as a topic; it showed up twice in 1992 and not at all in 1993. In 1994 the association gave a major press award to a magazine article arguing that fathers are not necessary in the home. In 1995 the word "marital" appeared only twice on the program, and "marriage" not at all. Noting the curious disappearance of "marriage" from the marriage counselors' vocabulary, *U.S. News & World Report* columnist John Leo writes: "The therapeutic custodians of marriage don't believe in it any more and seem determined not to bolster, promote or even talk about it much."[4]

Members of the divorce establishment could demonstrate their commitment to children by taking leadership in divorce prevention. Therapists, lawyers, and other professionals who profit from divorces involving children might, through their professional associations, support projects specifically designed to reduce divorce among families with children. Others could make important contributions as well.

Scholars might put marriage back on their research agenda and thereby add to our knowledge of what makes marriages succeed or fail.[5] Clergy might renew their commitment and redouble their efforts to provide pastoral care to married couples with children, especially at times when marriages are likely to be stressed. Within religious communities, older married couples might serve as mentors to younger couples.

A serious and sustained effort at divorce prevention would send an important message about marriage as a valuable but vanishing social resource which must be prized and protected. Such a message might encourage couples, husbands especially, to be more vigilant about the maintenance and care of their marriages. Indeed, if Americans treated their marriages as tenderly as their family cars, there might be more commitment to repairing rather than junking marriages. There might also be greater recognition of the need for special maintenance and care of marriages that are fragile, including second marriages and marriages with handicapped children. Finally, there might be greater honor attached to marriage as a human pursuit requiring struggle, intention, and work.

Rethinking Marriage

It is futile, however, to call for better and stronger marriages without addressing the fundamental problem of a growing separatism between men and women. In recent decades, men and women have moved toward greater equality in education and occupation, greater flexibility in work roles, and greater androgyny in general. In the daily commerce between the sexes, there is less deference and conscious division than in the past. Yet despite these more comradely relationships in work and learning, the intimate partnerships between women and men have become increasingly fragile, conflict-ridden, and subject to breakdown. Perhaps never before in the nation's history has there been such pessimism, even cynicism, about the ability of men and women to live together in lasting marriages and to share a common life.

This pervasive decline in the ideal and expectation for long-lasting marriage was perhaps predictable. In every other domain of life, Americans are moving away from lasting relationships and toward limited and contingent commitments. The world of work offers little hope of permanent ties; the entire ethos of the American workplace has shifted toward a short-term, performance-based, limited-benefits, ten-career-changes-in-a-lifetime model. Increasingly too, the workplace rewards individuals who are mobile, unattached, unrestricted by family commitments. The public commitment to both our oldest and our youngest citizens is also becoming more limited and contingent, as is the public commitment to public servants themselves. We live in an age of term limits. And of course, the marketplace thrives in an environment where there are few fetters to the free flow of capital. For years the Prudential Insurance Company asked Americans to seek an affiliation with a durable and dependable company, to buy a "piece of the Rock." Now, in a new advertising campaign, Prudential tells its customers: "Be Your Own Rock."

In a society swiftly applying the principle of "term limits" to every other dimension of life, therefore, it is not surprising that this notion should pervade family relationships as well. More to the point, it is only to be expected that the values exalted and rewarded in the marketplace should become those in family life as well. Yet precisely because other social bonds are becoming more undependable and impermanent, the need for strong and lasting family bonds increases, even as the environment that would support strong family bonds weakens. This means that there must be a sustained effort to strengthen marriage bonds and to create a social and cultural environment supportive of the commitment to marriage.

Because marriage and parenthood are part of our affectional and private lives, this effort is largely a matter for the civil society rather than for government. To be sure, public policy and the bully pulpit can be used to support and encourage an effort toward strengthening marriages with children.[6] But the breakdown of marriage was not caused by changes in the tax code or divorce laws, and it is unlikely to be resolved by the legislative actions of Congress or the states. If men and women are to find a way to share the tasks of parenthood in marriage, that way can come about only through a change of heart and mind, a new consciousness about the meaning of commitment itself, and a turning away from the contemporary model of relationships offered by Madison Avenue, Wall Street, or Hollywood.

A first step toward that goal will involve recapturing a sense of the purposes of marriage that extend beyond the self. This will require a philosophy and language that offer a richer and more challenging conception of marriage than the one that now dominates our discourse. Our contemporary secular thinking about marriage is a blend of psychotherapy and politics, and its language is one of rights and needs. As the personal ads suggest, the task of finding a partner involves finding someone who will both meet your emotional needs and refrain from infringing on your individual rights. This approach accepts the self as sovereign; a truly "healthy" marriage is one in which neither spouse gives up prerogatives or freedoms. The popular notion of marriage as a fifty-fifty deal is not so much an affirmation of a partnership between equals as a treaty negotiated between two sovereigns who must share space in one castle. And like such arrangements in the political sphere, this kind of domestic arrangement is vulnerable to boundary disputes and border skirmishes, a kind of sniping over whose rights have been violated and who holds advantage. A marital partnership founded on such terms is likely to be both tense and unstable. More centrally, the notion of protecting the essential properties of the self from incursions by another is antithetical to marital commitment in which one must desire and accept as a matter of faith the giving over of oneself to another.

Nonetheless, this conception of marriage owes much to what is best in our traditions. We share an abiding optimism in the perfectibility of both individuals and institutions. To a remarkable degree, over the course of the nation's short history, we have been able to achieve greater perfection in many of our most important personal relationships and social institutions. Our political ideals and aspirations for equality, independence, and individual happiness have helped shape our expectations and ideals of marriage and helped us criticize and correct its abuses. In the vow to marry "for better, for worse," we have been keenly attuned to the "for better."

Yet precisely because of our aspirations for improvement, we may have neglected the challenges and requirements of the second half of the vow. That second half is what we implicitly accept when we become parents, pledging ourselves to a biological or adopted child for all of our lives, without certain knowledge of that child's health, capacities, or destiny. It is also a pledge we freely make to a chosen beloved, without certain knowledge of what lies ahead. A voluntary pledge taken in abject ignorance of the future, imposing lifelong obligations and secured only by mutual affections, is an extravagant thing, impossible and unsustainable without the cultivation of certain beliefs, habits, and shared understandings about the nature and purpose of such voluntary bonds.

The basis for such understandings cannot be found in the language of relationships that dominates contemporary American discourse. The notion of marriage as a union between two sovereign selves affirms virtues like independence, initiative, and self-reliance. Yet while attending to the virtues associated with the integrity of the individual, our contemporary discourse on marriage entirely neglects the virtues that are essential to the integrity of bonds—virtues like fidelity, kindness, forgiveness, modesty, gratitude, loyalty, patience, generosity, and selflessness. Indeed, in many popular psychotherapies, these virtues are not virtues at all but rather psychological blocks or hang-ups that must be overcome through therapy.

It has been the argument of this book that a model of family relationships based on marketplace notions of unfettered choice, limited warranties, and contingent obligations undermines the strength and durability of family bonds. The model of family relationships cannot be identical to the model offered by the marketplace. Indeed, if the family does not exist to some degree in opposition to the marketplace as the source of a competing set of values, such as solidarity, loyalty, and binding obligation, then it will be unable to shape and foster the individual competencies required in the political and economic domains of life. It is the experience of dependable and durable family bonds that shapes a child's sense of trust and fosters the development of such traits as initiative, independence, and even risk-taking. Without these traits, it is extremely difficult to cultivate other personal characteristics such as resourcefulness, responsibility, and resilience which are essential in a pluralistic society and a demanding global economy.

If we are to strengthen marriage as the central institution for child-rearing, therefore, it may be necessary to recover fluency in the language and ideas of another American tradition, one deriving from our civic and religious life and our identity as a nation of immigrants. It is in this tradition that our aspirations toward individual perfectibility and happiness are linked to the pursuit of the well-being of others. It is this tradition that recognizes the entirety of a "for better, for worse" commitment in our lives as family members, neighbors, and citizens, summoning us together in bad as well as good times. Without such abiding commitments, we would not be able to endure the disasters, losses, and personal tragedies that befall us and that are part of our human condition. Our civic and religious traditions offer a vision of the obligated self, voluntarily bound to a set of roles, duties, and responsibilities, and of a nation where sacrifice for the next generation guides adult ambitions and purposes and where wholeness of self is found in service and commitment to others.

Notes

INTRODUCTION: THE MAKING OF A DIVORCE CULTURE

1.   An analysis of income data provided by The Northeastern University Center for Labor Market Studies shows the following distribution by education and marital status:

MEDIAN INCOMES FOR U.S. FAMILIES WITH CHILDREN, 1994

Education of household head	Married Couple Families	Single Parent Families
College Graduate	$71,263	$36,006
High School Graduate	$40,098	$14,698

Based on 1994 Current Population Statistics. Families with one or more children under 18. Age of household head: 22–62.

CHAPTER ONE: THE PROBLEM OF DIVORCE

1.   Roderick Phillips, *Untying the Knot: A Short History of Divorce* (Cambridge, England: Cambridge University Press and Canto, 1991), 38–39.

2.   Nancy F. Cott, "Divorce and the Changing Status of Women," in *The American Family in Social-Historical Perspective*, 2d ed., ed. Michael Gordon, (New York: St. Martin's Press, 1978), 116.

3.   Merril D. Smith, *Breaking the Bonds: Marital Discord in Pennsylvania, 1730–1830* (New York: New York University Press, 1991), 34.

4. Ibid., 15.

5. Jay Fliegelman, *Prodigals and Pilgrims: The American Revolution Against Patriarchal Authority, 1750–1800* (Cambridge, England: Cambridge University Press, 1982), 125–26.

6. "Reflections on Unhappy Marriages," in Thomas Paine, *Complete Writings of Thomas Paine*, ed. Philip S. Foner, 2 vols. (New York: Citadel Press, 1945), vol. 2, 1119.

7. Fliegelman, 126.

8. Paine, 1120.

9. Fliegelman, 125.

10. Cott, 119.

11. Phillips, 45. More liberal divorce laws probably also helped regularize the "poor man's divorce"—desertion. America was a vast and unsettled nation, where it was easy to get lost and stay lost. Early American divorce records tell of wayward husbands who set out to look for jobs or join the army or ship out to sea and never returned. Desertion was much more difficult for women with children, because husbandless families attracted public attention and concern. It was more economically and legally hazardous as well: a wife was guilty of desertion and therefore nonsupport if she abandoned her husband's household, whereas a husband could leave "bed and board" as long as he continued to provide for his wife and children. Nonetheless, wives did sometimes desert.

12. Cited in Michael Grossberg, *Governing the Hearth: Law and the Family in Nineteenth-Century America* (Chapel Hill: University of North Carolina Press, 1985), 3.

13. Cited in Fliegelman, 127.

14. Paine, 1120.

15. Edwin Post, *Truly Emily Post: A Biography* (New York: Funk & Wagnalls, 1961), 156.

16. Nelson Manfred Blake, *The Road to Reno: A History of Divorce in the United States* (New York: Macmillan Company, 1962), 122.

17. "Divorce in South Dakota," *Nation* 56 (January 26, 1893), 61.

18. Ibid.

19. Phillips, 238.

20. Cited in Theodore Caplow and others, *Middletown Families: Fifty Years of Change and Continuity* (Minneapolis: University of Minnesota Press, 1982), 48.

21. Cited in Morris Ploscowe, *The Truth About Divorce* (New York: Hawthorn Books, 1955), 219.

22. Cited in Robert S. Lynd and Helen Merrell Lynd, *Middletown: A Study in American Culture* (New York: Harvest Book, 1956), 128.

23. Phillips, 191.

24. Elaine Tyler May, *Great Expectations: Marriage and Divorce in Post-Victorian America* (Chicago: University of Chicago Press, 1980), 145.

25. Ibid., 140.

26. Lynd and Lynd, 126.

27. Samuel Preston adds complexity to this argument by noting that in addition to the wife's reported level of satisfaction with a husband's income, a husband's income relative to his wife's father has been important in setting women's income and consumption expectations in marriage. There seems to be a higher risk of marital disruption when the husband ranks lower than the wife's father in income and related socioeconomic factors. See his discussion in "The Incidence of Divorce with Cohorts of American Marriages Contracted Since the Civil War," *Demography* 16 (February 1979), 1–25, especially 16–20, passim.

28. May, 149.

29. Cited ibid., 147.

30. Lee Rainwater, Richard P. Coleman, and Gerald Handel, *Workingman's Wife: Her Personality, World and Life Style* (New York: A Macfadden Bartell Book, 1959), 91.

31. Cited in Lynd and Lynd, 127.

32. Blake, 124–25.

33. "Divorce Too Difficult," *Nation* 82 (June 21, 1906), 505.

34. Robert Grant, "A Call to a New Crusade," *Good Housekeeping* 73 (September 1921), 42.

35. Cynthia Griffin Wolff, *A Feast of Words: The Triumph of Edith Wharton* (Oxford: Oxford University Press, 1978), 226.

36. Ibid., 227.

37. Carl N. Degler, *At Odds: Women and the Family in America from the Revolution to the Present* (New York: Oxford University Press, 1980), 333.

38. Phillips, 232.

39. Wolff, 228.

40. Ibid., 249.

41. Ibid., 247.

42. Ibid., 249.

43. Ibid., 249–50.

44. Conduct literature became a popular genre in the nineteenth century. For a rich cultural history of nineteenth-century manners, see John F. Kasson, *Rudeness and Civility: Manners in Nineteenth-Century Urban America* (New York: Hill and Wang, 1990), and on the sheer volume of etiquette literature, 44–47.

45. Post, 203–04.

46. Ibid., 235–36.

47. *Dictionary of American Biography*, ed. John A. Garraty, supplement 6 (New York: Charles Scribner's Sons, 1980), 514.

48. *Dictionary of American Biography*, Kenneth T. Jackson, ed., supplement 9 (New York: Charles Scribner's Sons, 1994), 824–25.

49. Post, 203.

50. Emily Post, *Etiquette* (New York: Funk & Wagnalls, 1922), 508.

51. Cited in Kasson, 61.

52. Emily Post, *Etiquette* (New York: Funk & Wagnalls, 1942), 896. Like the law, etiquette involved a corpus of practice and opinion. Consequently, Emily Post devoted much of her time to research, searching through the literature for precedents. Only as a last resort would she invent a rule. Edwin Post, 216.

53. Emily Post, 1922 ed., 2–3.

54. Emily Post, 1945 ed., 596.

55. Edwin Post, 146.

56. Emily Post, *Etiquette* (New York: Funk & Wagnalls, 1960), 628.

57. Ibid., 628.

58. Emily Post, *Children Are People and Ideal Parents Are Comrades* (New York: Funk & Wagnalls, 1940), 195.

59. Emily Post, *Etiquette* (New York: Funk & Wagnalls, 1965), 678.

60. Ibid., 677.

61. Elizabeth L. Post, *The New Emily Post's Etiquette* (New York: Funk & Wagnalls, 1975), 933.

62. Emily Post, 1965 ed., 678.

63. Emily Post, *Etiquette*, 1942 ed., 145.

64. Emily Post, *Etiquette* (New York: Funk & Wagnalls, 1957), 225.

65. Emily Post, *Children Are People*, 192–3.

66. Ernest R. Groves, *Marriage* (New York: Henry Holt and Company, 1933), 494.

67. Ibid., 509.

68. Ernest R. Groves, *Conserving Marriage and the Family: A Realistic Discussion of the Divorce Problem* (New York: Macmillan Company, 1945), 101.

69. Ibid., 104–05.

70. Ibid., 9.

71. Ibid., 508.

72. Those who married just before or during the Depression had a higher divorce rate than would be expected from the long-term trend lines, suggesting that severe economic hardships may have irreparably damaged some marriages, leading couples to divorce once economic conditions improved. Andrew Cherlin, *Marriage, Divorce, Remarriage*, rev. ed. (Cambridge, Mass.: Harvard University Press, 1992), 23.

73. Larry Bumpass and James Sweet, *American Families and Households* (New York: Russell Sage Foundation, 1987), 178.

74. John Mariano, *The Veteran and His Marriage* (New York: Council on Marriage Relations, 1945), 232.

75. Ibid., 233.

76. Edward O. Laumann et al., *The Social Organization of Sexuality: Sexual*

Practices in the United States (Chicago: University of Chicago Press, 1994), 498.

77. Cherlin, 21–22; see also William J. Goode, *World Changes in Divorce Patterns* (New Haven: Yale University Press, 1993), 139.

78. Cherlin, 24.

CHAPTER TWO: THE RISE OF EXPRESSIVE DIVORCE

1. As the Belgian scholar Ron Lesthaeghe explains, periods of sustained economic growth that foster greater attention to individual aspirations are likely to generate a variety of emancipation movements. His theory sheds light on the relationship between the postwar economy and the emergence of the civil rights and women's rights movements in the 1960s as well as the cultural emancipation movements—the sexual revolution and the divorce revolution. See his discussion in "A Century of Demographic and Cultural Change in Western Europe: An Exploration of Underlying Dimensions," *Population and Development Review* 9 (September 1983), 411–35.

2. "How Changes in the Economy Are Reshaping American Values," in *Values and Public Policy*, ed. Henry J. Aaron, Thomas E. Mann, and Timothy Taylor (Washington: Brookings Institution, 1994), 18–19.

3. Joseph Veroff, Elizabeth Douvan, and Richard Kulka, *The Inner American: A Self-Portrait from 1957 to 1976* (New York: Basic Books, 1981), 57–58. At the same time, the authors note, occupational concerns—the satisfactions and future security of the job—became more important sources of unhappiness, especially for men.

4. Ibid., 485.

5. William J. Doherty, *Soul Searching: Why Psychotherapy Must Promote Moral Responsibility* (New York: Basic Books, 1995), 6.

6. Harry Specht and Mark Courtney, *Unfaithful Angels: How Social Work Has Abandoned Its Mission* (New York: Free Press, 1994), 8.

7. Ibid., 4.

8. Ibid., 15.

9. J. Richard Udry, *The Social Context of Marriage* (Philadelphia: J. B. Lippincott, 1966), 547.

10. Specht and Courtney, 13.

11. I am indebted to Don S. Browning for his elucidation of the impact of psychology on religious thought and practice in post–World War II American society. Professor Browning points out that some conservative religious denominations have remained strongly antidivorce, even in recent years. These denominations include the Church of Christ, the Mennonites, and the Mormons. For a rich and illuminating consideration of modern psychologies as "practical moral philosophies," see Don S. Browning, *Religious Thought and the Modern Psycholo-*

gies: A Critical Conversation in the Theology of Culture (Philadelphia: Fortress Press, 1987).

12. Joseph Veroff, Richard A. Kulka, and Elizabeth Douvan, *Mental Health in America: Patterns of Help-seeking from 1957 to 1976* (New York: Basic Books, 1981), 8.

13. Robert N. Bellah et al., eds., *Individualism and Commitment in American Life: Readings on the Themes of Habits of the Heart* (New York: Harper & Row and Perennial Library, 1987), 184; also cited in Doherty, 10.

14. Many people forget that Friedan's book was based on the lives of her Smith College classmates, talented college graduates who had spent years raising children and were reaching the end of their child-rearing careers. The empty-nest syndrome may have contributed to the restlessness of these upper-middle-class women as much as the empty-marriage syndrome.

15. Jessie Bernard, *The Future of Marriage* (New York: World Publishing, 1972), 51.

16. Ibid., 294.

17. Norval D. Glenn, "The Contribution of Marriage to the Psychological Well-being of Males and Females," *Journal of Marriage and the Family* 37 (August 1975), 594.

18. Veroff, Douvan, and Kulka, 181.

19. Ibid., 180–81.

20. Phillips, 249.

21. Earl A. Grollman and Marjorie L. Sams, *Living Through Your Divorce* (New York: Beacon Press, 1978), 37.

22. Abigail Trafford, *Crazy Time: Surviving Divorce and Building a New Life*, rev. ed. (New York: Harper-Perennial, 1992), 64.

23. J. Randall Nichols, *Ending Marriage, Keeping Faith: A New Guide Through the Spiritual Journey of Divorce* (New York: Crossroad Publishing Company, 1991), 9–22, passim.

24. Christopher L. Hayes, Deborah Anderson, and Melinda Blau, *Our Turn: Women Who Triumph in the Face of Divorce* (New York: Pocket Books, 1993), 70.

25. Trafford, 160.

26. Catherine Kohler Riessman, *Divorce Talk: Men and Women Make Sense of Personal Relationships* (New Brunswick, N.J.: Rutgers University Press, 1990), 165.

27. Ibid., 170.

28. Timothy J. Horgan, *Winning Your Divorce: A Man's Survival Guide* (New York: Plume Book, 1995), 136.

29. Ibid., 69.

30. Jacques Bacal and Louise Sloane, *ABC of Divorce* (New York: E. P. Dutton, 1947), 7.

31. Hayes, Anderson, and Blau, 41.

32. Stephanie Marston, *The Divorced Parent: Success Strategies for Raising Your Children After Separation* (New York: Pocket Books, 1994), 13; Trafford, 3; Catherine Napolitane with Victoria Pellegrino, *Living and Loving After Divorce* (New York: Signet, 1977), 3.

33. Trafford, 58.

34. See, for example, Elie Wymard, *Divorced Women, New Lives* (New York: Ballantine Books, 1990), 29.

35. See, for example, Lynette Triere with Richard Peacock, *Learning to Leave: A Woman's Guide*, rev. ed. (New York: Warner Books, 1993), 50; and Hayes, Anderson, and Blau, 118.

36. Triere, 19.

37. Shoshana Alexander, *In Praise of Single Parents: Mothers and Fathers Embracing the Challenge* (Boston: Houghton Mifflin, 1994), 47.

38. Ann Swidler, "Love and Adulthood in American Culture," in *Themes of Work and Love in Adulthood*, eds. Neil J. Smelser and Erik H. Erikson (Cambridge, Mass.: Harvard University Press, 1980), 124.

39. Ibid., 129.

40. Hayes, Anderson, and Blau, 35.

41. Linda Gordon, *Pitied but Not Entitled: Single Mothers and the History of Welfare, 1890–1935* (New York: Free Press, 1994), 31.

42. Norman M. Lobsenz, "How Divorced Young Mothers Learn to Stand Alone," *Redbook* 138 (November 1971), 140.

43. Frances Slade, *Divorce If You Must* (New York: Coward-McCann, 1938), 116.

44. William J. Goode, *After Divorce* (Glencoe, Ill.: Free Press, 1956), 309.

45. Lobsenz, 140.

46. Alan L. Otten, "Divorce Doesn't Damp Mothers' Lives," *Wall Street Journal*, August 12, 1994, B1.

47. Hayes, Anderson, and Blau, 109.

CHAPTER THREE: THE DIVORCE ETHIC

1 Goode, *World Changes*, 144.

2. Mary Ann Glendon, *Abortion and Divorce in Western Law: American Failures, European Challenges* (Cambridge, Mass.: Harvard University Press, 1987), 81.

3. Donald S. Moir, "No Fault Divorce and the Best Interests of Children," *Denver University Law Review* 69 (1992), 679.

4. Elizabeth Post, 15th ed., 155.

5. Kenneth Dressel and others, "Professional Intervention in Divorce: The Views of Lawyers, Psychotherapists, and Clergy," in *Divorce and Separation: Con-*

text, Causes and Consequences, eds. George Levinger and Oliver C. Moles (New York: Basic Books, 1979), 258.

6. Albert Martin, *One Man, Hurt* (New York: Ballantine Books, 1975), 244.

7. Doherty, 31.

8. Melvin G. Goldzband, M.D., *Quality Time: Easing Children Through Divorce* (New York: McGraw-Hill Book Company, 1985), 58.

9. Constance Ahrons, *The Good Divorce: Keeping Your Family Together When Your Marriage Comes Apart* (New York: HarperCollins, 1994), 13; in other contexts, she associates stigma with ostracism, rootlessness, and the absence of social models.

10. Ibid., 40, but also 1–46, passim.

11. Ibid., 13.

12. Ibid., 12.

13. An Orange County, California, jeweler, credited with coining the term "divorce jewelry," adds a do-it-yourself dimension to this business by providing blowtorches and goggles to customers. At least eight other jewelers in this conservative county offer divorce jewelry services. Anne H. Soukhanov, *Word Watch: The Story Behind the Words of Our Lives* (New York: Henry Holt and Company, 1995), 24.

14. Ahrons, 70.

15. Ibid., 46.

16. Ibid., 1–2.

17. Ibid., 21.

18. Cited in Riessman, 203.

19. Robert Coles, "On Divorce," *New Oxford Review* LXI (July–August 1994), 24.

CHAPTER FOUR: DIVORCE "FOR THE SAKE OF THE CHILDREN"

1. Bacal and Sloane, 16.

2. Arland Thornton, "Changing Attitudes Toward Family Issues in the United States," *Journal of Marriage and the Family* 51 (November 1989), 880–81.

3. Joannie M. Schrof, "Outlook," *U.S. News & World Report* (October 23, 1995), 29.

4. Goode, *World Changes*, 149.

5. Sara McLanahan and Gary Sandefur, *Growing Up with a Single Parent: What Hurts, What Helps* (Cambridge, Mass.: Harvard University Press, 1994), 2.

6. As a representative example of this line of argument, see Stephanie Coontz, *The Way We Never Were: American Families and the Nostalgia Trap* (New York: Basic Books, 1992), 183–84.

7.   Susan Gettleman and Janet Markowitz, *The Courage to Divorce* (New York: Simon & Schuster, 1974), 86–87.

8.   Ibid., 104.

9.   Ibid., 94.

10.   Ibid., 95.

11.   Ibid., 220.

12.   Mel Krantzler, *Creative Divorce: A New Opportunity for Personal Growth* (New York: Signet, 1974), 211.

13.   Cited in Joseph Epstein, *Divorced in America: Marriage in an Age of Possibility* (New York: E. P. Dutton, 1974), 256.

14.   Sharon Kraus, "The Crisis of Divorce: Growth Promoting or Pathogenic?," *Journal of Divorce* 3 (Winter 1979), 111.

15.   A 1973 review of the research on fatherless families, for example, concluded that most of the damage done to children by father absence was probably explained by differences in social class rather than by the mere presence or absence of a father. McLanahan and Sandefur, 13–14.

16.   Judith S. Wallerstein and Sandra Blakeslee, *Second Chances: Men, Women, and Children a Decade After Divorce* (New York: Ticknor & Fields, 1989), xiv.

17.   McLanahan and Sandefur, 24.

18.   Nicholas Zill and Christine Winquist Nord, *Running in Place: How American Families Are Faring in a Changing Economy and an Individualistic Society* (Washington, D.C.: Child Trends, 1994), 15–17.

19.   McLanahan and Sandefur, 86–88.

20.   Sally C. Clarke, "Advance Report of Final Marriage Statistics, 1989 and 1990," Monthly Vital Statistics Report, vol. 43, no. 12, suppl. (Hyattsville, Md.: National Center for Health Statistics, 1995), 3.

21.   National Center for Health Statistics, "Developmental, Learning and Emotional Problems: Health of Our Nation's Children, United States, 1988," *Advance Data*, no. 190 (November 16, 1990), 8–9.

22.   McLanahan and Sandefur, 88–91.

23.   Eleanor E. Maccoby and Robert H. Mnookin, *Dividing the Child: Social and Legal Dilemmas of Custody* (Cambridge, Mass.: Harvard University Press, 1992), 294.

24.   McLanahan and Sandefur, 30–31.

25.   See, for example, Andrew J. Cherlin's critical comments in *Marriage, Divorce, Remarriage*, 75–76.

26.   American Academy of Pediatrics, "The Pediatrician's Role in Helping Children and Families Deal with Divorce," policy statement, November 1983; and "The Pediatrician's Role in Helping Children and Families Deal with Separation and Divorce," policy statement, July 1994.

27.   Alexander, 132.

28. Triere, 275.

29. Alexander, 289–90.

30. In the earlier research on father absence, see especially Anna Freud's observations on the precocious and persistent worries about absent fathers among English children institutionalized in nurseries outside London during wartime bombing raids in *Infants Without Families and Reports on the Hampstead Nurseries, 1939–45* (London: Hogarth Press and the Institute of Psychoanalysis, 1974), 635–49.

31. Alexander, 290.

32. Ibid.

33. National Commission on Children, *Speaking of Kids: A National Survey of Children and Parents* (Washington, D.C.: National Commission on Children), 23–25.

34. McLanahan and Sandefur, 60.

35. "The Diversity and Strength of American Families," Hearing, Select Committee on Children, Youth and Families, House of Representatives, 99th Congress (Washington, D.C.: U.S. Government Printing Office, 1986), 78.

36. Coontz develops her point with this example: "Researchers at the University of North Carolina report that women are more likely to have a drinking problem *prior* to divorce or separation than after it, and that divorce reduces the risk of alcohol dependence among women who were problem drinkers before. Is it worse to end up an adult child of divorced parents or an adult child of an alcoholic?" This is a striking example of false choices. *Way We Never Were*, 224.

CHAPTER FIVE: THE CHILDREN'S STORY OF DIVORCE

1. Joanne E. Bernstein, *Books to Help Children Cope with Separation and Loss* (New York: R. R. Bowker, 1977), and Joanne E. Bernstein and Masha Kabakow Rudman, *Books to Help Children Cope with Separation and Loss*, 3 vols. (New York: R. R. Bowker, 1989). In 1994 *The Horn Book Guide*, an annotated critical bibliography published by one of the nation's leading journals of children's literature, gave its highest recommendations to a crop of 1994 books on family breakdown and pathology, including a "horror novel" about two girl pen pals, one "struggling with an abusive older brother" and the other a liar and institutionalized felon; a "survival" story of a boy abused by his father and stepmother; an animal-loving girl who rescues a reclusive neighbor despondent over his failed marriage; a boy whose "only contact with his dad has been intermittent forays to ride roller coasters"; and a young girl's coming to terms with her unwed sister's decision to give up her baby for adoption. See *The Horn Book Guide to Children's and Young Adult Books: Review of Books Published July–December 1994*, vol. VI, no. 1 (Boston: Horn Book, 1995).

2. Beverly Cleary, "Newbery Medal Acceptance," *Horn Book Magazine* LX (August 1984), 434.

3. Richard Peck, *Love and Death at the Mall: Teaching and Writing for the Literate Young* (New York: Delacorte Press, 1989), 128–29.

4. Judy Blume, *Letters to Judy: What Kids Wish They Could Tell You* (New York: Pocket Books, 1986), 89–90.

5. Erica Jong, *Fear of Fifty: A Midlife Memoir* (New York: Harper Paperbacks, 1994), 227.

6. Judith Vigna, *Grandma Without Me* (Niles, Ill.: Albert Whitman & Company, 1984), np.

7. Judith Vigna, *Mommy and Me by Ourselves Again* (Niles, Ill.: Albert Whitman & Company, 1987), np.

8. Edith Nesbit, *The Railway Children* (New York: Bantam Books, 1993), 10.

9. Barbara Shook Hazen, *Two Homes to Live In: A Child's-Eye View of Divorce* (New York: Human Sciences Press, 1983), np.

10. Kathy Stinson, *Mom and Dad Don't Live Together Any More* (Toronto: Annick Press Ltd., 1984), np.

11. Ken Rush, *Friday's Journey* (New York: Orchard Books, 1994).

12. Judy Blume, *It's Not the End of the World* (New York: Dell, 1972), 91.

13. Norma Simon, *I Wish I Had My Father* (Niles, Ill.: Albert Whitman & Company, 1983), np.

14. Maria Gripe, *The Night Daddy* (New York: Delacorte Press, 1971), 23.

15. Eric Rofes, ed., *The Kids' Book of Divorce: By, For and About Kids* (New York: Vintage Books, 1982), 97.

16. Anne Scott MacLeod, "An End to Innocence: The Transformation of Childhood in Twentieth-Century Children's Literature," in *Opening Texts: Psychoanalysis and the Culture of the Child*, ed. Joseph H. Smith and William Kerrigan (Baltimore: Johns Hopkins University Press, 1985), 108–10.

17. Ibid.

18. The girl in one such book dreams of growing up and living in the same house with "no suitcases." C. B. Christiansen, *My Mother's House, My Father's House* (New York: Puffin Books, 1989).

19. Karin Calvert, *Children in the House: The Material Culture of Early Childhood, 1600–1900* (Boston: Northeastern University Press), 135–36; also Kasson, 170.

20. Calvert, 141.

21. Beth Goff, *Where Is Daddy? The Story of a Divorce* (Boston: Beacon Press, 1969), np. This book was the winner of a Special Citation from the Child Study Association of America.

22. Linda Walvoord Girard, *At Daddy's on Saturdays* (Niles, Ill.: Albert Whitman & Company, 1987), np.

23. Gripe, 149.

24. Blume, 121.

25. Richard A. Gardner, *The Boys and Girls Book About Divorce* (New York: Bantam Books, 1971), 73.

26. Anne Scott MacLeod, *American Childhood: Essays on Children's Literature of the Nineteenth and Twentieth Centuries* (Athens: University of Georgia Press, 1994), 204.

27. Beverly Cleary, *Dear Mr. Henshaw* (New York: A Yearling Book, 1983).

28. In her acceptance speech Cleary spoke movingly of the changes in children's correspondence in the preceding seven or eight years and especially of the way children's letters today reflect "the dark and lonely side of childhood." "Newbery Medal Acceptance," 433–34.

29. Ibid., 434–35.

30. Ibid.

31. Beverly Cleary, *Henry Huggins* (New York: Avon Camelot Books, 1950).

32. Bernard Wishy, *The Child and the Republic: The Dawn of Modern American Child Nurture* (Philadelphia: University of Pennsylvania Press, 1968), 176–78, passim.

33. Beverly Cleary, *Otis Spofford* (New York: Avon Camelot Books, 1963). One critic notes that Otis's mother does not maintain the traditional standards in cooking and housekeeping: "[H]is mother feeds [Otis] canned dinners and, because she is pressed for time, puts off ironing and neglects sorting the laundry so that Otis's underwear turns an embarrassing pink." Barbara Chatton, "Ramona and Her Neighbors: Why We Love Them," *Horn Book Magazine* LXXI (March–April 1995), 300.

34. Peter Mayle, *Why Are We Getting a Divorce?* (New York: Harmony Books, 1988), 1–2.

35. I have received personal letters from young adults who report that they could close their eyes and experience the exact sensations they felt years ago at the moment their parents announced the decision to divorce.

36. Kai Erikson, *Everything in Its Path: Destruction of Community in the Buffalo Creek Flood* (New York: Touchstone Books, 1976), 212.

37. Jeanne Warren Lindsay, *Do I Have a Daddy?: A Story About a Single-Parent Child* (Buena Park, Calif.: Morning Glory Press, 1991), np.

38. Lee Salk, *What Every Child Would Like Parents to Know About Divorce* (New York: Harper & Row, 1978), 25–26.

39. Cited by MacLeod, "An End to Innocence," 107.

40. Gardner, 140.

41. Peggy Mann, *My Dad Lives in a Downtown Hotel* (New York: Doubleday & Company, 1973), 87.

42. Richard Peck, *Unfinished Portrait of Jessica* (New York: Dell Publishing, 1991), 143.

43. Mayle, 21.

44. John P. Brogan and Ula Maiden, *The Kids' Guide to Divorce* (New York: Fawcett Crest, 1986), 120.

45. Steven L. Nickman, *When Mom and Dad Divorce* (New York: Simon & Schuster, 1986), 25.

46. Apparently some children still have this capacity: One third-grader going through a difficult divorce read and reread Beverly Cleary's Ramona books because "they were stories about the way her family used to be, and she could laugh and remember and, she said wisely, 'they comfort me.'" Chatton, 299.

47. Interestingly, the children in *Half Magic* live in a broken home themselves. Their mother is a widow and also a "nontraditional" working mother. During the summertime the children are left with a cranky housekeeper whose rules and supervision they routinely subvert and escape. But the adult world is distinct from the children's world, which is filled with excitement and adventure. Edward Eager, *Half Magic* (New York: An Odyssey Classic, 1954).

48. Brogan and Maiden, 76.

49. Cleary, *Dear Mr. Henshaw*, 81.

50. Brogan and Maiden, 76–77.

51. Laurene Krasny Brown and Marc Brown, *Dinosaurs Divorce: A Guide for Changing Families* (New York: Little, Brown, 1986), np.

52. Sheila A. Egoff, *Thursday's Child: Trends and Patterns in Contemporary Children's Literature* (Chicago: American Library Association, 1981), 3.

53. MacLeod, "An End to Innocence," 103.

54. Ibid.

55. Ibid., 107.

56. Ibid., 112.

57. Mayle, 26–27.

58. Joy Berry, *Good Answers to Tough Questions About Divorce* (Chicago: Children's Press, nd), 41.

59. Elizabeth Wurtzel, "Parental Guidance Suggested," in *Next: Young American Writers on the New Generation*, ed. Eric Liu (New York: W. W. Norton & Company, 1994), 202.

CHAPTER SIX: MORE PERFECT UNIONS?

1. "The Diversity and Strength of American Families," Hearing, Select Committee on Children, Youth, and Families, House Ninety-ninth Congress, Second Session, February 25, 1986 (Washington, D.C.: U.S. Government Printing Office, 1986), 74.

2. For example, sociologist Judith Stacey links the rise and fall of the nuclear family to the rise and fall of industrial capitalism. See her discussion of the

"ephemeral modern family," in *Brave New Families: Stories of Domestic Upheaval in Late Twentieth Century America* (New York: Basic Books, 1990), 6–16, passim.

3. Lawrence Stone, "The Historical Origins of the Modern Family," the Fifth Annual O. Meredith Wilson Lecture (Salt Lake City: Department of History, University of Utah, 1982), 1. For a fuller discussion, see Stone, *The Family, Sex and Marriage in England: 1500–1800* (New York: Harper & Row, 1977).

4. Steven Ruggles, "The Transformation of American Family Structure," *American Historical Review* 99 (February 1994), 109. Ruggles notes that in the nineteenth century the predominant extended family structure was the "stem" family, in which one child typically remained in the parental household.

5. Zill and Nord, 25.

6. Stone, "Historical Origins," 14.

7. Cited in Grossberg, 9.

8. Daniel Scott Smith, "Parental Power and Marriage Patterns: An Analysis of Historical Patterns in Hingham, Massachusetts," *Journal of Marriage and the Family* 35 (August 1973), 426–27.

9. Alexis de Tocqueville, *Democracy in America*, ed. J. P. Mayer (Garden City, N.Y.: Anchor Books, 1969), 596.

10. Stone, "Historical Origins," 10.

11. David Schneider, *American Kinship: A Cultural Account* (Englewood Cliffs, N.J.: Prentice-Hall, 1968), 37.

12. Ibid., 91.

13. Ibid., 33–34.

14. Stone, "Historical Origins," 11.

15. Schneider, 54.

16. Ploscowe, 7.

17. Nichols, 63.

18. Moir, 675.

19. David Knox and Caroline Schacht, *Choices in Relationships: An Introduction to Marriage and the Family*, 3d ed. (New York: West Publishing, 1991), 31.

20. Alexander, 314.

21. Jane Mattes, *Single Mothers by Choice: A Guidebook for Single Women Who Are Considering or Have Chosen Motherhood* (New York: Times Books, 1994), 53.

22. Anne Lamott, *Operating Instructions: A Journal of My Son's First Year* (New York: Pantheon Books, 1993), 38.

23. Ibid., 41.

24. Mattes, 156.

25. Alexander, 285.

26. Ibid., 291.

27. Bryan Strong and Christine DeVault, *The Marriage and Family Experience* (St. Paul, Minn.: West Publishing, 1992), 16–17.

28. Trafford, 267.

29. Alexander, 322.

30. Barbara Kingsolver, "The New American Family: A Revealing Look at Who We Are," *Parenting* (March 1995), 74–81, passim.

31. Ibid., 81.

32. "The American Family: There Is No Normal," *Life* 15 (June 1, 1992), 4.

33. "Letters," *Cleveland Plain Dealer*, October 23, 1994, 5-C.

34. Massachusetts Mutual Family Values Study, June 1989. Telephone survey conducted by Mellman and Lazarus among a national sample of twelve hundred adults.

35. *American Heritage Dictionary*, 3d ed. (Boston: Houghton Mifflin, 1992), 659.

36. Mary Ann Schwartz and Barbara Marliene Scott, *Marriages and Families: Diversity and Change* (Englewood Cliffs, N.J.: Prentice Hall, 1994), 3.

37. Gretchen Super, *What Kind of Family Do You Have?* (Lafayette, La.: Twenty-first Century Books, 1991), 55.

38. Cited by Alan Otten, "People Patterns," *The Wall Street Journal*, June 15, 1993, B-1.

39. In Focus, "Most Believe Dan Quayle Was Right: Kids Do Fare Best in Two-Parent Families," Family Research Council publication. The survey was conducted during September 1993 among a sample of eleven hundred randomly selected adults. The margin of error is plus or minus three points.

40. Jean Ferris, *Looking for Home* (New York: Farrar, Straus & Giroux, 1993), 166.

41. Carol Shields, *The Republic of Love* (New York: Penguin Books, 1992), 224.

42. William A. Galston, "The Reinstitutionalization of Marriage: Political Theory and Public Policy," a paper presented to the Marriage in America Symposium. Institute for American Values, New York, 1992.

CHAPTER SEVEN: COMING APART

1. Nicholas Zill, Donna Ruane Morrison, and Mary Jo Coiro, "Long-Term Effects of Parental Divorce on Parent-Child Relationships, Adjustment, and Achievement in Young Adulthood," *Journal of Family Psychology*, 7 (1993), 96.

2. McLanahan and Sandefur, 25.

3. Ibid.

4. "Money Income of Households, Families and Persons in the United

States: 1990," Bureau of the Census, Current Population Reports, Consumer Income, Series P-60, No. 174 (Washington, D.C.: U.S. Government Printing Office, August 1991).

5.   Frank Furstenberg and Christine W. Nord, "Parenting Apart: Patterns of Childbearing After Marital Disruption," *Journal of Marriage and the Family*, 47 (November 1985), 894.

6.   Frank Furstenberg, Jr., and Andrew J. Cherlin, *Divided Families: What Happens to Children When Parents Part* (Cambridge, Mass.: Harvard University Press, 1991), 35–36.

7.   "Parenting Together and Parenting Apart," a Council on Families in America Working Paper, Institute for American Values, New York City, May 1993, 31–32.

8.   Jill Radsken, "Debate over 'Deadbeat' Dads," *Boston Herald*, July 18, 1993, 5.

9.   National Commission on Children, 22.

10.   Wallerstein and Blakeslee, 238.

11.   Ibid., 157–58.

12.   Timothy J. Biblarz and Adrian E. Raftery, "The Effects of Family Disruption on Social Mobility," *American Sociological Review* 58 (February 1993), 97.

13.   McLanahan and Sandefur, 35.

14.   Zill and Nord, 7–8.

15.   Teresa M. Cooney and Peter Uhlenberg, "The Role of Divorce in Men's Relations with Their Adult Children After Mid-Life," *Journal of Marriage and the Family* 52 (August 1990), 685–86.

16.   Alice S. Rossi and Peter H. Rossi, "Normative Obligations and Parent-Child Help Exchange Across the Life Course," a paper prepared for a conference on Parent-Child Relations Across the Life Span, University of New Hampshire, May 1989, 16.

17.   Wallerstein and Blakeslee, 187.

18.   McLanahan and Sandefur, 28.

19.   Ibid., 103.

20.   Zill, Morrison, and Coiro, 96.

21.   Maccoby and Mnookin, 187.

22.   Arland Thornton, "The Influence of the Family on Premarital Sexual Attitudes and Behavior," *Demography* 24 (August 1987), 335.

23.   Alexander, 269.

24.   Martin Daly and Margo Wilson, *Homicide* (Hawthorne, N.Y.: Aldine de Gruyter, 1988), 89.

25.   See, for example, discussions in McLanahan and Sandefur, 28, and Weiss, 20–22.

26.   Maccoby and Mnookin, 218–19.

27.   Dorothy Rabinowitz, "The Sex Crime of the Season," *Wall Street Journal,* October 17, 1994, A12.

28.   Sally Blakeslee Ives, David Fassler, and Michele Lash, *The Divorce Workbook: A Guide for Kids and Families* (Burlington, Vt.: Waterfront Books, 1985), 69.

29.   Carla B. Garrity and Mitchell A. Baris, *Caught in the Middle: Protecting the Children of High-Conflict Divorce* (New York: Lexington Books, 1994), 159–60.

30.   Ibid.

31.   Edward Kruk, "Psychological and Structural Factors Contributing to the Disengagement of Noncustodial Fathers After Divorce," *Family and Conciliation Courts Review* 30 (January 1992), 95.

32.   Children's Letters to Oprah, *The Oprah Winfrey Show,* December 26, 1994, transcript by Burrelle's Information Services (Chicago: Harpo Productions, 1994), 15–16.

33.   Pepper Schwartz, "New Bonds: Para-Dads, Para-Moms," *The New York Times,* November 9, 1995, C1.

34.   Cited in Jill Bauer, *From "I Do" to "I'll Sue": An Irreverent Compendium for Survivors of Divorce* (New York: Plume Book), 72.

35.   McLanahan and Sandefur, 30.

36.   Sandra Hofferth, "Kin Networks, Race and Family Structure," *Journal of Marriage and the Family* 46 (November 1984), 795.

37.   Ibid., 803.

38.   See, for example, Alexandra Peers, "The Hornet's Nest of Divorce: The House," *Wall Street Journal,* September 29, 1995, B1.

39.   Andrew J. Cherlin, "The Weakening Link Between Marriage and the Care of Children," *Family Planning Perspectives* 20 (November–December 1988), 303.

40.   However, the majority of children do not have a second home to visit. According to the National Survey of Children, 58 percent said they never visited their nonresidential parent at all. Furstenberg and Nord, 896.

41.   Bernard Bailyn, *The Peopling of British North America: An Introduction* (New York: Vintage Books, 1988), 21–22.

42.   Ibid.

43.   Furstenberg and Cherlin, 79–82.

CHAPTER EIGHT: DISMANTLING THE DIVORCE CULTURE

1.   Catherine Napolitane with Victoria Pelligrino, *Living and Loving After Divorce* (New York: Signet, 1977), 236.

2. This freedom was particularly cherished by those who had been denied it. One of the ways black Americans marked their emancipation was to rush out to have their marriages registered and legalized. For example, in Vicksburg, Mississippi, between 1864 and 1866, 4,638 couples who had been married during slavery had their marriages registered. Of the 843 couples who registered their marriages in Washington, D.C., in the year 1866–67, 3 had been married for more than fifty years. Andrew Billingsley, *Climbing Jacob's Ladder: The Enduring Legacy of African-American Families* (New York: Simon & Schuster, 1992), 102.

3. Alan S. Stone, "Calculation and Emotion in Marriage," in *Contemporary Marriage: Comparative Perspectives on a Changing Institution*, ed. Kingsley Davis (New York: Russell Sage Foundation, 1985), 404.

4. John Leo, "Where Marriage Is a Scary Word," *U.S. News & World Report* (February 5, 1996), 22.

5. Two recent, empirically based studies offer useful insights and approaches. See John Mordechai Gottmann, *Why Marriages Succeed or Fail: What You Can Learn from the Breakthrough Research to Make Your Marriage Last* (New York: Simon & Schuster, 1994); Judith S. Wallerstein and Sandra Blakeslee, *The Good Marriage: How and Why Love Lasts* (Boston: Houghton Mifflin Co., 1995).

6. See, for example, the concluding discussion in David Popenoe, *Life Without Father* (New York: Free Press, 1996).

Index